A WORLD WITHOUT TYRANNY

TURNING POINT Christian Worldview Series
Marvin Olasky, General Editor

Turning Point: A Christian Worldview Declaration
by Herbert Schlossberg and Marvin Olasky

Prodigal Press: The Anti-Christian Bias of the American News Media
by Marvin Olasky

Freedom, Justice, and Hope:
Toward a Strategy for the Poor and the Oppressed
by Marvin Olasky, Herbert Schlossberg,
Pierre Berthoud, and Clark H. Pinnock

Beyond Good Intentions: A Biblical View of Politics
by Doug Bandow

Prosperity and Poverty: The Compassionate Use
of Resources in a World of Scarcity
by E. Calvin Beisner

The Seductive Image: A Christian Critique
of the World of Film
by K. L. Billingsley

All God's Children and Blue Suede Shoes:
Christians and Popular Culture
by Kenneth A. Myers

A World Without Tyranny:
Christian Faith and International Politics
by Dean C. Curry

Prospects for Growth:
A Biblical View of Population,
Resources and the Future
by E. Calvin Beisner

A WORLD WITHOUT TYRANNY

Christian Faith and
International Politics

Dean C. Curry

CROSSWAY BOOKS • WESTCHESTER, ILLINOIS
A DIVISION OF GOOD NEWS PUBLISHERS

A World Without Tyranny.

Copyright © 1990 by Dean C. Curry.

Published by Crossway Books, a division of
Good News Publishers, Westchester, Illinois 60154.

Published in association with the
Fieldstead Institute
P.O. Box 19061,
Irvine, California 92713

Cover photo: Comstock, Inc. / Michael Stuckey

First printing, 1990

Printed in the United States of America

Library of Congress Catalog Card Number 89-81259

ISBN 0-89107-509-7

Unless otherwise noted, all Bible quotations are taken from *Holy Bible: New International Version*, copyright © 1978 by the New York International Bible Society. Used by permission of Zondervan Bible Publishers.

For Jean Marie

TABLE OF

CONTENTS

ACKNOWLEDGMENTS

---

*B*ooks and the ideas contained in them are never the product of one person. I would like to thank Marvin Olasky for his thorough reading of my manuscript. His comments and suggestions have made this a better book, I am sure. A number of individuals have significantly influenced my own intellectual journey; in particular, Ted Prescott, Ken Myers, Walter Kansteiner, George Weigel, Peter Berger, Richard Neuhaus, Mark Amstutz, Brian O'Connell, Michael Cromartie, James Hunter, Alberto Coll, and Kent Hill. These people deserve special thanks, but none of the responsibility for any of my book's shortcomings. Thanks also to Messiah College for its support of my work. Finally, my children, Ashley and Peter, are a constant reminder of what is really important in life. And, Jean, for everything—this book is for you.

INTRODUCTION

Challenged by Pilate to identify Himself lest He be falsely accused, Jesus responded that "My kingdom is not of this world. If it were, my servants would fight to prevent my arrest by the Jews. But now my kingdom is from another place."[1] Immediately before His arrest and appearance before Pilate, Christ prayed that the Father would now be with His disciples, "for they are not of the world any more than I am of the world."[2] After His resurrection His disciples asked Him, "Lord, are you at this time going to restore the kingdom to Israel?" To which Christ responded, "It is not for you to know the times or dates the Father has set by his own authority. But you will receive power when the Holy Spirit comes on you; and you will be witnesses in Jerusalem, and in all Judea and Samaria, and to the ends of the earth."[3]

Throughout the Gospels Christ reminds His disciples that His Kingdom is an alien kingdom, a kingdom not of this world. It is rather a spiritual kingdom of redemption and righteousness. Consequently, those who follow Christ are themselves "aliens and strangers on earth" who long "for a better country—a heavenly one."[4] This reality that the Christian's ultimate loyalty is to a spiritual city "whose architect and builder is God"[5] has forced Christians since the time of the Early Church to wrestle with the implications of their heavenly citizenship for their earthly sojourn. Certainly God has placed His people *in* the world, but He also reminds them throughout the Scriptures that they are not *of* the world. The Kingdom of God is not coextensive with the kingdom of this world.

But what does this mean practically? Should Christians separate themselves completely from worldly ambitions, institutions, and responsibilities? Does citizenship in God's city mean that Christians should ignore what goes on in the city of man? Is the Christian's sole earthly responsibility to lead people into the Kingdom of God, to "make disciples of all nations"?[6] Are not Christians to pray without ceasing for the coming of God's Kingdom?[7]

These questions have elicited different responses from Christians throughout nearly 2,000 years of Christian history. Some Christians, like many of the early Christians and the later Anabaptists, have indeed interpreted the Scriptures as a command to literally "come out from them and be separate."[8] For others, such as John Calvin and those who have followed in the Reformed theological tradition, Christ's words have been viewed as a mandate to subdue the earth, a command to transform the world.[9] For still other Christians—Lutherans, Roman Catholics, and pietists of many kinds, for example—the relationship between the Christian's citizenship in the Kingdom of God and the Christian's citizenship in the kingdom of the world is more ambiguous.[10]

But what about the more broadly defined world of different peoples and cultures, the world beyond our national borders? What is the Christian's responsibility to *this* world? Is the Christian's responsibility simply, as the "Great Commission" suggests, to share the Good News of God's Kingdom to others, with the goal of making disciples of all nations and perhaps also, along the way, through acts of charity to help meet the material needs of human beings? In other words, is this the only justification for Christian engagement of the larger world?

In raising these questions we are really asking a much more specific kind of question; namely, is there any justification for a Christian's interest and involvement in the great issues of international politics and foreign affairs? God's Word is clear in its assertion that the state is ordained by God and that we are to give to Caesar what is rightfully his.[11] But beyond paying taxes and obeying the civil authorities, are the politics among nations of concern to Christians?

These questions have always been important. However, they have taken on new urgency in recent years. Major changes in international relations have brought about new opportunities as well as new dangers. Nuclear weapons, terrorism, and global interdependence have made the great issues of international politics more personal to everyone. International politics affects every American to one extent or another. From the Soviet Union to the Middle East to Asia, Africa, and Latin America, the world has become a web of interdependent relationships in which every nation is intertwined.

The question of Christian involvement in international politics is sharper now because of the nature of the issues confronting us, and because of the important events that have been taking place around the world. In the Soviet Union, the dramatic domestic and international reforms of Mikhail Gorbachev have raised the possibility of a new era of peaceful cooperation between the United States and the Soviet Union. For the first time since the end of the Second World War, people are beginning to talk about the end of the Cold War. Some people are even proclaiming the death of Marxism.

There are indeed signs of a new dawn in American-Soviet relations as the Soviet Union undergoes a metamorphosis of possibly historic dimensions. The Soviet press is experiencing unprecedented freedom to publish; dissidents are being allowed to voice their criticisms; Soviet troops have left Afghanistan; the number of religious believers in Soviet labor camps is at its lowest level in many years. All of these changes, and others, signal that the Soviet Union may be evolving into a more pragmatic and stable world power. Moreover, the ratification of the Intermediate Nuclear Forces Treaty in late 1988 and the subsequent destruction of a whole class of nuclear weapons has generated optimism that nuclear disarmament may no longer be just a dream.

In the Middle East, potentially dramatic events are unfolding also. In December 1988, the United States agreed for the first time to begin diplomatic contact with Yasir Arafat's Palestinian Liberation Organization. The United States decision was made against the backdrop of steadily increasing Palestinian violence in Israel's occupied territories. Hence, at a time when the threat of another Arab war against Israel is unlikely, the Israelis find themselves confronted with an internal problem that has the potential to tear apart that nation, and the Middle East.

Elsewhere in the Middle East, the Iranian revolution enters its second decade. While many have held on to a hope that Iran would become less militant as time wore on, there is little evidence that this has happened. There is strong evidence that, along with Libya, Iran continues to be a major sponsor of international terrorism. And while Iran and Iraq have begun the process of ending their bloody war, which has cost over one million lives, there are disturbing indications that Iran has no interest in becoming a peaceful member of the international community.

The situation in Africa is distressing, even tragic. Africa remains the only region of the world that still is not able to feed its rapidly multiplying millions. The hunger and poverty endemic to most of that continent continues to be fueled by governments that are economically and politically repressive. South Africa remains the focus of most international attention, and the future of this wealthy and strategically important country is characterized by uncertainty. In most other parts of Africa—Kenya being a prominent example—the trend of recent years has been a movement *away* from democracy and a deterioration of basic human rights. Africa is a precarious continent whose destiny, for better or for worse, is likely to be decided during the 1990s.

In Asia, the pace and the nature of change is exhilarating. For over a decade China moved steadily away from Marxist orthodoxy as economic liberalization gave rise to pressures for democracy. The movement for political freedom, however, was dealt a brutal setback in the Spring of 1989 as an aging Communist leadership groped for ways to maintain its total control of Chinese life. Taiwan, South Korea, Singapore, and Hong Kong—just three decades ago poor, underdeveloped nations—now boast some of the fastest-growing economies in the world. Japan continues to be the economic miracle of the world and promises to further extend its economic power into new technology areas such as supercomputers and semiconductors. Indeed, some people believe Asia is on the verge of global economic domination. The implications of Asia's economic might for the United States are momentous.

In other parts of Asia, politics, not economics, promises to bring major changes. The future of the Philippines is very much up in the air as a ruthless Communist movement known as the New People's Army contends with the new Filipino democracy which is the product of Corrie Aquino's "people power." At stake is the future of a country which has had close historic ties with the United States. In Cambodia, the Vietnamese, who have occupied Cambodia for more than ten years, have left. However, there is much anxiety in Cambodia and elsewhere that the Vietnamese departure will bring about the return of the brutal regime of Pol Pot, which in the early 1970s was responsible for the deaths of over one million Cambodians.

Closer to the United States, Central America is as unstable as it has ever been. The Arias peace plan has not brought peace to that troubled region. Nicaragua is in shambles, while El Salvador, under pressure from Marxist rebels, appears to be headed in the same direction. In other parts of Latin America democracy is more entrenched than ever; but many Latin American nations, such as Mexico and Brazil, face major economic problems. These problems, including massive debt, threaten not only the economic viability of these nations, but their political stability as well.

Western Europe, too, faces an unprecedented threat to its post-World War II cohesion. For fifty years, fear of Soviet aggression against Europe has acted like a glue holding together countries with a long history of mutual animosity (for example, France and Germany). With the prospects of a less-aggressive Soviet Union, many analysts believe old European hostilities will surface once again. At the same time, 1992 will see the complete integration of the western European economies. The political and economic implications of a fully operational Common Market both for Europe and the rest of the world are uncertain.

These issues, and many others, will shape the course of world history into the twenty-first century. How, then, as American Christians should our faith inform our understanding and approach to international politics? Historically, American Christians have responded to this question in different ways. During the American Revolution, Christians embraced the cause of American independence as being consistent with Biblical teaching. During the nineteenth century, as the American nation overspread the North American continent, Christians saw this as a manifestation of God's divine destiny for the United States.

During the First and Second World Wars of this century, Christians enthusiastically joined the fight against the tyranny of the Kaiser and the evil of Hitler. More recently, Christians have in the main endorsed the United States' post-World War Two role as leader and protector of the Free World.

Some American Christians have followed the separatist path of their Anabaptist forebears and shunned any involvement with global politics. Other American Christians, however, have somewhat uncritically identified the interests of the Church with the interests of the nation. Many Christians still see the United States as having special status as an agent of God's Kingdom in the world.

However, a second approach—the mirror image antithesis of the first—has gained popularity among some Christians in recent years. With roots in the progressive reform movement of the late nineteenth century and the Christian Socialist movement of the 1930s, the contemporary version of this approach views the United States as a deeply flawed society, an unjust society with injustices reflected in a malevolent foreign policy. The United States is thus characterized as an imperialistic and exploitative nation with interests and agenda radically different from those of God's Kingdom. Consequently, the role of the Church must be to stand in "prophetic" opposition to the "principalities and powers" of this world—meaning U.S. foreign policy.

Both approaches teach that the Christian faith demands involvement in the world of international affairs. It is ironic that both approaches see themselves as being true to the demands of Christian discipleship. Indeed, both define their positions as being Biblical. But that is where the similarity ends. The two approaches begin with different theological moorings and have fundamentally different understandings of international politics and the nature of Christian responsibility in the world. Patriotism, power, national interest, peace, freedom, justice, democracy, liberation—each of these is construed differently by supporters of the two approaches.

Rarely, however, do Christians discuss these bedrock theological and political assumptions. It is much more common for Christians to join the larger public debate over specific foreign policy issues as committed partisans for one point of view or another. There is little deliberate reflection upon questions of hermeneutics and epistemology—how we interpret the Bible, how we know what we know, how these in turn relate to politics among nations. Moreover, often even less careful attention is given to the nature of international politics itself, particularly the relationship among ethics, power, and national purpose, as well as the essence of and relationship among peace, freedom, justice, and national security.

Unlike Roman Catholics, American Protestants do not have a hoary tradition of systematic social thought to guide them in their engagement of international politics.[12] Contemporary foreign policy issues such as U.S.-Soviet relations, arms control, trade protectionism, aid to the Nicaraguan *contras*, and South African sanctions—to name just a few—are more often than not fiercely debated along partisan lines while given, in an *a priori* manner, the imprimatur of being *the* Biblical or Christian approach. Rarely is careful consideration given to the fundamental question of the relationship between the Christian faith and the world of international politics. It is frequently assumed that there is a relationship, but again rarely is this assumption the product of a consciously articulated Biblical exegesis or theological hermeneutic. Yet, such issues cannot be addressed responsibly in a presuppositional void—that is, in an exegetical or hermeneutical vacuum.

Furthermore, much discussion of foreign policy issues which comes from a "Christian or Biblical perspective" does not exhibit a thorough understanding of the issues themselves. For this reason—although not for this reason alone—the Christian discussion of foreign policy is often considered irrelevant in those influential opinion, academic, and policy circles that are ultimately responsible for the formulation and implementation of U.S. foreign policy. Clearly, therefore, a keen knowledge of history, an understanding of the dynamics of international relations, and sensitivity to the realities of politics constitute the starting point for any Christian perspective of international politics that should be taken seriously or could have an impact on foreign policy itself.

In short, a Biblically faithful and effective Christian engagement of foreign policy issues can only emerge from a sound understanding of Biblical Christianity, international politics, and the relationship between the two. This task constitutes the purpose of this book, as well as one of its theses. In recent years, hosts of books written by Christians have discussed specific issues such as war and peace and have addressed international politics in the context of social ethics. But there have been few attempts to do what this book does; namely, to analyze systematically the connection between Christianity as a Biblically-based theological system and the world of international politics. As such, this book deals with issues of theology, politics, and morality. It does not claim to represent *the* Biblical view of international politics. It does not sanctify partisan positions on specific contemporary foreign policy issues as being the "Biblical" positions. The overarching objective is to articulate a Christian theology of international politics and to relate that theology to the application of Biblical principles in the arena of global politics.

The present volume confronts the pressing contemporary international issues of our day: issues of war and peace, freedom and tyranny, wealth and poverty. These issues, however, can be responsibly approached only within the context of an awareness of the pervasiveness of sin. Adam's sin, and the long, dark shadow it casts over the history and pretensions of mankind, must be the starting point of Christian reflection about politics among nations. Yet, contemporary international politics is rooted in a general crisis of faith that has led to the rise of ideology as an animating force. We will see how the decline of a Christian consensus in the West, and the supplanting of this consensus with other ideologies—secular and non-secular, has contributed to twentieth-century brutality.

Each of these ideas, and others, will be developed in the three parts of this book. Part One begins with a discussion of the foreign policy debate during the 1988 American presidential campaign, and then continues with an examination of the state of freedom and tyranny in the contemporary world. Part Two develops a Biblical framework for a Christian approach to international politics. Part Three uses that framework to define an agenda for Christian engagement of the world.

A final observation is in order. Many inside and outside the Christian community have questioned the value of attempting to articulate a Christian understanding of international politics.

Behind this point of view is the assumption that Christianity really has nothing important to say to the world of politics and public policy; at best, Christianity is irrelevant to the "real world" of politics and foreign policy. It is my belief that such a view could not be further from the truth. As a community of faith, Christians continually need to talk to each other about what it means to be "in the world, but not of the world." We need to struggle continually with the question of what belongs to God and what belongs to Caesar. We need to grapple continually with the ambiguity inherent in citizenship in both heavenly and earthly kingdoms.

Christians should not abandon their faith commitments as they enter the public square, the world in which foreign policy is made and carried out, but should instead become even more sensitive to the implications of faith for their earthly sojourn. It is my hope that this book will contribute, however humbly, to that goal.

PART ONE

THE STATE OF THE WORLD

O N E

AMERICA IN THE WORLD: THE ROLE OF POLITICS AND IDEAS

S tudents of American government have long observed that American voters make many political decisions according to the logic of economic self-interest. Indeed, the United States was born out of a passionate commitment to the principle that there should be "no taxation without representation." "Pocketbook" issues such as taxes, the federal deficit, and government spending directly affect every citizen. The proliferation of taxpayer revolts during the past decade, most notably California's Proposition 13 which drastically limited property taxes, and the popularity of Reaganomics with its goal of lower federal taxes and less government spending attest to the importance the American public gives to the economic policies of their elected representatives.

The 1988 presidential campaign demonstrated that economic issues are still a major concern of the American electorate. At the same time, however, the 1988 campaign established that the American voting public is paying even more attention to the foreign policy views of those aspiring to the White House. The campaign battle between Republican George Bush and Democrat Michael Dukakis confirmed that domestic policy is no longer the sole key to presidential elections.[1]

A SHRINKING WORLD

There was a time, not too many years ago, when Americans lived their lives with little awareness of other nations or dependence on them. North America's geographical isolation and its abundant natural resources allowed the United States to develop apart from foreign influences. The realities imposed by geographical insularity were reinforced by an American abhorrence of power politics. In his Farewell Address, George Washington encouraged his fellow-citizens to be "constantly awake [to] the insidious wiles of foreign influence." The United States, warned Washington, should "steer clear of permanent alliances with any portion of the foreign world" and should have "as little political connection as possible" with other nations.

Washington's exhortation was quite understandable to his contemporaries. By the late eighteenth century, Americans saw their experiment in democratic society as unique in the annals of human history.[2] These Americans were influenced both by New England Calvinism (and its belief that America was God's New Jerusalem) and by Virginia Deism (with its Enlightenment-rooted faith in man's ability to forge a political community void of the shortcomings associated with past societies). Thus early Americans saw their nation as a *Novus Ordo Seclorum*—a new order of the ages.[3] America was clearly a different nation. In the words of Reinhold Niebuhr, an "innocent nation" that had successfully "turned its back upon the vices of Europe and made a new beginning."[4]

This sense of American "exceptionalism" directly affected the way in which Americans viewed their role in the world. America was to be, in the words of seventeenth-century Puritan John Winthrop, "a city on a hill," a beacon to the rest of the world. However, the light generated by this beacon was to be one of example. In other words, America's influence *on* the world was to be accomplished without American involvement *in* the world. The machinations of international politics were the "insidious wiles" of which Washington spoke. To preserve its innocency, to preserve its purity as a nation set apart, the United States for most of its history disavowed any desire to participate in world politics. When the realities of national interest finally forced the United States to exercise its responsibilities of power—for example, during the Spanish-American War and

World War I—America's involvement was defined and justified in terms of America's mission as the agent of a new age. Thus, as U.S. troops marched off to Europe in 1917, President Wilson announced that Americans were fighting to "make the world safe for democracy."[5]

The United States emerged from the First World War a major world power, and from the Second World War a super-power without equal. After 1945 the United States assumed leadership of the Free World and accepted responsibilities commensurate with its economic, military, and ideological power. However, the United States continues today to define its engagement of international relations—as it has done since Wilson—in moral terms. Though it has assumed the responsibilities of the great nations and empires of the past, the United States still does not act like a traditional great power. No American president has articulated U.S. foreign policy goals in the language of *realpolitik*; to do so would be to betray America's historical sense of uniqueness and moral mission.

What has changed in the past forty years, therefore, is not America's view of America, but rather of the world itself. The larger historical forces at work at the turn of this century and during the 1940s made the United States a major international actor. By mid-century, other political and nonpolitical forces had eroded the insularity provided by geographical isolation. Advances in communication and travel technology, growing economic interdependence, and the existence of nuclear weapons have been the most significant of the new forces influencing U.S. foreign policy. Very simply, the world has shrunk. It is no longer possible for the United States to withdraw from the larger world or to ignore what happens elsewhere. The isolationist inclination persists, rooted as it is in the very character of the American national soul. But the nature of the world in which Americans live has been altered dramatically and irreversibly.[6] Today political and economic events in Japan, Chile, Syria, Argentina, Great Britain, South Africa—indeed everywhere—have the potential to impact all Americans.

Americans are more interested in the foreign policy views of their elected leaders than at previous times in American history. Presidents now are measured by their ability to handle foreign crises as well as day-to-day affairs.[7] Increasing congressional scrutiny of the Executive branch's conduct of foreign policy, the zealotry of the media, and the widespread attention given to recent foreign policy imbroglios such as the Iran-*contra* affair have reinforced the public's impression that the president's ability to govern America in every area can be judged by his handling of foreign policy.

AMERICAN POWER AND PURPOSE

Foreign policy has become not only a lens through which to assess the managerial competency of American presidents, but also a prism through which Americans assess what the late Catholic theologian John Courtney Murray called the "American Proposition"—that matrix of beliefs, values, and ideals which has come to define democracy in America.[8] Throughout American history there has existed a consensus regarding the essential meaning and purpose of the American experience, which historians and political scientists have called the American political tradition.[9] That there has existed a consensus of values and ideals throughout American history is not to argue that conflict and struggle have been absent from the American experience. This is obviously not the case. However, such conflict has been primarily about the *means* to achieve a common vision, not about the vision itself.[10]

During America's 200-year history, a remarkable continuity of values and ideals has led to consensus regarding national purpose. Even though U.S. foreign policy has vacillated between periods of isolation and intervention, belief in the legitimacy of American political and economic institutions has remained steady as well. So has the concurrent belief that American democracy is worth emulating throughout the world. In other words, the historical consensus about the value of American democracy has translated into an American consensus about the universal value of the American democratic experience for the rest of the world.

The American consensus regarding the legitimacy of American values, institutions, and ideals remained unchallenged until recently.[11] Americans believed that the United States, even with its flaws, was a force for good in the world. Since the 1960s, however, the American political tradition has been challenged by influential elements of American society. For example, early in the present century the Communist Party was influential among certain segments of American society, primarily literary intellectuals. However, the direct influence of these people on American society at large was small and their impact short-lived.[12] Within a decade after the Second World War, the Old Left, as the members of the Communist Party and their fellow-traveling friends were called, was dying because of its close ties to Stalinism. Yet, many of its ideas lived on in the New Left of the 1960s.

It is difficult to generalize about a phenomenon so diverse as the New Left. It did not emerge as a single organization, nor was it associated with one particular issue.[13] Its roots were diverse as well. For many, the New Left was primarily a political movement. For others, it represented a protest against the traditional values and beliefs of American society. Ultimately it was both a political and cultural movement. What united the various strands was repudiation of the legitimacy of traditional American political, economic, and social values. The New Left came to represent what University of Chicago sociologist Edward Shils has called a new antinomianism. Shils clearly defines the essence of the New Left worldview:

> At its innermost core resides, first, the fundamental and all-overriding value of the emancipation of the individual from the burden of obligations and, second, the unremitting insistence on his rights. This is the root of the matter. The highest ideal of antinomianism is a life of complete self-determination, free of the burden of tradition and conventions, free of the constraints imposed by institutional rules and laws and of the stipulations of authority operating within the setting of institutions. Neither God nor man is to be set over self. . . . The traditions of individualistic and constitutional liberalism—equality before the law, equality of opportunity, equality of electoral power, equality in the freedom of expression in the representation of ideals and interests—are not only negated by this anarchistic liberalism; *their postulates are denied.* (emphasis added)[14]

The New Left's repudiation of the core principles of the American Proposition, what Shils above refers to as the postulates of constitutional liberalism, has had a direct impact on its approach to United States foreign policy. New Leftists purport, continues Shils,

> to distinguish themselves from the "Old Left" by criticism of the Soviet Union and their refusal to subordinate themselves to the Communist Parties of their respective countries. This disavowal is specious. It is not just on a tactical calculation that the collaboration rests, but rather on a fundamental agreement of values and ideas, with variations of emphasis. . . . [The New Left] have opposed American society no less vehemently than did the Old Left. . . . A very important feature of [the New Left is their readiness], in discussion about the relation between the Soviet Union and the United States, invariably to give to the Soviet Union the benefit of the doubt.[15]

While a central theme or single emphasis does not appear in the New Left's foreign policy agenda, their agenda is a wide-ranging and complex mosaic of what *Partisan Review* editor William Phillips characterizes as "outworn Marxist notions, vaguely progressive ideas, trendy causes like environmentalism and various liberation movements, sympathy for something called the Third World, pacifism, anti-Americanism, [and] an obsessive fear of nuclear power."[16]

The New Left coalesced in the 1960s and was closely identified with the Vietnam War, student activism, and the "counterculture." The two decades since the heyday of the Sixties have seen the end of the Vietnam War, as well as the demise of the counterculture and widespread student protest. However, the mellowing of America's student generation in recent years has not brought an end to the animating ideas of the New Left or an end to its agenda. In this sense the phenomenon of the New Left is different from that of other radical groups—Left and Right—in American history. Historically most radical movements have been transient, as shown in the early twentieth century in the rapid rise and fall of the American Socialist movement and the Ku Klux Klan. But the influence of the New Left has not been transient; to the contrary, the fundamental beliefs of the New Left germinated in those of the Sixties generation who moved into positions of influence, particularly in the universities and the media.[17]

Once on the outside, the ideas and values of the New Left have become an integral part of the belief system of that segment of the middle class which sociologists call the "New Class" or "Knowledge Class." This class consists of those, in the words of Boston University sociologist Peter Berger, "whose occupations deal with the production and distribution of symbolic knowledge . . . people who are employed in the educational system, the communications media, the vast counseling and guidance networks, and the bureaucratic agencies planning for the . . . needs of society."[18]

The rise of the New Class is of special significance to us for two reasons. First, the New Class exercises disproportionate influence on American politics and culture, not by virtue of its size, but because of its dominant role in American higher education and the American media. Second, the value and belief system of the New Class is inherently secular and anti-religious, and is politically far to the left of the mainstream of traditional American politics.[19]

The obvious manifestations of the youthful rebellion and insolence of the Sixties are now historical curiosities; yesterday's counterculture has become today's "establishment." But the worldview which animated the Sixties counterculture was not shorn along with its hair, bell-bottom jeans, and peace symbols. The values, ideals, and agenda of the Sixties New Left has been carried into the "establishment"—the universities, media, governmental bureaucracies, and centers of culture—through a New Class who find themselves not on the outside of American life, but in a position to redefine the soul of the American nation—its very meaning and purpose.

The 1988 presidential campaign brought the conflict between the historic American political tradition and the New Class's alternative vision to the forefront of American politics. Nowhere was this conflict more apparent than in the debate over U.S. foreign policy. Republicans and Democrats have sometimes disagreed over foreign policy issues, but there was always a common, bipartisan affirmation of certain bedrock principles. In the post-World War Two period, this bipartisan consensus revolved around a commitment to democratic values and institutions, an opposition to communism, and a belief that the United States must exercise its unilateral responsibilities as the leader of the Free World. Moreover, transcending these principles was the accepted understanding that the United States' involvement in international relations has been, on balance, positive in terms of its impact on other nations.

The specifics of how these foundational principles should be worked out was the subject of disagreement between political parties and within them. The principles themselves, however, went unchallenged in any serious way—until the 1988 presidential campaign.[20] To be sure, Michael Dukakis, the 1988 Democratic presidential candidate, is personally committed to democracy and opposed to communism. In this general sense, Dukakis's approach to U.S. foreign policy was within what is frequently called the "mainstream" of American politics.

But these generalizations do not in themselves tell us much about the underlying worldview assumptions Dukakis brought to his *interpretation* of the principles. For rarely, if ever, had there been a presidential campaign in which the underlying worldview assumptions of the candidates were so dissimilar. Indeed, Dukakis was the first major party presidential candidate—with the possible exception of George McGovern—whose assumptions about the purpose of American foreign policy represented a radical departure from the post-World War bipartisan consensus in the foreign policy realm. Dukakis, in turn, sought through his stump speeches and symbolic appearances at meetings of veterans' groups and defense industries to demonstrate his commitment to the traditional values and agenda of American foreign policy.[21] But behind the campaign theatrics of both candidates lay real, fundamental differences in their respective understandings of U.S. foreign policy.

George Bush's foreign policy speeches fell within the traditional bipartisan mainstream in terms of his understanding of the purpose and obligations of U.S. foreign policy. But Michael Dukakis's outlook was more in tune with the perspective of the Sixties Left than with the mainstream of traditional American politics.[22] Two commentators with ties to the Democratic Party succinctly described the essence of Dukakis's worldview:

Dukakis has faithfully represented the views of post-Vietnam Democrats who are skittish about the use of force, opposed to much of this decade's military buildup, strongly inclined to multilateral rather than unilateral action abroad, eager to strike new arms control agreements with the Soviets, and dedicated to the neo-Wilsonian promotion of global human rights.[23]

To be sure, Dukakis's foreign policy rhetoric and specific policy positions did not represent the most radical extremism associated with the Sixties Left. Yet, his understanding of the way the world works and his approach to U.S. foreign policy reflected the five foundational assumptions of the Sixties Left and the "post-Vietnam Democrats":[24]

(1) The anti-Soviet posture of U.S. foreign policy during the Cold War has been an excessive, paranoid reaction on the part of the United States. The idea of an ideologically-driven, expansionistic Soviet Union determined to conquer the world is a product of Cold War mythology. In reality Soviet foreign policy has been motivated by legitimate defensive concerns. When Soviet foreign policy has been overly aggressive and expansionistic, such as in Afghanistan, it has been no more so than U.S. foreign policy. Moreover, the United States' obsessive preoccupation with the Soviet Union and communism has led to excesses and distortions in its foreign policy, among which the most egregious have been fueling the nuclear arms race, illegal intervention in the affairs of sovereign nations (e.g., Vietnam and Nicaragua), and the toleration of dictatorships (e.g., the Shah of Iran and Pinochet of Chile).

(2) Because of its preoccupation with communism and the Soviet Union, the United States has not been sensitive to the progressive revolutionary forces at work in the Third World. In the post-World War period, U.S. policy toward the Third World has been seen as an extension of U.S. policy toward the Soviet Union. In reality, the problems of the Third World have little or nothing to do with ideology and everything to do with poverty and exploitation. The United States' fixation on communism has therefore placed it "on the wrong side of history" in its relationship with the Third World nations of the southern hemisphere. This explains the fiasco of U.S. policy toward such countries as South Africa,

Angola, Mozambique, El Salvador, and Nicaragua. A progressive U.S. foreign policy would in turn reorient itself toward the problems of the Third World. North-South relations—the relationship between the wealthy, industrialized nations of the northern hemisphere and the poor and the exploited countries of the southern hemisphere—must be at the top of the American foreign policy agenda.

(3) The American experience in Vietnam demonstrated not only the bankruptcy of a policy built on anti-communism, but it also proved there are limits to American power. Not only should the United States not attempt to impose its ideology on other countries, the United States does not have the power and the influence to do so. The notion of American omnipotence is another part of the American Cold War mythology. The legitimate role for the U.S. military is to protect the immediate borders of the United States.

(4) The limits of American power, the necessity of rejecting the Cold War-inspired temptation to use American power arrogantly, and the reality that international peace, justice, and stability are not solely an American concern mandate that the United States forego unilateral action in the world. Multilateral diplomacy must replace military force as the primary instrument of U.S. foreign policy. Whether in Central America, the Persian Gulf, or Africa, the United States should cast aside its failed unilateral policies and work closely with the United Nations, the Organization of American States, the Organization of African Unity, and our allies to promote peace and justice. International peace and justice are not solely an American concern, nor an American responsibility.

(5) The United States is a nation in decline.[25] Like the great nations and empires of the past, the United States has overextended its global commitments and must now begin the process of military retrenchment if it is going to continue to meet the minimal economic expectations of its citizens. If the United States fails to reorder its priorities—away from global military commitments—the United States will accelerate its fall as a great power.

In sum: the 1988 presidential campaign saw foreign policy concerns receive more attention than in past presidential contests. Perceptions of growing American dependency on other nations, questions of leadership competency, and competing visions of the national purpose came together in the 1988 presidential contest in an unprecedented manner. Of these three factors, by far the most important for the future of American politics and, by extension, the world is the last.

The issue of what America is and what it should be to the rest of the world will have far-reaching consequences for the future of humankind. In this sense, the 1988 campaign marked a crucial juncture in American history. Certainly for the first time since 1945, and arguably for the first time in the nation's history, Americans began to debate the underlying legitimacy of the American Proposition as that proposition has been understood for 200 years. A common vision of the purpose and use of American power has been replaced by conflicting visions. The traditional vision remains, but the new vision, represented by Michael Dukakis and the so-called "McGovern wing" of the Democratic Party, established itself as a contender for what has been called the "mainstream" of thinking regarding United States foreign policy.

IDEAS HAVE CONSEQUENCES

Looking back at the 1988 campaign, it is tempting to conclude that it was all "politics as usual." The overblown rhetoric, the putative lack of sustained substantive discussion between the candidates, the emphasis on symbolic media opportunities were sound reasons for concluding that while other things may change, American electoral politics has a kind of predictable permanence that is as old as American electioneering. There is, to be sure, truth in this observation; electoral politics in the United States has remained remarkably constant since the rowdy days of Andrew Jackson in the early nineteenth century.

But this historical observation about the manner in which campaigns are conducted should not lead us to the conclusion—as it frequently does—that the ideas separating candidates and parties are insignificant or not really that important. Sometimes that is the case. As we have noted, American politics, in contrast to what is found in many other democracies around the world, is generally consensual and moderate in nature. Radicalism, of the Left or

Right, has never found a home in the United States. At the same time, it is equally true that America is not a country without an ideology or with no concern for ideology.

The republican idea gave birth to the American experiment in democracy. That idea, with its commitment to liberty, equality, and virtue, sustained those ideals which have been at the heart of American political culture for the past two centuries.[26] Yet, throughout these 200 years there have emerged and coexisted alternative visions—or competing ideologies—that have sought to replace the republican ideology of the Founding Fathers as the defining vision of the American nation.[27] Certainly the most significant of these alternative visions, though not the only one, was the Southern antebellum political tradition articulately defined and defended by the likes of John C. Calhoun.[28] Abraham Lincoln understood that the Civil War was ultimately not a war about slavery, but in a more fundamental sense a contest between two different visions of what America was all about; it was a struggle to see "if this nation or any nation, *so conceived*, can long endure."

Throughout American history we can find other examples of alternative visions vying for ascendancy. Sometimes they are rejected, as in the case of the Southern political tradition, and sometimes they subtly transform America's traditional republican ideology, as was arguably the case with Franklin Roosevelt's New Deal. The point here—and it is a very important point—is that ideas are important. Our perceptions of men, government, and the world itself are not, as Richard Weaver wisely noted, "mere rationalizations of what has been brought about by unaccountable forces. They are rather deductions from our most basic ideas of human destiny, and they have a great, though not unobstructed, power to determine our course."[29] In short, ideas have consequences.

Americans are by their very nature a pragmatic people. They find what works and they do it. Because of this pragmatic spirit, Americans are reluctant to acknowledge the importance of ideas. But, as we have stressed, the United States was born out of an idea, and that idea is what brought the American nation through a cataclysmic civil war. Moreover, along the way there have been other ideas which have challenged and modified the founding idea of the country's Framers. Ideas about politics, about economics, about education, about all spheres of human existence are important; to one extent or another, they ultimately determine how we and all of humanity live our lives. In politics, the way in which we *choose* to order our society—that ordering being a reflection of a guiding idea or vision—is all-important in terms of how we actually *do* live our lives.

The bottom line is simple and important: ideas count, and the ideas that divide our political candidates are not always insignificant, particularly when the candidates reflect different visions of what America is and what it should be about. Nowhere is this observation of more consequence than in the realm of foreign policy. While a bipartisan foreign policy consensus once existed in the United States, in the aftermath of the Vietnam War this consensus has moved far in the direction of dissolving. The competing visions that have replaced this consensus, represented in the 1988 presidential race in the differing worldviews of George Bush and Michael Dukakis, appear to be a permanent fixture of the American political landscape. But they are not simply "political" disagreements between Democrats and Republicans. They are fundamentally different understandings of world politics and America's role in the world.

The foreign policy debates conducted during the 1988 presidential campaign raised in bold relief the underlying alternative visions which now confront the United States and its policymakers. What is the nature of communism? Is the Soviet Union a threat to the United States? Is the United States "on the wrong side of history"? Are there limits to American power? What constitutes the national interest of the United States? Is the United States a nation in decline? These are momentous questions, the answers to which will have a major impact not only on America's future, but the future of the rest of the world. This is not an exaggerated statement of national hubris, but rather a recognition of the important role which the United States plays in international relations.

How these questions are answered—in other words, which guiding idea or vision we choose to answer them—will bear directly on the great global problems of our time: the problems of war and peace, wealth and poverty, freedom and tyranny, justice and injustice. It is to these problems that we now turn our attention.

FREEDOM vs. TYRANNY: THE STATE OF THE WORLD

*B*efore his election and during the 1988 campaign, George Bush proclaimed that "peace is breaking out all over." The causes and long-term implications of this blooming "global spring" are subject to different interpretations, but the reality is that the world in the last decade of the twentieth century is experiencing unprecedented peace and prosperity. This is, of course, a relative statement. Poverty, war, and oppression are still common throughout the world. Yet, at no time since the end of the Second World War have the signs of global peace and material prosperity been more positive. The facts are impressive.

For nearly half a century the world has not witnessed a major war between the dominant world powers—the United States and the Soviet Union. This fifty years of peace between global powers is all the more impressive when we realize that not since the second century A.D. has the world experienced fifty consecutive years of peace.[1] Even more encouraging are signs that the basis of the peace between the world's superpowers is changing. For most of the last five decades the peace between the United States and the Soviet Union has been secured by a "balance of terror" grounded in the nuclear-weapons capability of both nations. More recently, great hope has been expressed that the domestic reforms of Soviet President and General Secretary

Mikhail Gorbachev will result in a more stable and less precarious long-term basis for peace.

The anticipation of a new relationship between the United States and the Soviet Union is not the only reason for optimism about the state of the world. Regional conflicts that have been going on for years and have cost millions of human lives are apparently coming to an end in the Middle East, Africa, and Asia. Since the end of the Second World War, over 100 "small" wars have been fought in which at least eighteen million persons were killed. In the early 1980s over forty regional conflicts—both civil and international—were being waged. By the time of George Bush's election, many of these long, costly wars—in the Persian Gulf, Cambodia, Afghanistan, and Southwest as well as Saharan Africa—showed promising signs of coming to an end.

Elsewhere in the world, another reason for hope lies in the tide of democracy that is sweeping much of the world. When the history of the present century is written, historians will be able to define it by reference to one monstrous reality: tyranny. For much of this century, the darkness of tyranny seemed to be triumphing as its shadow extended over ever-greater numbers of the world's peoples and nations. During the 1980s, however, the forces of freedom have seemed to be turning the tide as many countries without a tradition of liberty began to embrace the values and institutions of democratic government.

From Asia to Latin America, democracy is on the move. In 1900 only one out of ten of the people in the world lived under democracy. By the late 1980s, that number was increasing as many formerly nondemocratic nations began the transition toward democratic government. In Latin America, for example, where in 1980 only 40 percent of the people lived under democratic rule, by the end of the Reagan presidency over 90 percent did. To be sure, some of these democratic governments are fragile, such as in El Salvador; and other nations are just beginning to democratize, as in Chile. But the trends are nonetheless moving in the right direction.

Economic freedom has grown alongside political freedom. Even Communist nations such as China and the Soviet Union have begun to understand that dramatic economic growth is only possible in an environment that allows economic freedom. The movement toward free open economic markets has been nothing less than profound. From Asia to Latin America to Eastern Europe to Africa, the decade of the 1980s has witnessed a steady erosion of state dominance over economic decision-making and a steady growth of market-driven economic decision-making. The results have been impressive, both in the developing nations—the so-called Third World—and among the developed, industrialized nations.

Thirty years after "state socialism" was proclaimed the economics of the future in the Third World, country after country has either jettisoned state socialism or has slowly begun to experiment with market capitalism. For those less developed countries that have done this, the results have been staggering. For example, the "four little dragons" of East Asia—South Korea, Taiwan, Singapore, and Hong Kong, all underdeveloped nations just thirty years ago—have seen their economies quadruple in size since 1960. The economically backward nations elsewhere in Asia, especially China, have taken note of the experience of these four little dragons. Indeed, the only examples of successful economic development are to be found among nations—such as the four little dragons, but also including countries such as Chile—that have renounced strict state control of economic decision-making in favor of economic privatization and rewards for private investment.[2]

The success of its four Asian neighbors have led the Communist leaders of China to proclaim that "it doesn't matter if a cat is black or white, only that it catches a mouse." In the Soviet Union also, Mikhail Gorbachev has embarked on a cautious program of economic liberalism, hoping to invigorate a stagnating Soviet economy.

While free market economies do not now dominate the world, the undeniable fact is that the trend of the last decade is away from socialism toward capitalism. As the comparative experiences of countries such as socialist Tanzania and capitalist Taiwan have demonstrated, market capitalism works and state socialism does not. Many Third World nations appear to have learned this lesson, although not all, as the experience of Central Africa illustrates.

But even apart from the development experience of specific nations, an additional reality of recent years is that poverty has decreased worldwide. There are a host of statistical or empirical numbers that bear out this reality. For example, food production has increased nearly everywhere during the past thirty years, and fertility rates have declined. In addition, the Third World has seen life expectancy increase by an average of seven years since 1950 and infant mortality drop by over 50 percent during the same period.[3]

These impersonal numbers are given life by the real improvements in quality of life that have occurred in nearly every Third World country over the past thirty years. Richard Critchfield, an American anthropologist and reporter, has spent the last three decades living for extended periods of time in villages throughout the Third World—in Africa, Asia, and Latin America. Critchfield's accounts of life in Third World villages are as interesting as they are insightful.[4] Returning as he does to the same villages year after year, Critchfield writes that almost without exception villagers throughout the Third World have seen a steady improvement in the quality of their lives during the past three decades.[5]

In sum, the global trends of the past ten years are encouraging. The world has become more peaceful, more prosperous, and more democratic. There is less violence, less poverty, and less tyranny evident in the world than at any other time during the twentieth century. Having stated this incontrovertible fact, it must also be reiterated that the relative material peace and prosperity that the world now enjoys falls far short of the perfect peace and prosperity of the future fulfilled Kingdom of God.

The reality is that the world has become a better place for most, though certainly not all, of its citizens. Yet, war, poverty, and oppression remain, as the effects of human sin continue to pervade all that man does. The notion of unending human progress is a myth born out of the humanist secularism of the eighteenth-century Enlightenment.[6] While the material conditions of human life have steadily improved over the past 200 years of human history, human nature itself has shown no improvement. The bloody carnage of the twentieth century—the bloodiest century in all of human history—bears testimony to this reality. Ultimately, the perfection of all things will be an extra-historical work, dependent on the work of the sovereign Lord of the universe.

While the perfect restoration of all things awaits the historically climactic work of God, it is also true that God, through His common grace, enables human beings to create the conditions for a more peaceful and prosperous world now. This means that nations which order themselves politically and economically in accord with Biblical principles, whether or not many of their citizens are Christians, can attain earthly peace and prosperity. Both the past 200 years of human history and recent events throughout the world demonstrate beyond a shadow of a doubt that peace and prosperity are inextricably linked to political and economic liberty, and that the ideal and promise of liberty has been most fully achieved through the values and institutions of democratic government.

No nation can identify itself with the Kingdom of God, nor can any modern nation-state claim to be God's chosen nation. Moreover, no political or economic system can be equated with God's Kingdom. However, as noted in Chapter One, the Framers of the American nation saw their work as historically unprecedented, nothing less than a new order of the ages. Abraham Lincoln defined the United States as an "almost chosen nation" and thus "the last great hope of mankind." It is easy, as many have done, to dismiss such beliefs as reflections of nationalistic hubris, especially since such beliefs have been used at times to justify policies not in accord with the nation's founding ideals.

On the other hand, the larger and more important reality is that this belief in American exceptionalism is grounded in an important truth about the United States: Prior to the American experiment in democratic government, political tyranny was the norm of human existence. With the birth of the American government, the ideal of freedom—a freedom rooted in an acknowledgment of the inalienable nature of human rights, the rule of law, limited government, and representative government—became a real historical possibility for mankind.

For most of its history, despite its flaws, the United States has stood as a beacon showing the rest of the world what is possible in human government.[7] America still stands as an example to the rest of the world, but unlike the late eighteenth and nineteenth centuries, the United States is no longer the world's only embodiment of the democratic ideal. America's role in the world, therefore, has been transformed in recent American history from that of symbolic example to that of symbol *and* leader of the Free World. This has been a role which, because of its historic isolationist inclinations, the United States has accepted reluctant-ly. In this role as leader of the Free World, the United States has been, on balance, a force for good in the world.

What if the United States had not assumed responsibility for keeping alive the promise of democracy? Very simply, the power of America gave many countries the opportunity to avoid tyranny. American power, by which we mean the United States' ability to influence events politically, economically, and militarily, checked tyranny while creating the political and economic conditions for growing (and unprecedented) international stability and prosperity. Like other great powers throughout history, the United States exercised its power to carry forth its national purposes. What distinguished the United States from other great powers in history was not the nature of American power, but rather the nature of American *purpose*. United States power was wed to the democratic proposition (namely, the idea that freedom can triumph over tyranny).

At times this democratic purpose has been betrayed. At times it has been made subservient to more selfish purposes. This is not surprising. All nations are communities of fallen men and women prone to sinful egotism. What is unique about the American experience is that in spite of periodic blind spots and wrong turns, the history of United States' involvement in the world has centered on defending an idea—the idea of freedom—against tyranny of any kind.

The world historical tide has recently begun to flow in the direction of increasing freedom, but this trend is by no means fixed. The forces threatening freedom, and by extension international peace and prosperity, are as alive today as at any time during the twentieth century. Therefore, the challenges facing United States foreign policy are as real and as important as they have ever been. The world has changed since the United States first assumed global responsibility for the preservation and perpetuation of the democratic idea nearly fifty years ago. What has not changed is the need for a strong, purposeful, and assertive role for the United States in international affairs.

HOW THE UNITED STATES ASSUMED LEADERSHIP

To understand the need for that strong role, we might return briefly to the morning of February 24, 1947. On that date, the course of history changed. On that date, the British Ambassador to the United States informed U.S. Secretary of State George C. Marshall that Great Britain could no longer support Turkey and Greece in their struggle against Soviet-sponsored aggression. The British ambassador made it clear that the British hoped the United States would assume the burden of aiding those two countries. Nearly three weeks after receiving the British request, President Truman stood before the Congress on March 12 and stated "that it must be the policy of the United States to support free peoples who are resisting attempted subjugation by armed minorities or outside pressure." As a result of this speech, Congress appropriated 400 million dollars to aid the Greek and Turkish governments and authorized the use of American personnel to supervise the distribution of American aid.

Even more importantly, the "Truman Doctrine" speech marked the beginning of a new era of American leadership in the world. The *New York Times* editorialized two days after Truman's speech that "The epoch of [American] isolation and occasional intervention is ended. It is being replaced by an epoch of American responsibility."[8] This was not a role the United States wanted, nor was it one the United States saw itself playing even a couple of years before.

It is true that the United States emerged from the Second World War the strongest nation in the world. Unlike Europe and Japan which lay in ruins, the United States' economy thrived during the war years. By the war's end, unemployment stood at just 1 percent of the labor force, while the total size of the U.S. economy more than doubled from 1939 to 1946.[9] Moreover, by August 1945, the United States had over fourteen million men and women under arms and was the only nation to possess the atomic bomb. The United States was at war's end arguably the world's first superpower.

The United States did not act, however, like a traditional great power. Even before the United States formally entered the Second World War, President Roosevelt was determined that the mistakes of World War I not be repeated. He was convinced as early as August 1941, when he signed the Atlantic Charter with British Prime Minister Winston Churchill, that the Second World War was the product of the failure of the peace treaty which had ended the First World War. Specifically, President Roosevelt believed, as did many other Americans, that the victor's peace imposed upon Germany in 1919 and the failure of the United States to join the League of Nations had headed the world toward another world war. Consequently, the idea of a United Nations, giving institutional expression to the idea of multilateral cooperation among the nations of the world, became a priority for Franklin Roosevelt throughout the years of the Second World War.

By the time of his death in April 1945, Roosevelt believed that his vision for a new era in global cooperation would shortly become a reality. Defeat of the Axis powers was imminent. The United States and the Soviet Union, the only countries capable of vying for hegemony after the war, were allies. After meeting with Soviet leader Josef Stalin several times during the war, President Roosevelt believed he had won Stalin's friendship and respect. At wartime conferences in Teheran and Yalta, the Big Three—Roosevelt, Stalin, and Churchill—laid plans for a new era in international relations. At home in the United States, Stalin was now "Uncle Joe," a trusted ally soon to be a friend and helper in the construction of a new world order.[10]

Roosevelt was convinced that the wartime alliance between the United States and the Soviet Union would survive the end of the war. Within a few months after his death, however, that alliance began to unravel as the Soviet Union balked on its wartime promises and began to consolidate its control over the nations of Eastern Europe. In the two years after 1945, Stalin began to pursue a relentless plan of Soviet expansion from Eastern Europe to the Baltic, to Iran, and to Greece and Turkey. With President Truman at his side, Winston Churchill addressed a group of college students in Fulton, Missouri in March 1946 and concluded that "an iron curtain has descended across the Continent" of Europe. The Cold War had begun.

ROOTS OF THE COLD WAR

The origins or causes of the Cold War have been the subject of intense study by historians. During the 1960s, it became fashionable in certain segments of the American intellectual community to blame the United States. While there were variations of this argument, the most common was that American policymakers fabricated the myth of Soviet expansionism in order to justify the United States' own goal of world domination.[11] This argument, with its Neo-Marxist assumptions, was popularized by the New Left in the 1960s. It is still embraced by those committed to the ideological agenda of the New Left, especially many within the American religious community.[12] The American historical community, however, has by and large dismissed the New Left interpretation of the origins of the Cold War as bad history and questionable scholarship.[13]

At root, the world after 1945 has been shaped by one dominant reality—the conflict between two mutually exclusive ideologies: democratic capitalism and Marxism-Leninism. The United States decided in the aftermath of World War II to forsake its isolationist tradition and lead the Free World in withstanding the tyranny of Marxism-Leninism. That has been *the* motivating objective of American foreign policy for the entire post-War period. Out of the ashes of the Second World War was born a new world—not one with the peaceful international cooperation Franklin Roosevelt had envisioned, but one torn along ideological lines.

THE COLD WAR HEATS UP

After 1945, "East" and "West" became synonymous with the struggle between fundamentally antagonistic worldviews. In the Soviet Union the historic expansionistic goals of the pre-Bolshevik Russian empire were legitimized by the eschatological vision of Marxism-Leninism.[14] The Soviet Union, defining itself as the vanguard movement of a worldwide revolution, began a relentless conquest of territories contiguous to its border. The United States, thrust into the unfamiliar position of global leadership, was unprepared for the threat posed by an ideologically-driven adversary bent on world domination. After numerous twists and turns, President Truman accepted the policy recommendation of a career Foreign Service Officer, George F. Kennan.

By the start of World War II, Kennan had a reputation as the United States' most knowledgeable expert on the Soviet Union. Because of his background, Kennan was assigned to the United States Embassy in Moscow, where in 1946 he dictated a telegram to the State Department spelling out his understanding of "the sources of Soviet conduct." Kennan's telegram, published under the pseudonym X in the influential journal *Foreign Affairs*, quickly became the single most authoritative analysis of Soviet intentions.

According to Kennan, the Soviet Union was driven by three factors: traditional Russian foreign policy objectives, the ideology of Marxism-Leninism, and the irrationality of its leader, Stalin. These three factors, Kennan argued, were inextricably intertwined, producing a volatile mix. The fusion of Russia's autocratic tradition with a secular ideology committed to the inexorable triumph of communism provided the Soviet Union with its justification for global expansion. In other words, expansionism was an inherent element of Soviet foreign policy. Because of this, Kennan proposed that U.S. foreign policy emphasize "a long-term, patient but firm and vigilant containment of Russian expansive tendencies."

American policymakers accepted Kennan's analysis and advice. The primary objective of American foreign policy became the containment of Soviet expansionism. During the late 1940s and throughout the 1950s, this policy brought the United States into direct confrontation with the Soviet Union in Berlin, Korea, the Middle East, and Eastern Europe as Stalin and his successor, Nikita Khrushchev, pressed on with their expansionistic global agenda. In 1962, Soviet designs on the Western Hemisphere brought the United States and the Soviet Union to the brink of actual war over the placement of Soviet nuclear missiles in Cuba.

Many historians see the 1962 Cuban missile crisis as the zenith of the Cold War, the ultimate test of the U.S. containment policy. In President Kennedy, Khrushchev believed he was confronting an inexperienced, weak leader who lacked the resolve to respond to a strong, aggressive Soviet move in the Western Hemisphere. Khrushchev was so sure of his ability to bully Kennedy that he was apparently willing to risk nuclear war to achieve a major Soviet victory. Subsequent events proved that Khrushchev's perceptions were far off the mark.

But who "won" the Cuban crisis? It has become something of an orthodoxy to conclude that the United States gained the most from President Kennedy's firm stand against the Soviets. Accordingly, it is sometimes believed, Khrushchev and the Soviet Union learned an important lesson about the willingness of the

United States to pay any price to contain the spread of communism. Hence, after 1962 Soviet global ambitions were muted.

The facts, however, do not support this interpretation. In one sense, the United States did "win" the missile crisis—the nuclear missiles were withdrawn. On the other hand, as part of the deal which led to the withdrawal of the Soviet missiles, the United States agreed not to attack or invade Cuba. A good case can be made that this was, in fact, one of the major objectives of Soviet policy from the start. In 1962 the Soviets had an interest in consolidating the success of Fidel Castro's Communist revolution. The placement of Soviet missiles alongside a large Soviet military presence on the island-nation was one way of guaranteeing that communism would not disappear from Cuba. Forced to withdraw the missiles because of an overwhelming U.S. military advantage, the Soviets shrewdly negotiated an agreement that gave them in treaty form what they could not coerce; namely, an American promise to accept the Communist status quo in Cuba.

Moreover, the missile crisis taught the Soviet Union an important lesson about the relationship between political power and military power. President Kennedy's threat to retaliate against the Soviet Union was made credible by the conventional and nuclear military superiority that the United States enjoyed. For the very reason that Soviet leaders did not have adequate military power, they were not able to carry forth on their political—i.e., foreign policy—goals. The almost geometrical growth in Soviet military nuclear and conventional capabilities in the seventeen years following the Cuban missile crisis strongly suggests that the Soviets were determined after 1962 never again to be caught in a position of military inferiority vis-a-vis the United States.[15] Thus, rather than 1962 marking the beginning of the end of the Cold War, the Cuban missile crisis signaled an intensification of the Soviet commitment to global expansion.

The period from 1962 to 1979 saw a dramatic growth in Soviet power around the world. In addition to possessing the largest conventional military force in the world, by the late 1970s the Soviets possessed the world's most powerful nuclear arsenal. This growth in military strength was coupled by increasing Soviet aggressiveness around the globe.

After a brief warming of relations associated with President Nixon's policy of detente in the early 1970s, Soviet foreign policy became bolder during the Carter years.[16] Seventeen years after the Cuban missile crisis, the Soviet Union aggressively expanded its influence to Angola, Ethiopia, Mozambique, Vietnam, Afghanistan, and Nicaragua. During these years, containment still stood as the centerpiece of American foreign policy. However, for a variety of reasons, including a Vietnam-induced reticence to use military power and a general wariness of global responsibility, the United States stood nearly immobile while the Soviet Union, under Leonid Brezhnev, extended its influence in Africa, Asia, the Middle East, and Central America.

THE REAGAN RESPONSE

The election of Ronald Reagan in 1980 represented a turning point in U.S.-Soviet relations. A major theme of the Reagan campaign was a promise to make America strong again. In particular, Reagan ran against policies of Jimmy Carter that had led to a retrenchment of American influence while the Soviet Union continued to score one foreign policy victory after another.[17] Referring to the Soviet Union as an "evil empire," Reagan pledged a return to a forceful American containment of Soviet expansionism. "If history teaches us anything," President Reagan stated in 1982,

> it teaches that self-delusion in the face of unpleasant facts is folly. We see around us today marks of our terrible dilemma—predictions of doomsday, anti-nuclear demonstrations, an arms race in which the West must for its own protection be an unwilling participant. At the same time, we see totalitarian forces in the world who seek subversion and conflict around the globe to further their barbarous assault on the human spirit.[18]

In light of this continuing threat, Reagan believed that the overarching objective of U.S. foreign policy must be "to preserve freedom as well as peace."

There were two key elements to the Reagan foreign policy. First, during the eight years of the Reagan Administration, over $2 trillion was spent on strengthening American military capabilities. In building a stronger military, President Reagan intended to make the U.S. conventional and nuclear forces a more credible deterrent. The Reagan Administration understood, as recent administrations had not, that the United States' political influence in the world was ultimately dependent on its relative military position vis-a-vis the Soviet Union.

In addition to strengthening the military, President Reagan demonstrated that the United States was willing to use force if American interests were threatened. Although the American invasion of Grenada in 1983 and the 1986 bombing raid against Libya were relatively minor military missions, they were important for symbolic reasons. In both instances President Reagan demonstrated his determination to cast off the so-called "lessons" of Vietnam (specifically the notion—so prominent in the Carter years—that American military power was useless). In using military force, even in such a minor way, President Reagan wanted to make a statement to the Soviet Union and the world that the Vietnam experience had *not* reduced the United States to a pitiful giant.

The second element of the Reagan foreign policy can be viewed as President Reagan's own unique contribution to post-World War II American foreign policy. The first element of the Reagan foreign policy—revitalizing American military strength—was designed to improve the United States' ability to contain Soviet expansionism. The second element took American foreign policy beyond containment only. Democracy, President Reagan emphasized early in his administration, "needs cultivation." While containment was a necessary element of American foreign policy, it was not a sufficient basis for it:

> If the rest of this century is to witness the gradual growth of freedom and democratic ideals, *we must take actions to assist the campaign for democracy*. . . . While we must be cautious about forcing the pace of change, we must not hesitate to declare our ultimate objective and to take concrete actions to move toward them. We must be staunch in our conviction that freedom is not the sole prerogative of a lucky few but the inalienable and universal right of all human beings.[19] (emphasis added)

In other words, the Reagan Administration believed that an aggressive policy of containing Soviet expansion must be supplemented by direct American support for democratic movements throughout the world. This policy, which became known as the "Reagan Doctrine," was grounded in the principle that peace and justice are the products of freedom, and that lasting global peace will only result from the growth of democratic values and institutions.

Through direct aid and through quasi-governmental initiatives such as the National Endowment for Democracy, the Reagan Administration supported democratic political parties, newspapers, and labor movements in Chile, Argentina, Poland, South Africa, the Philippines, and elsewhere. The Reagan Doctrine was also the basis for American military support of the Nicaraguan *contras* and the Afghan *mujahadeen* in their struggles against Soviet-supported communism. Overall, despite some foreign policy failures (such as the Iran-*contra* fiasco), the Reagan presidency saw:

(1) Restoration of American confidence, an intangible but essential ingredient for a strong America and an effective foreign policy;

(2) eradication of the military imbalance that contributed to the diminishing of American influence in the world;

(3) increasing cohesion among the United States' NATO allies, a direct result of the growth of American confidence and resolve;

(4) diminution of Libyan-sponsored terrorism as a result of direct military action against Colonel Qaddafi;

(5) maturation of democratic values and institutions in South Korea, Taiwan, and elsewhere;

(6) the birth of democratic institutions in Argentina, El Salvador, the Philippines, and elsewhere;

(7) an agreement to withdraw Cuban troops from Angola and to settle peacefully the twenty-year-old Namibian crisis;

(8) the withdrawal of Soviet troops from Afghanistan, an historically unprecedented retreat for the Soviet Union;

(9) the first real nuclear arms reduction since the dawn of the nuclear age;

(10) the demise of Soviet socialism as a viable political and economic movement.

Of all the positive changes during the Reagan years, the last may be the most important. Ronald Reagan entered the White House an outspoken foe of a bold, arrogant, expansive Soviet Union. Eight years later the Soviet Union, according to its own admission, lay in virtual shambles. In the words of one noted student of the Soviet Union, "the most dramatic political experiment of the century is collapsing before our eyes—slowly, but certainly."[20] What this means for the United States and for freedom in the world is wrapped up in the enigma of Mikhail Gorbachev.

THE GORBACHEV RIDDLE

Recent changes and trends in the Soviet Union are so dramatic that there is widespread speculation that the Soviet Union may be evolving into a more democratic and thus less threatening nation. "The news from the Soviet Union," states Robert Kaiser, "is enthralling."[21] There is even talk, for the first time in the post-World War II period, of an end to the Cold War. The victory of democratic capitalism over Soviet communism is "within sight," observes one astute observer of U.S.-Soviet relations; "the ideological war has been won."[22]

These observations are the result of changes that have taken place in the Soviet Union under the leadership of Mikhail Gorbachev. Words and ideas such as *glasnost*, *perestroika*, and "new thinking" have become closely associated with the style and substance of Gorbachev's rule in the Soviet Union. But are the Soviet changes really historically unprecedented? Is Gorbachev a different kind of Soviet leader? What are the sources of Gorbachev's reforms, and what are his goals? Can Gorbachev be trusted? Are his policies something the United States should encourage and even support? Is communism dead? Is the world on the verge of a new historical era of global peace?

One more quick historical overview will help suggest answers to these questions. After Stalin's death in 1953, the Soviet Union was led by Nikita Khrushchev, who ruled until 1964. After Khrushchev's "retirement," Leonid Brezhnev governed, until his death in 1982. While both Khrushchev and Brezhnev ruled in less overtly terroristic ways than Stalin, they were still ruthless dictators committed to policies of Stalin that had governed Soviet economic and political life since the mid-1920s.

In 1956 Khrushchev stunned the Soviet Communist Party and the world by denouncing atrocities that Stalin had committed against Party members during his nearly three-decade rule of the Soviet Union. Khrushchev even went so far as to initiate a program of de-Stalinization. History books were rewritten, and Stalin's name—and thus his memory and legacy—was removed from the official Party encyclopedia. Khrushchev's de-Stalinization program was significant; yet, Khrushchev's gripe with Stalin was personal, not ideological. Khrushchev attacked Stalin precisely because Stalin had nearly destroyed the Communist Party in order to consolidate his own total control of the Soviet Union. Khrushchev's famous 1956 speech lamented the death of hundreds of thousands of Party members, not the millions of non-Party members who were murdered in order to bring about Stalin's vision of socialism.

Neither Khrushchev nor Brezhnev ever repudiated the Stalinist economic and political system which they inherited—a brutal, dictatorial system of total Party control over political and economic decision-making.

In the realm of foreign policy, Khrushchev and Brezhnev continued the Stalinist goal of expanding Soviet influence around the world. As did Stalin before them, both leaders saw Soviet foreign policy as the revolutionary vehicle through which the struggle against capitalism would be carried out. However, deferring to the realities of the nuclear age, both resurrected the old Leninist idea of "peaceful coexistence"—the belief that Soviet expansion would occur without direct armed conflict with the United States. For Khrushchev and Brezhnev, foreign policy was a tool of their Marxist-Leninist ideology. The triumph of communism and the defeat of capitalism was inevitable. Soviet expansion was a necessary element in the eventual worldwide triumph of communism. Peaceful coexistence was a strategy of victory without nuclear war.[23]

In the years immediately preceding Brezhnev's death, it became increasingly clear that the Stalinist system had created economic and political problems of such magnitude that the Soviet Union's status as a world superpower was jeopardized. In particular, the Soviet economy, which serves as the engine driving Soviet political and military goals, was stagnant and backward, while the Soviet political apparatus, dominated by the Communist Party, was corrupt and moribund. During the 1970s, while still a Party leader at the provincial level, Mikhail Gorbachev began to believe that change was needed if the Soviet Union was to remain domestically and internationally strong.[24] Just as importantly, Gorbachev saw economic and political reform as a necessary component of revitalizing Soviet Marxism-Leninism. Sovietologist Thane Gustafson points out in this regard that "Gorbachev himself is a true believer in Marxism-Leninism, determined to revive faith and pride in a just, cleansed, and modernized socialism."[25]

However, early on Gorbachev did not publicly challenge the Stalinist basis of Soviet life. To have done so would have meant almost certain political suicide.[26] Working his way up the Party organizational ladder, Gorbachev became a member of the elite Party Secretariat in 1978 and, following the deaths of Brezhnev's two successors, Yuri Andropov and Konstantin Chernenko, became General Secretary of the Soviet Union in March 1985. Because of the political risks, Gorbachev was slow to criticize the growing failures of the Soviet system. When he assumed leadership of the Soviet Union, he spoke initially of the need to "accelerate" (*uskoreniye*) the development of the Soviet economy. During these initial days, Gorbachev's criticisms were nuanced and oblique. As he consolidated his own political position within the Party, he began to become more forthright. By 1987 the terms *perestroika* and *glasnost* summarized the Gorbachev agenda.

The Soviet Union, Gorbachev stressed, was in crisis. Soviet life was characterized by "a condition of stagnation and somnolence, threatening society with ossification and social corrosion."[27] Social problems, like diseases, have to be cured, Gorbachev stated: "If you drive a disease into an organism's depths, the disease only worsens." The solution to the Soviet disease, or social crisis, required not "partial improvements," but "radical reform"—a restructuring (*perestroika*) or transformation of all of Soviet society—"not only the economy but . . . social relations, the political system, the spiritual and ideological sphere." Moreover, Gorbachev has made it clear that such a radical restructuring of society can only take place in an atmosphere of openness (*glasnost*): "It is necessary that everywhere things be arranged so that the people who are searching, creative, and in the vanguard of restructuring breathe more easily, work more fruitfully, and live better."

The failures of the Soviet economic system of which Gorbachev speaks and which he is attempting to address are monumental. Seventy years after the revolution that brought the Soviets to power, meat and butter are rationed in much of the Soviet Union.[28] Twenty percent of the Soviet urban population continues to live in communal apartments in which whole families live in just one room and share kitchen and bathroom facilities with other families. Living standards of the average Soviet citizen have fallen below those of the citizens of neighboring Communist countries. Half of the elementary and high schools in the Soviet Union are not heated and do not even have electricity or indoor sewage systems. Labor productivity and technological knowledge is rapidly falling below that of the West, while, according to Gorbachev himself, Soviet national income has not grown at all in the past twenty years. To make matters worse, life expectancy in the Soviet Union was until very recently falling. Infant mortality rates, on the other hand, have been rising. In 1988, the Soviet Union ranked only 32nd in the world in life expectancy and was 50th in infant mortality.

Gorbachev's call for *perestroika* or a restructuring of Soviet life is an historically unprecedented admission by a Soviet leader that the Stalinist system itself brought about the current crisis. The outward signs of crisis, however, are only symptomatic of a deep-seated pathology which pervades all of Soviet life. It, too, is the product of the Stalinist system, and its effects, as Gorbachev understands, have the potential to destroy Soviet society, and thus even the future of Marxism-Leninism.

In other words, the root problem confronting the Soviet Union is not susceptible to a quick fix. "We are like a seriously ill man," quips a Soviet economist, "who after a long time in bed, takes his first step with the greatest difficulty and finds, to his horror, that he has almost forgotten how to walk."[29] As several other Communist and non-Marxist Socialist countries have come to see, communism destroys any sense of initiative and responsibility and eventually produces a fatalistic citizenry completely dependent on the capricious and frequently brutal power of the state.

It is interesting in this regard that while Gorbachev's call for increased openness or *glasnost* has been warmly received by Soviet intellectuals, there is little evidence of overwhelming enthusiasm for his reforms among the common people, even the young.[30] It is instructive, as well as sobering, that as Gorbachev presses ahead with his reform, there is a growing nostalgia among Soviet citizens for Stalin and his way of doing things.[31]

There are many sound reasons, therefore, for pessimism about the ability of Mikhail Gorbachev to effect the kinds of fundamental changes needed to truly transform Soviet society. Apart from the obstacles associated with the Stalinist legacy itself, Gorbachev's reforms are opposed by powerful leaders within the Communist Party who have much to lose personally if *perestroika* is eventually successful. Whether or not Gorbachev succeeds in the long run—and his reforms can only be accomplished, if at all, in the distant future—many believe that Gorbachev's personal style and policies have no precedent in the history of the Soviet regime. Gorbachev is an original; in temperament and philosophy, he is not in the same mold as his predecessors. Very simply, he is different and—relative to what has come before him—he is remarkable.

The reality is that heretofore unimaginable things have been taking place in the Soviet Union since Gorbachev embarked on his *perestroika* and *glasnost*. Dissidents and intellectuals, such as Andrei Sakharov, have been given unheard-of freedom to criticize the Soviet system and even the Communist Party itself. National groups such as the Estonians have been allowed to proclaim openly their yearnings for national autonomy. For the first time since the Cold War began, Soviet officials are allowing Radio Free Europe and other Western radio networks to be broadcast without interference. The crimes and corruption of some Party leaders are being publicly exposed with an honesty that before 1985 would have been unthinkable. American journalists have been allowed to visit labor camps. American military planes regularly make verification flights over Soviet military installations unaccompanied by Soviet officials. Indeed, Gorbachev's *glasnost* has brought extraordinary changes to the nation of Lenin, Stalin, Khrushchev, and Brezhnev.

All of this is true. The fact that Gorbachev is different and that he is attempting to bring about unprecedented change to the Soviet Union cannot be denied, nor should its implications be underestimated. But having acknowledged this, the more essential question is, What does it all mean? We know that Gorbachev wants to restructure the Soviet Union, but to what end? Without a doubt, *perestroika* and *glasnost* are intended to economically strengthen the Soviet Union and to reinvigorate its citizens. It is less certain, however, what Gorbachev's ultimate objectives are as they relate to the Soviet Union's relationship to the rest of the world.

Throughout its history, Soviet foreign policy has been motivated by Marxist-Leninist ideology and its axiomatic belief in the inevitable global triumph of socialism over capitalism. Some in the West suggest, citing statements by Soviet officials, that this has all changed. Mikhail Gorbachev has spoken of a "new thinking" that animates Soviet foreign relations. In June 1987, Soviet Foreign Minister Eduard Shevardnadze defined the contours of this "new thinking" when he explained that "the main thing is that [the Soviet Union] not incur additional expenses in connection with the need to maintain its *defensive* capacity and protect its *legitimate* foreign policy interests"[32] (emphasis added).

Recent signs might signal an historic move away from an expansionistic Soviet foreign policy. The Soviet decision to withdraw from Afghanistan, for example, as well as Gorbachev's pledge made before the United Nations to reduce the Soviet military by 500,000 troops and to remove 10,000 battle tanks from Eastern Europe, are unprecedented retrenchments for the Soviet Union. Gorbachev, with his personal charisma and flair for the dramatic, has made the most of these announcements, suggesting that the "new thinking" portends a friendlier Soviet Union, one the West need not fear.

The Western press and Western leaders have generally responded favorably to Gorbachev and have hailed his promises as presaging a new dawn in international relations. West German Foreign Minister Hans Dietrich Genscher has praised Gorbachev for creating the promise of a peaceful, prosperous, and common European culture from the Atlantic Ocean to the Ural Mountains. In his enthusiasm for Gorbachev, Genscher has stated that Western Europe and the United States has an "historical duty" to help Gorbachev achieve his goals.[33]

Genscher may be more enthusiastic than his counterparts throughout Western Europe and the United States, but many do believe that Gorbachev and his reforms need to be encouraged. Optimism about the birth of a new Soviet Union is reflected in the increased willingness of Western business firms and financial institutions to do business with the Soviet Union.[34] From 1982 to 1984, Western banks loaned the Soviet Union a little more than $2 billion. After Gorbachev assumed power and introduced his reforms, Western bank loans increased to almost $9 billion for the years 1985–1987.[35]

The prevailing wisdom in the West is most likely on target in assuming that Gorbachev is interested in paring back Soviet international commitments out of need to shore things up at home. Soviet overseas commitments have become financially costly, inefficient, and—as the Soviet Afghanistan experience demonstrates—politically unpopular at home. It is estimated, for example, that with an economy half the size of the United States, the Soviet Union spends as much as 20 percent—compared to 6 percent for the United States—of its Gross National Product on the military. Unlike his predecessors, Gorbachev understands that the Soviet Union cannot have all the guns it wants *and* all the butter it wants. The future of the Soviet Union depends on its ability to restart its dying domestic society. Hence, for the first time in the post-Stalin era, domestic interests are taking priority over international interests. Gorbachev's chief preoccupation is to galvanize a moribund economy and mobilize an apathetic and fatalistic public.[36]

This much we can be reasonably sure of. It is, however, premature to conclude that the Soviet Union is no longer a threat to freedom and world peace. In fact, *nothing that Gorbachev has said or done conclusively suggests that the leadership of the Soviet Union has turned away from the historical goals of Marxism-Leninism.* Gorbachev's talk of peace has yet to be matched by a commensurate commitment to scale back dramatically the size and offensive configuration of Soviet military forces. One critic of Gorbachev has equipped that "*glasnost* and *perestroika* have certainly resulted in disarmament—but of the U.S., not of the Soviet Union."[37] Yes, Gorbachev has committed to reduce the size of the Soviet military by half a million troops while reducing the number of Soviet tanks in eastern Europe by

10,000. But even with a reduction of 500,000 troops, the Soviet armed forces are far and away the largest and best-equipped in the world.

A respected U.S. analyst of Soviet military forces has concluded that "no state in the world rivals the U.S.S.R. in its combination of size, sophistication, and command and control of military forces."[38] Soviet ground forces include more than two hundred divisions consisting of over five million troops and fifty-five million reservists. The Soviets have more than 50,000 tanks, 48,000 pieces of artillery, and 4,500 helicopters.[39] The Soviet air force includes nearly 5,000 aircraft. The Soviet air defense system has another 2,000 defensive aircraft, in addition to 10,000 early warning systems and 9,000 surface-to-air missiles. The Soviet navy has nearly 400 submarines and over 250 surface ships, with an additional component of nearly 400 bombers and 200 fighter aircraft. The total Soviet strategic nuclear force—including ICBMs, intermediate and mid-range missiles, submarine-launched ballistic missiles, and bombers—is over 4,000. In every major category of weapons and personnel, Soviet forces far outnumber those of the United States.

Viewed from another perspective, from 1978 to 1988 the Soviet Union produced 25,300 battle tanks compared to the U.S.'s 7,600. In the single year 1988—during the height of Gorbachev's "new thinking"—the United States produced 600 tanks to the Soviet Union's 2,500. The same disparities are evident with respect to artillery pieces, fighter planes, and nuclear-capable rocket launchers. The Soviet Union also has come a long way in the overall *quality* of its forces. The Soviet officer corps is highly educated. The technical quality of Soviet weapons is as good or better than that produced by the United States.[40] In short, for all of his talk of disarmament and peace, the Soviet military capability is stronger under Gorbachev than it has been at any time in Soviet history. Parts of the Soviet military under Gorbachev are leaner, but perhaps meaner.

As noted earlier, military power has both military utility as well as political utility. Military force does not actually have to be used to give political advantage. The mere existence of a credibly strong military force translates into the ability to influence political outcomes.

Gorbachev apparently understands this dynamic relationship between military strength and political influence. Gorbachev's response to the Afghanistan imbroglio suggests that the Soviets will not, at least in the short term, pursue a policy of bold military expansion. At the same time, his rhetoric aside, Gorbachev's actions in building a *more* powerful Soviet military machine provides compelling evidence that he is not willing to give up the Soviet Union's status as a global power.

Hence, *perestroika* and *glasnost* ultimately represent a strategy for reinvigorating a moribund Marxist-Leninist empire. In our weariness from standing vigilant against Soviet expansion during the past half-century, we must guard against wishful thinking which distorts our ability to read Soviet intentions accurately. To the extent that Gorbachev is a rational leader who understands the dangers of pursuing reckless adventures, his reforms should be welcomed, and even encouraged. But we must never lose sight of the fact that Gorbachev's reforms are meant to strengthen, not weaken, the Soviet Union.

THE FUTURE OF TYRANNY

It is premature and dangerous to pronounce the death of the Cold War. The past decade has witnessed a positive change in the nature of U.S.–Soviet relations. Chronic confrontation between the United States and the Soviet Union, which throughout the first three decades of the Cold War frequently hemorrhaged into major international crises, has been replaced by a less bellicose relationship. The vigilance of the United States in standing against Soviet expansion has paid off, confirming George Kennan's prescience in 1947 that "the United States has it in its power to increase enormously the strains under which the Soviet policy must operate, to force upon the Kremlin a far greater degree of moderation and circumspection."[41]

Recent events in the Soviet Union, as well the blossoming of the "global spring" discussed earlier, have demonstrated beyond a shadow of a doubt the superiority of the democratic idea. Recent events have also vindicated the global leadership role that the United States has played as the primary bearer of the democratic idea in the post-War era. Today, the political and economic trends in the world are more favorable than they have been at any time in this century. The United States and the forces of democracy have won the first phase of the post-War conflict against modern tyranny. In this sense, much has changed during the past decade. And yet nothing has changed, for human nature has not been transformed.

What we are witnessing, therefore, is not the end of tyranny, but the demise of a particular manifestation—or, as I refer to it above, a particular phase—of an ongoing conflict between freedom and tyranny. Tyranny is not dead, nor is the Marxist variety of tyranny dead. The threats to human freedom and dignity are greater today than they have ever been—and they are increasing, not diminishing. The central problem of international relations today, as it has been since the eighteenth century, is religious. For modern tyranny is an inevitable product of modern man's loss of the sense of transcendent reality. A Christian approach to contemporary international relations must begin with this basic truth.

PART TWO

INTERNATIONAL RELATIONS AND THE BIBLE

INTERNATIONAL POLITICS: A BIBLICAL STARTING POINT

*T*he rivalry between the United States and the Soviet Union has influenced most people's overall perception of international politics. Since the end of World War II, nearly everything that has taken place in international politics has been in some way related to the conflict between the United States and the Soviet Union. Regional conflicts (for example, the conflict between Israel and its Arab neighbors), relations with allies, involvement in international organizations such as the United Nations, economic relationships, and relations with ex-colonial nations (now called the Third World) have all been connected to the struggle between the superpowers.

Because of this, the recent changes taking place in the Soviet Union under Gorbachev have raised hopes for a new era in international politics.[1] These hopes fall along a continuum. For some, the hope is for a general lessening of tensions between the United States and the Soviet Union, providing a new basis for peaceful competition between the two countries. For others, the hope is more grand: the end of international conflict altogether. This latter hope flows from the assumption that the source of post-World War tension in international politics has been removed by reform in the Soviet Union and a less ideological, more pragmatic American approach to international affairs. Because of these events, we are poised to witness the birth of a new dawn in human relations.

This optimism about the future must, however, be challenged on two counts. First, there is a human tendency to want to see our current activities as new, unique, and better than the old. The sense of euphoria that has lately overspread much of the West about a new dawn of peace actually represents something very old. Throughout history, there have been other periods when men believed they stood on the verge of a new and better world. Earlier in this century, for example, Woodrow Wilson believed that his Fourteen Points would build the foundations of a new world order.

The second observation, related to the first, is that the current euphoria, like other euphorias of the past two centuries, is a manifestation of an eighteenth-century Enlightenment notion. That notion, so pervasive and destructive in its influence in the West, asserts that human beings through their *own* actions (apart from God) are capable of bringing about unlimited progress. This Enlightenment lie becomes especially pernicious whenever it is coupled with the belief that "the present moment" is an opening to a new Eden. That is wrong thinking, for while much has changed for the good throughout the centuries, the undeniable constant has been the inherent evil of human nature. To argue otherwise is to deny what both history and God's Word teach us. The central problem of international politics, therefore, is what it has always been: the nature of man himself.

SIN AND HUMAN NATURE

Tyranny is an inevitable by-product of human nature—that is, of man's sin. Selfishness, egotism, greed, lust for power, and other innate qualities of the human condition are rooted in man's rebellion against his Creator, the sovereign Lord of the universe. Man's fundamental problem, therefore, is not intellectual or rational; it has nothing to do with ignorance or lack of knowledge. Rather, man's problem is fundamentally spiritual in nature. Having rebelled against God, seeking to be like Him,[2] man's relationship to his Creator was severed, with ominous personal consequences.[3] Henceforth, an unbridgeable chasm would exist in man's relationship with God.

Moreover, the sin of the first man became the inescapable inheritance of his progeny everywhere and throughout history.[4] Only through the reconciling death and resurrection of Jesus Christ can man's vertical relationship to God be restored.[5]

The effects of sin, evident in the lives of each human being who has ever lived, also have horizontal consequences. In other words, just as man's rebellion against God ruptured man's relationship with God, so man's rebellion against God ruptured man's relationship with other human beings. All of creation bears the scar of man's sin.[6] The first manifestation of sin recorded in the Scriptures after the Fall was Cain's murder of Abel. Cain, an angry, selfish, jealous young man, chose to snuff out the life of another human being. In this brutal act we see a foreshadowing of the ongoing interpersonal consequences of man's rebellion against God.

The behavior of Cain has been repeated countless times with countless permutations throughout history. If the history of mankind demonstrates anything, it shows that the blood of Cain runs through us all. To this fact, the most brutal century in all of history—our own twentieth century—stands as a testimony. Man's propensity and ability to inflict pain and injustice on other human beings is not limited by time, geography, ethnicity, or education. This basic, elemental truth must be the starting point of any approach to international politics. Politics among nations reflects, as do all human endeavors, the effects of sin.

GOD'S COMMON GRACE

This truth, however, must be considered alongside another elemental truth, also attested to in Scripture and in history: The effects of sin are pervasive; but God, by His grace, has tempered the impact of sin on every person and on society itself. Were it not for the restraining effect of God's grace, human life would be impossible. Man's disobedience against God has made him totally depraved, incapable on his own of doing any good work. But God, through His grace, which is extended to all men—regenerate as well as unregenerate—restrains the full impact of sin and enables human beings to discern truth and do what is right.

It must be stressed that this knowledge of truth is not salvific; human beings cannot spiritually save themselves from the eternally destructive effects of sin. That is accomplished only by God's special grace through faith.[7] But this knowledge is useful in allowing human beings the *possibility* of living peacefully, decently, and justly.[8] It is in this context that God has given the institution of government to mankind as a means of orderly and just living during man's sojourn on earth.[9]

The dual reality of the pervasive nature of human sin and God's restraining grace frame a Biblical approach to international politics. Sin and its effects are an ever-present fact of human nature that cannot be wished away or worked away. Only through the blood of Jesus Christ is man reconciled to God and his sins forgiven. And only when Christ returns and establishes His eternal rule will sin be banished forever. Before that time, however, through the gift of His common grace, God has given to all human beings the wisdom and the ability to experience peace. Not the salvific peace of what Augustine called the eternal "celestial city"—that is available only to those who accept Christ as Savior and as the Lord of their lives—but a relative peace of earthly tranquillity and order. That is, because of sin, human beings cannot forge a world of perfect peace and perfect justice. But because of God's gift of common grace, human beings can forge a relatively more just and more peaceful world.

For the Christian, this is the basis of our Biblical responsibility for involvement in international politics. To be sure, God has not called every Christian to be a politician, a foreign diplomat, or a scholar of international relations. God does not expect all of us to be experts on American-Soviet relations, trade policy, or defense appropriations. Nor should we ever allow ourselves to feel guilty for our inability to solve the world's problems. At the same time, however, Christians are not to wash their hands of the affairs of the world. Having created man, God commanded him to subdue the earth and to rule over its every dimension.[10] *Everything*, says the Psalmist, has been placed by God under our feet.[11] As all of the earth is the Lord's,[12] so God is the sovereign Lord of history, and He is the Lord of every area of human life as well.[13]

Every human endeavor, whether it be education, the family, business, aesthetics, or politics, falls under the Lordship of Christ. Furthermore, God has called each and every Christian to specific tasks in life. For some, it is to preach and evangelize, for others to teach, to engage in business activity, to create works of art; yet for others, it is to be mother, father, husband, or wife. Regardless of the tasks to which God has called an individual Christian, those tasks should be entered into with one purpose—to glorify God. All that the Christian does for God's glory constitutes full-time Christian service.

CONFUSING BIBLICAL TASKS

Everything the Christian does should be informed by faith for the glory of God, but not every task has the same function or purpose. The purpose of politics is not the same purpose as the Church. Both politics and the Church (like every other sphere of human endeavor) fall under the Lordship of Christ; both perform tasks that are mandated by God. But their tasks are very different. The Church's prime responsibility is to spread the Good News of Jesus Christ to a world of sinners—to bear witness to the Heavenly Kingdom. The purpose of politics, on the other hand, is to address mankind's problems during his sojourn in the earthly kingdom. Politics is concerned with mankind's temporal well-being, while the Church is concerned with mankind's eternal well-being.[14] These two tasks are not the same, nor should they be confused.

A prominent example of confusing these tasks is found in a recent theological movement known as liberation theology. Liberation theology emerged in the early 1970s among a group of dissident Latin American Catholic priests, most notable among them Gustavo Gutierrez.[15] Since its emergence in Latin America, the influence of liberation theology has spread to North America and Europe, where its ideas have come to dominate theological thinking not only among theological liberals, but among some segments of the theologically conservative evangelical world as well.[16]

Liberation theology is a diverse movement with no one individual leader or institutional leadership. Nonetheless, there is a core set of themes which characterize what is often called the theology of liberation.[17] Liberation theology begins with the premise that all theology is biased,[18] that theology reflects the social and economic class of those who develop it. Accordingly, the traditional theology of North America and Europe is said to represent the class, race, and gender interests of those do it.[19] In other words, North American and European theology is seen as a theological system meant to perpetuate the interests of white, North American/European, capitalist males. Furthermore, liberation theologians argue, this North American/European theology supports and legitimates a political and economic system—democratic capitalism—which is responsible for exploiting and impoverishing the Third World.

Starting from the premise that traditional Christian theology is biased, and that North American and European countries are *directly* engaged in the conscious rape of the Third World, the theology of liberation maintains that true Christian theology must arise from the experiences of the poor in the Third World. When it does, it will inevitably reflect "a preferential option" for the poor.

Certainly traditional Christian theology would affirm the need for the Church to be concerned for the material needs of the poor. However, liberation theology goes way beyond that affirmation in constructing a theological system that is more grounded in the politics of Marx and Lenin than in the teachings of Jesus. Liberation theology actually equates Biblical salvation with political liberation.

Liberation theology understands the Biblical message as a political manifesto calling the poor to struggle, even violently, against the rich. Sin is rooted not in man's personal rebellion against God, but in exploitation by one class (the rich) against another (the poor). Thus, the heart of Christian theology is reduced to a Marxist conflict between socioeconomic classes. Biblical salvation, therefore, is defined in terms of political and economic liberation, Christ is the model political revolutionary, and revolution is the vehicle for the creation of the Kingdom of God—a classless society.

In short, liberation theology takes the story and message of Christianity and politicizes it, using a Marxist framework. The fundamental message of the Bible—man's sin, salvation through Jesus Christ, and the promise of the fulfilled Kingdom of God—is made part of a political agenda. This is not conjecture; these themes pervade the writings of liberation theologians and have been adopted in countries—particularly Nicaragua, South Africa, and the Philippines—where liberation theology has had a real political impact.[20]

The ideas of liberation theology have in recent years become more influential among American Catholics and Protestants, including (in subtle ways) some evangelicals.[21] For example, recent surveys suggest that evangelicals increasingly believe social action (i.e., addressing social ills through political action) and evangelism/discipleship are *equally* important missions for the Church.[22] A Biblical approach of Christianity would never posit that Christians avoid social involvement. And yet, this distinction is crucial: social action and evangelism are not theologically equivalent. The former is a task for the political sphere, while the latter is *the* central mission of the Church.

The politicization of Christianity represented by liberation theology constitutes a false religion, and not the faith of Paul, Augustine, Luther, and saints throughout history. Liberation theology and its variants, so influential today, deform the message of the Scripture in the interest of a secular, partisan political agenda.[23] There is no greater danger to Christian orthodoxy today than the threat posed to it by the politicization of the Christian faith. As the Dutch theologian H. M. Kuitert so powerfully reminds us: ". . . the dead are not raised by politics. There is no political route to the messianic kingdom."[24]

OTHER CHALLENGES TO BIBLICAL CHRISTIANITY

The purposes of politics and the Church cannot and should not be confused. To do so, as liberation theology illustrates, is to make earthly well-being the essence of Christianity. It needs to be stressed, however, that earthly well-being is important; hence, politics is important. The task of politics is as important as any other which God has given to man. The error comes in confusing tasks. Politics is not theology, just as theology is not politics. And yet, the Bible teaches that Christ is Lord of *all* of life. Just as it is wrong to confuse the the political task with the task of the Church, it is also wrong to view the heavenly and the spiritual as good and the earthly and the physical as evil.

This tendency to denigrate earthly endeavors is an old problem within Christianity. It originated with the influence of Platonic thought on Christian thinking. Plato believed that ideas are pure and perfect, representing the ultimate reality. Material things, on the other hand, were seen as flawed and imperfect.

Plato's philosophy was dualistic in that it postulated that the world of ideas is good, while the material world is evil. Unfortunately, some Christians fell prey to the influence of Plato in the first century when the Gnostic heresy arose, and others have been seduced since then.[25]

When Christians are taught to flee the world, and earthly pursuits such as politics are seen as "worldly," Platonic dualism is at work. This dualistic approach to Christianity (associated with what is often called Fundamentalism) is not as widespread in America as it was fifty years ago. However, there still exists a propensity among Christians to belittle earthly activities that are not directly related to "spiritual" matters such as personal evangelism.

This dualistic understanding of Christianity is at variance with the full-orbed nature of Biblical Christianity. According to God's own Word, "God saw all that he had made, *and it was very good*"[26] (emphasis added). God is the Creator and the Sustainer of the material world. Sin distorted the perfection of that which God created, but nowhere in the Scripture does God teach that sin negated the inherent goodness of His creation. Nowhere does the Bible say that the material world or man as a material being is evil. To the contrary, "the heavens declare the glory of God; the skies proclaim the work of his hands. . . . The earth is the Lord's, and everything in it; the world, and all who live in it."[27]

In summary: both Marxized Christians and Platonized Christians distort the Bible. We need to understand that the purpose of politics is earthly, while the purpose of the Church is heavenly; but the tasks of Heaven and the tasks of earth are both good. Each kingdom, H. M. Kuitert points out, "has an indissoluble value of its own. The doctrine of the two kingdoms is concerned with the two ways in which God is occupied with man and the world."[28] God has given His people two mandates for their sojourn in this world: first, to subdue or rule over God's good creation; second, to spread the gospel to all people. God has provided the cultural mandate for man's earthly well-being. He has provided the evangelical mandate for man's eternal well-being. Rather than flee this world, Biblical obedience demands that we engage it.

But how? As stated above, God calls His people to different

vocations. Moreover, God provides the possibility for earthly well-being through the tasks unique to each of these vocations. Through the nurture of the family, for example, people learn the importance of trust, honesty, caring, and social responsibility. Through education, human horizons about man and the universe are broadened. Through art, human creativity is unleashed. Through the enterprise of business, man's material needs are provided. Likewise, through the task of politics God has given man the possibility of escaping the tyranny of sin as it manifests itself in man's inclination to practice injustice toward others. None of these tasks or the vocations associated with them can transform the world or human nature. But they can and do make a difference in terms of earthly well-being.

It is for this reason that Christians should be interested in the task of politics—including international politics. Sin is the root cause of tyranny. But God's common grace allows man the possibility of checking tyranny and living peacefully, freely, and justly. Man's ability to forge a *perfect* world is thwarted by his total depravity. But God's restraining grace provides man with the capacity to build a *better* world.

Politics is a gift which God has given to man to provide for his earthly well-being. Because we are citizens of the Heavenly Kingdom, Christians know the Giver of this gift and understand its importance in God's created order. Christian faith and international politics are not antithetical. To the contrary, the Christian's engagement of international politics derives directly from our Biblically-grounded faith. The specific relationship between our Biblical faith and international politics is the subject to which we now turn.

INTERNATIONAL POLITICS: A BIBLICAL FRAMEWORK

The Closing of the American Mind has been one of the most talked-about books published in recent years.[1] In it, Allan Bloom, a professor at the University of Chicago, argues that contemporary American culture believes in only one value: relativism. The purpose of Professor Bloom's book is to warn our society of the dangers of teaching relativism. At stake, says Bloom, is the moral fabric of American society and the future of democracy.

Professor Bloom's book has been very controversial, primarily because of his call for a return to the teaching of values in American education. The hostile reaction to the book at many universities illustrates that relativism has become a value which influential segments of American society believe needs to be defended at all costs. Relativism is the core value of the religion of secular humanism.[2] And secular humanism is the religious worldview that dominates the thinking of the media, academic, legal, and cultural elites in the United States.

The general popularity of Bloom's book, however, shows that large numbers of Americans want to fight the erosion of morality that has been slowly undermining society and, ultimately, American democracy itself.[3] In sounding the alarm, Allan Bloom has done us and future generations a great service. Yet Bloom does not have a satisfactory answer to the problem which he identifies, for the crisis of American democracy is the inevitable product of God-denying humanism. Freedom, justice, and peace—the fruits of American democracy—are the inevitable product of belief in a God who sustains His creation. When that belief fades, democracy fades.

In other words, the solution to the problems which confront our nation can never be solved apart from God and the universal and absolute principles He has set forth in His Word, the Bible. The same is true for the problems that confront us in the realm of foreign policy. God's plan for His creation is found in His Word. It is through the Word of God that the Christian faith is anchored in Jesus Christ. And it is in God's Word that the Christian's engagement of international politics must be anchored as well.

SOLA SCRIPTURA

True Christianity is a Biblical religion rooted in God's special revelation of Himself in the written pages of the Old and New Testaments. Christians from the beginning of Church history have maintained that the Word of God is fully and finally authoritative in matters of faith and conduct. During the Protestant Reformation in the sixteenth century, *sola Scriptura* (or literally, "Scripture only") became the doctrine around which the Reformers rallied. The Christian is bound by no authority, no truth apart from that contained in the Bible. Apart from the Bible, Christianity would be inconceivable; indeed, apart from God's self-revelation in the Bible all of life loses its meaning and purpose.

It cannot be emphasized too strongly that the Bible is central to the Christian faith. The Bible constitutes the final reference point for all of man's thinking and acting. Attempts to water down the authority of the Scripture—as theological liberals do—comprise another form of humanism, denying the Lordship of Christ and establishing man as the subjective source of authority. We cannot serve two masters; either we will serve God or we will serve man. Obedience to Christ demands that we not be conformed to the world's way of thinking and acting, but that we rather be transformed, according to the Apostle Paul, by the renewing of our minds in order that we might accomplish

God's perfect will.[4] It is through God's revelation in His Word, in conjunction with the ministry of the Holy Spirit, that the Christian's mind is so transformed.

Christian faith, therefore, is built upon the revelation of God provided in the Holy Scriptures. What we know of God, life, and history is revealed to us there. God's revelation is a history of man's disobedience and God's redemptive work. But it is more than a factual story; it is a God-breathed account that, in Paul's words to Timothy, is "useful for teaching, rebuking, correcting and training in righteousness, so that the man of God may be thoroughly equipped *for every good work*[5]" (emphasis added).

Christians usually have little difficulty accepting the final authority of Scripture in their own personal walk with God. But what does it mean to say that the Bible is authoritative in every area of human activity? How is the Bible authoritative in the realm of American foreign policy and international politics?

WHAT THE BIBLE IS NOT

The Bible is a historical document. The events described in it, from the creation of the world in Genesis to the final consummation of the Kingdom in Revelation, are historical. That is, they have either already taken place or they will take place at some future time. Christians take the historicity of the Biblical record very seriously. All of the doctrines of the Christian faith, including man's fall, the virgin birth of Christ, and Christ's bodily resurrection from the dead, stand or fall on their historicity. Christianity is true because the events described in the Old and New Testaments really happened.

The Bible tells of God's redemptive plan in the context of the lives of real people. The Bible is replete with the full panoply of human personalities, institutions, and relationships. Moreover, the Biblical story, from the creation of the nations in Genesis 10 to the coming of the New Jerusalem in Revelation 21, is told against the backdrop of real nations and empires. The Bible teaches that God created the nations and uses them to work out His purposes in history.[6] Throughout the Old Testament, God's purposes for His chosen nation (Israel) are accomplished through the actions of other nations. The Bible also establishes that God judges the nations,[7] exalting those that honor Him and disgracing those that dishonor Him.[8]

The Biblical account of God's sovereignty over the nations is an integral part of the redemptive story of the Bible. However, these Biblical narratives are not about politics per se. The Bible is not a textbook of political science, nor is it a political manifesto. The Bible is the special revelation of God's redemptive work in history. The Bible does not speak directly to specific foreign policy issues; that is not its purpose.

Nowhere in the Bible can we find *direct* answers to the urgent foreign policy problems confronting the United States. For example, in our policy toward South Africa, should the United States follow the advice of Bishop Desmond Tutu and strengthen sanctions against his country, or should we listen to Zulu Chief Gathsa Buthelezi and abolish all sanctions? With regard to the Soviet Union, is U.S. foreign policy best served by increasing financial assistance to the Gorbachev government or by pursuing a more cautious wait-and-see policy? Should the United States press South Korea harder to improve its human rights situation, or does our goal of deterring North Korean aggression preclude such a tough stance by the United States? Should the Bush Administration push for the resumption of military aid to the Nicaraguan *contras*, or is the Arias peace plan the most likely route to democratization in that Central American nation?

On these important issues and all of the others confronting American foreign policy the Bible is silent—at least directly. It is not that the Bible is irrelevant to twentieth-century America or contemporary international politics. It is simply that the Bible is not a manual of foreign policy or of international politics, just as it is not a manual of dentistry or astrophysics. If a person wants to learn dentistry, he would not study dentistry using the Bible; if a person wants to understand the movement of the stars, he would not find a scientific discussion of astronomy in the Bible. Likewise, the answers to the pressing problems confronting American foreign policy are not explicitly spelled out in the Bible.

Theologian Henry Van Til clearly describes the relationship between God's special revelation and man's earthly tasks when he writes:

> [T]he prophet Isaiah tells us that the farmer learns to prepare his soil under the direct instruction of God (Isa. 28:24-29),

while David confesses that God teaches his hands to war (Ps. 18:34). Man does not need a special revelation for acquiring the arts of agriculture or of war, the techniques of science and art: these things are learned from nature through the inspiration of the Spirit.[9]

In those matters relating to earthly well-being, therefore, "God's gifts are not restricted to the elect but are [also] given to the children of Cain."[10]

This gift of God to His elect as well as to the children of Cain—or to the unregenerate—is God's common grace.[11] Sometimes common grace is called general revelation since it is available to all men, even unbelievers. It is, as discussed in the previous chapter, the grace which restrains the consequences of man's sin and enables human beings to have earthly well-being. This general revelation does not bring spiritual well-being; such saving grace is found only through God's special revelation. Moreover, general revelation does not stand on its own. In other words, man's ability to cultivate the soil, to understand the scientific makeup of the universe, to create objects of beauty, and to build free, just, and prosperous nations is not the result of man's inherent goodness, reasonableness, or decency. Rather, man's earthly abilities are gifts from God. General revelation, or common grace, is not independent from God, just as man himself is not autonomous. As man and the universe presuppose the existence of God, so general revelation (or common grace) presupposes special revelation.

There is, then, a relationship between the Bible and foreign policy issues. Ultimately there is no knowledge, truth, meaning, or earthly well-being apart from God. While not a textbook, God's Word does have something to say to international politics. As the Creator and the Sustainer of all that is, Christ's Lordship extends over the Heavenly Kingdom as well as the earthly kingdom. The Bible provides the Christian with three pillars upon which a Christian approach to international politics must be built. We will consider those now.

EARTHLY RESPONSIBILITY

First and fundamentally, the Bible gives us a God-given mandate for our responsibilities in the world. The Christian lives in a constant state of tension and expectation, longing for the fullness of God's Kingdom, but living in the here and now of the earthly kingdom. Christ has instructed us to occupy that earthly kingdom until He comes, knowing that *all* of our labors are not in vain.[12] Christ's promised Second Coming will bring the restoration of all things—including our physical bodies and our earthly home. Man's physical being is not evil, nor is the earth evil. They are good. They have been deformed by sin, but one day will be healed. The Creator loves His creation, and for this reason God expects His children to be caretakers of that which He created.

We must not, therefore, flee from the world. There is an old saying that some Christians are so heavenly-minded that they are no earthly good. Sadly, this is true. The earth *is* the Lord's, and as His spiritual progeny it is ours as well. A Pharisee confronted Christ out of impure motives and asked Him which was the greatest of the commandments. Jesus replied, "'Love the Lord your God with all your heart and with all your soul and with all your mind.' This is the first and greatest commandment. And the second is like it: 'Love your neighbor as yourself.'"[13] This is the essence of Biblical faith: we are to love God *and* our fellowman.

The order in which Christ stated the two great commandments is important. Because of sin, human beings are prone to self-centeredness and love of self. Hence, loving God with all that we have and are—i.e., with heart, soul, and mind—is a prerequisite to true love of neighbor. Only when we deny ourselves and understand our total dependence on Christ is genuine love for other human beings possible, and love of others is the only true basis of earthly well-being. C. S. Lewis poignantly captured this truth when he wrote: "Those who want Heaven most have served earth best. Those who love man less than God do most for man."[14] Such love, says Paul in Romans 13, is nothing less than the fulfillment of the Law.

As Christians, therefore, we derive our earthly responsibility toward the world—toward our neighbors—from our love of God, which is the core of the Christian faith. It is the faith of the Kingdom of God which motivates us to care for the earthly kingdom. On the evening of His resurrection, Christ appeared before His disciples and gave them instructions for the "meanwhile" in which we live. Christ said, "As the Father has sent me, I am sending you."[15] Christ came to seek and save those who were lost. He came to preach the Good News. But in witnessing to the salvation found in the Heavenly Kingdom, Christ showed great compassion for the well-being of those who hurt in the earthly kingdom. Indeed, in both His life and His message He demonstrated that Heaven and the earth are the Lord's.

We are to do the same, remembering that earthly well-being is not the same as eternal salvation. Political activism (or social action) is not to be confused with the Kingdom of God, nor is it a route to the Kingdom of God. We are to tend to the affairs of this world and we are to care for our neighbor *because* of our faith in and love for God.

The Scriptures make it clear that when we care for the well-being of God's creation, we show our love for Him.[16] This is not a suggestion from God; it is an unambiguous command. In the "meanwhile" in which we now live, we have one foot in the earthly kingdom and one in the heavenly. We serve only one Master, the Lord Jesus Christ. But we do so in two ways: through evangelism, and through obedience to God's cultural mandate.

Christianity is not an escapist religion. We have heavenly responsibilities as well as earthly ones. Just as it is inconsistent with Biblical teaching to equate political activism (or social action) with the Heavenly Kingdom, so it is also wrong for Christians to wash their hands of the affairs of this world.[17]

The responsibility of the Church in the affairs of this world is one of maintaining the integrity of its message and mission. The Church makes its most important contribution to earthly well-being not by taking part in partisan politics, but *by being the Church*. As such, the Church in three ways plays an important role in the affairs of this world.

(1) It witnesses to the transcendence of God, and thus the penultimate nature of politics.

(2) It teaches those Biblical principles by which we should live our lives.

(3) It acts as God's vehicle through which individual people and, as a consequence, society are ultimately transformed by Jesus Christ.

The Church's task is first and foremost a spiritual one. The Church stands as a witness to the transcendent nature of the Kingdom of God. The individual Christian's responsibility is twofold: first, to love God; and second, to love his or her neighbor. The central concern of politics is earthly well-being. Specifically, politics addresses issues concerning how people should live and to what ends they should live.

Foreign policy also deals with these latter questions, but on a different scale. For example, United States military might can be used to influence the outcome of events. Since the end of World War II, the presence of the military power of the United States has been used to prevent (or deter) Soviet aggression around the world. From time to time the United States has actually used its military power, as in the 1986 bombing raid against Libya. In both situations the United States has had a reason or purpose for using its military power. Military might is not the only source of a nation's power, however. Natural resources, the size of a nation's economy, even the value of a nation are sources of national power. In the early 1970s, Americans experienced firsthand the power of natural resources when the Arab nations embargoed oil shipments to our country. More recently, Japan's ability to influence the American economy has demonstrated the realities of economic power. But how should power be used, and to what end?

There is no escape from the use of power or the ability to influence. God created us as purposeful beings, and we accomplish our purposes through our ability to influence people and events. National power is not inherently immoral. The power that the United States possesses by virtue of its economic strength, the size of its military, its abundant natural resources, and its values is not in and of itself good or bad. The morality or immorality of American national power as it is used as an instrument of American foreign policy around the world is determined by American goals (or purposes) and the means that are used to achieve those goals. If the purposes for which American power is utilized are unjust, then American foreign policy is unjust. If the means that are used are unjust, then American foreign policy is also unjust.

To cite an example, it would be immoral for the United States to use its vast power to conquer another nation simply so it could subjugate that nation. However, the use of U.S. military power to free people subject to tyranny against their wishes would be a moral use of American power. This was exactly what happened in 1983 when the United States invaded the Caribbean island of Grenada. In the months prior to the invasion, the government of Grenada had been taken over by an avowedly Marxist revolutionary movement intent on imposing a Marxist-Leninist tyranny on the population.[18] Not only were the lives of innocent Grenadians at stake, but the presence of American medical students convinced the Reagan Administration—as well as the leaders of several other Caribbean islands—that an American military invasion could succeed in restoring democracy to that island-nation. Subsequent developments on Grenada showed that the American invasion was a success: a tyrannical government was removed, democracy was restored, and the island is prospering once again.

The Grenada invasion illustrates how power, means, and purpose relate to one another in foreign policy. American power was used to further purposes that were just and moral. Moreover, the means that were used to achieve those purposes were themselves moral. It is in the context of national purpose and the means which nations use to achieve those purposes that the Bible provides the second pillar upon which to build a Christian approach to international politics. Not only does the Bible provide the Christian with a mandate for involvement in the affairs of this world, the Bible also provides the Christian with a set of principles to guide us in establishing and assessing foreign policy goals and the means that are used to achieve those goals.

BIBLICAL PRINCIPLES AND APPLICATIONS

We noted earlier that the Bible is not a textbook of foreign policy. The Bible does, however, lay down authoritative principles that are absolute because they are God-given. This is important because while it is true that the unregenerate can distinguish right from wrong—through common grace—right and wrong derive from God. For example, while we cannot go to the Bible and point to chapter and verse that will tell us exactly what to do regarding South Africa's apartheid policy, we find in the Scripture principles which clearly teach us that God deplores racial discrimination. The Bible teaches that every man and woman is created equal in the sight of God. For one man to deny another his God-created dignity is an abomination. On this basis, apartheid is a form of tyranny which is clearly condemned in the Scripture. Christians, therefore, should be in the forefront of those who are opposed to this policy of the South African government.

In a similar vein, Christians should condemn Libya's Colonel Qaddafi because he is responsible for terrorist policies which kill and maim innocent human life, thus cheapening its value. According to God's infallible Word, every human life is sacred. Because the Scriptures teach that God abhors evil, values human life, and expects human beings to treat each other justly, Christians should condemn tyranny wherever it exists. Further, Christians should support policies which seek to build a world without tyranny.

As Christians, then, we have a crucial role to play in our nation's foreign affairs. It is our responsibility to witness to the Biblical source of those principles which should guide American foreign policy. If our nation should ever lose sight of the absolute nature of its guiding principles, tyranny will be the *inevitable* result. This is precisely what has happened in modern totalitarian societies where the meaning of justice and freedom have been relativized and perverted. The novelist George Orwell captured this problem brilliantly in his novel *Nineteen Eighty-Four*. In Orwell's totalitarian society of Oceania, history and language are given new meaning in order to serve the tyrannical interests of the state. Oceania's "Ministry of Truth" has the responsibility of giving new meaning to traditional values. In this redefinition, called "Newspeak," "War is Peace. Freedom is Slavery. Ignorance is Strength."

If the United States is to remain true to its historic principles, and if the purposes of American foreign policy are to reflect those principles, it is imperative for the Christians of America to remind our nation that those principles did not emerge out of thin air. Liberty and justice for all derive from God. Such principles are inalienable, as our Founding Fathers understood, because they are given by God. This is the *only* source of freedom and the *only* protection against tyranny. For this reason we must turn to the Scriptures to discern those God-given principles upon which earthly well-being is only possible.

AN UNDERSTANDING OF HISTORY

There is a third way in which the Bible speaks directly to international politics. In addition to authoritatively defining our responsibilities and the principles by which we carry out those responsibilities, the Bible provides us with an authoritative understanding of the purpose and destiny of history.

Every worldview has an understanding or perspective of history. The ancient Greeks, for example, believed history is cyclical—i.e., characterized by recurrent cycles of birth, maturation, and decay. Marxists believe history is inexorably marching through economic stages and will culminate in the worldwide triumph of communism. Existentialists believe history has no meaning and is going nowhere.[19]

The Christian view of history is fundamentally different from all of these, because it comes from the Bible. In the Scriptures we learn that God is the Creator and Sustainer of the universe. We also learn of man's sin, God's redemption through the death and resurrection of Christ, and the final restoration of all things in the Second Coming of Christ. History, therefore, is linear. It begins with the creation of man and moves toward the Second Coming. God is in control of history, which means that *nothing* happens in history apart from God's will.[20] Every act of history is meaningful and purposeful, because each is part of God's plan for the ultimate redemption of His creation. The Christian view of history is therefore optimistic, no matter how tragic current events might be, because God is in control.

The Christian view of history precludes any form of triumphalism such as is found in secular humanism and Marxism. Both of these worldviews believe that man, through his own work, can solve all mankind's problems and usher in an earthly utopia. The secular humanist believes this can be done through reason, education, and the power of the state, the Marxist through the revolutionary activity of the working class. But Christians know from God's Word that the restoration of all things awaits the extra-historical work of God through the Second Coming of Christ.[21] With this realization, all human activity, including foreign policy, is placed in proper, Biblical perspective.

For example, a great deal of attention has been given to the power of nuclear weapons to destroy all life on earth—what is called "omnicide." The possibility of this has led some people to the brink of despair, while other influential voices have urged mankind to sacrifice everything in the interest of one thing: the biological survival of human life.[22] This survivalism is an inevitable outgrowth of a humanistic worldview with its belief in the finality of the material world and its sole reliance on man's reason.

Survivalism is not taught in the Bible. In fact, the central message of the Bible is that man is more than a biological organism. He is in fact one who has been created in God's image. As a consequence, good and evil, right and wrong, freedom and tyranny are of ultimate significance to human life. These values, and others, define our humanness; that is, these things reflect the fact that we are created in the image of God.[23] Survivalism is un-Biblical because it denies the spiritual nature of man[24] and because it denies God's Lordship over the course of history.

As we look around our world, there is reason to be sad and concerned. Countless people suffer in innumerable ways. But as Christians, the Bible teaches us that we are never to despair. God promises to always be with us;[25] Christ promises us He will one day return.[26] These promises should be a tremendous source of encouragement as we occupy until that time. If the global problems of injustice, war, and poverty were solely up to us to resolve, there would be real reason for pessimism about the future. However, the Christian knows that we worship, in the words of Francis Schaeffer, "the God who is there." We believe in God, who assures us that our labors are not in vain; that no matter how awful things might be, He is in control. Moreover, we are a people of faith who anticipate with certainty that day when good will triumph over evil.

THE BIBLE AND PRUDENCE

Christians are a people of the Word. The Bible is our final authority, an invaluable guide for the Christian citizen as well as the Christian statesmen. This is not to say that unbelievers have no capacity for discernment when it comes to foreign policy issues. This is simply not the case. The reverse is also true: just because a person is a Christian does not guarantee that he is discerning in the realm of international politics. Martin Luther once quipped, in his own unique way, that it is better to be wooed by a wise Turk than a dumb Christian. While this is an important insight, it is also true that the unbeliever's understanding of earthly matters is incomplete. The Bible is a necessary element of a Christian approach to international politics. The Bible contains principles to guide us; and yet it does not contain specific policy recommendations. Moreover, the Bible does not tell us how to directly *translate* principles into policies.

Using the example of South Africa, the Bible does not tell us what United States foreign policy toward South Africa should be. There is little disagreement that Biblically American policy should condemn apartheid. But how? Publicly? Privately? Should the United States make the eradication of apartheid a priority foreign policy issue, or is it less important than other issues (such as American-Soviet relations)? Should the United States aggressively seek to end apartheid through undermining the current government of South Africa, or should the United States pursue a more passive policy of encouraging reform within the present status quo?

Obviously, the Bible does not provide us with specific answers to any of these questions. There is no "Biblical foreign policy" if we mean by that a foreign policy that is neatly and directly spelled out in the Bible. In recent years a oft-heard refrain from some influential segments of the evangelical world has been that Christians should formulate a *distinctively* Biblical approach to foreign policy. This notion of a Biblical third way is appealing, but Christians must resist this seduction.[27] There is nothing wrong with Christians having different points of view with respect to specific foreign policy issues. What is wrong is for Christians to claim that such positions represent *the* Biblical position.

Having said that, it is possible for Christians to advocate policies which are un-Biblical. Such policies would be those which are obviously antithetical to established Biblical principles. Christians can never, for example, be advocates of Nazi-like fascism or of Marxism-Leninism—ideologies which are anti-Christian to their very core. Similarly, it would be un-Biblical for Christians to support the indiscriminate and intentional killing of innocents or noncombatants. Christians need to be very careful that they never step over this line. Unfortunately, many Christians have crossed that line by supporting Marxist-Leninist movements and governments from Cuba to Nicaragua to Vietnam.[28]

A sad and tragic example of this problem is illustrated in the story of Armando Valladares. In the early 1960s, following Castro's Communist revolution in Cuba, Valladares, a young man in his early twenties, was arrested for his opposition to Castro—a charge that was not true. For the next two decades Valladares experienced the brutal horrors of Castro's prisons.[29] While in prison, Valladares and his fellow-inmates were often told by their captors of the visits of American religious leaders to Cuba and of the praise which those same religious leaders had for all the "good" things Castro was doing. These leaders not only praised Castro's accomplishments while on their visits to Cuba, but returned to the United States criticizing our national leaders for their harsh stance against Castro. For Valladares and the other inmates in Castro's gulag, being told of the praise of the American church leaders for Castro was worse punishment than any of the heinous physical tortures which Castro's henchmen were then inflicting regularly upon them. In Valladares' own words,

> During those years, with the purpose of forcing us to abandon our religious beliefs and to demoralize us, the Cuban Communist indoctrinators repeatedly used the statements of support for Castro's revolution made by some representatives of American Christian churches. Every time that a pamphlet was published in the United States, every time a clergyman would write an article in support of Fidel Castro's dictatorship, a translation would reach us and that was worse for the Christian political prisoners than the beatings or the hunger. While we waited for the solidarity embrace from our brothers in Christ, incomprehensibly to us, those who were embraced were our tormentors.[30]

This is a pathetic episode in the life of contemporary American Christianity. Sadly, it is not an isolated incident.[31] But it illustrates how Christians can advocate foreign policy views which clearly violate Biblical principles.

This story also illustrates that the process of translating Biblical principles into policy applications is not always easy, even for the Christian. The Church's role in international politics is to be the Church, to witness to principles contained in God's Word. As individual believers, our task is no different. We must learn to cultivate the ability to wisely apply Biblical principles to the specific issues of international politics. This ability is in fact *prudence*—the capacity to make wise and discerning decisions. Although prudence is not a monopoly of Christians, it is God-given. Shortly after Solomon became king, God approached him and told him that He would give him whatever he wanted. Solomon responded, "Now, O Lord my God, you have made your servant king in place of my father David. But I am only a little child and do not know how to carry out my duties. . . . So give your servant a discerning heart to govern your people and to distinguish between right and wrong."[32] The Lord "was pleased that Solomon had asked for this."[33] Alberto Coll, a Christian political scientist at the Naval War College, points out that prudence

has strong biblical roots in the Books of Proverbs and Ecclesiastes; in Jesus' clear differentiation between the work of the Kingdom of God, which he enjoined, and political activism, about which he was curiously indifferent; and in St. Paul's repeated acknowledgments of the special character of the political realm, in which rulers were to guide their policies, not by a literalist application of the Sermon on the Mount, but through a careful balancing of the demands of justice with the need to maintain order in a turbulent world. [In addition], the political indispensability of prudence was recognized by Augustine, by the medieval theologians who considered it the highest of the four cardinal virtues, and by Luther and Calvin.[34]

In short, prudence is a Biblically-grounded *Christian* virtue. Prudence is the process by which Biblical ideals are applied to real-world situations. Human rights policy, for example, illustrates the process of translating principles into policy. It is unlikely that any American president would resist the idea that the protection of human rights should be a priority item on the agenda of American foreign policy. Respect for the dignity and inalienable rights of all human beings is a foundational Biblical principle that Christians as well as non-Christians should embrace. However, translating this principle into an effective policy is not so easy. Here prudence plays an important role.

This point is illustrated in the human rights policy of President Jimmy Carter. When he assumed office in 1977, President Carter publicly stated that human rights would be the cornerstone of his administration's foreign policy. Carter proclaimed that America's tradition as a free, Christian nation demanded that human rights receive top priority.[35] As Carter discovered, however, affirming the principle is not the same thing as achieving it. In South Korea, for example, Carter was forced to moderate his human rights policy because the United States had other interests there (specifically, the protection of South Korea from North Korean aggression). This foreign policy objective was (and still is) more important than our concern about the human rights situation in South Korea. It is not that Carter was any less concerned about human rights—it was simply that another more important interest came into play.

In Iran, Carter painfully discovered the foolishness of pursuing a human rights policy without regard to other foreign policy considerations. There Carter was convinced that nothing could be worse than the Shah. Unfortunately, subsequent events proved that Carter was wrong. Even though the Shah was an authoritarian leader, and was at times brutal, a prudent American policy would have accepted the Shah as a lesser of evils. Had the United States pursued that policy, the human rights situation in Iran would be much better than it is today and, arguably, even better than it was at the time of the Shah's removal.[36]

Prudence, the translation of Biblical principles into concrete results in the real world, requires the careful, discerning weighing of competing means and ends. It also involves choosing between less than optimal alternatives. Prudence frequently requires the choice of a lesser evil in order to bring about a larger (or long-term) good.

Being a disciple of Jesus Christ during our earthly sojourn means that we are to act responsibly in light of Biblical teaching. This is what faithfulness to Christ and His Kingdom is all about.

Essential to being a faithful disciple is a realization of the role which prudence plays in all politics, including foreign policy. Christians who simply proclaim the great principles of Scripture without concern for how these principles can be implemented in the real world might claim the mantle of prophet. But by acting in this manner with disregard for the ambiguities inherent in a fallen world, such prophets ignore God's mandate that Christians act prudently. A Biblical foreign policy—a good, responsible, and moral foreign policy—will be at root a prudent foreign policy.

CULTIVATING CHRISTIAN PRUDENCE

The Bible and prudence: these are the two elements of a Christian approach to international politics, the two indispensable tools of Christian discipleship in matters relating to foreign policy. Orthodox Christianity, which in the United States is often called evangelical Christianity, has never had any problem affirming the centrality of the Bible to the Christian faith. Indeed, it is its Bible-centeredness that distinguishes evangelical Christianity from more theologically-liberal Christianity. Evangelicals, however, do not have a tradition of cultivating practical wisdom. How is this to be done?

First, Christians need to understand the importance and value of practical wisdom in the affairs of this world. Second, like Solomon, Christians need to prayerfully ask God for discernment. Third, Christians need to develop political savvy; that is, Christians must learn to be wise and astute about international affairs.

Practical wisdom does not just happen. It is not something one finds simply by reading the Bible. It requires that Christians seriously study history and learn its lessons. It requires that Christians have a keen sense of the great questions and answers of political philosophy. It requires that Christians be knowledgeable about foreign affairs; that they understand political systems, ideologies, and the dynamics of different cultures. Further, it requires insight and perceptiveness.

In short, practical wisdom requires both factual knowledge and discernment as well as the ability to understand how the two relate to one another.

INTERNATIONAL POLITICS: A CHRISTIAN AGENDA

The Bible and practical wisdom are foundations to understanding the relationship between our Christian faith and international politics. From the study of God's Word and the study of history, we discern seven elements of a Biblically-based Christian approach to foreign affairs:

First, a Christian understanding of international politics begins with the affirmation that the world belongs to God, that man is created in His image, and that both stand under God's judgment.

Second, a Christian understanding acknowledges the sinfulness of every human being. Sin can be forgiven, but its effects cannot be erased.

Third, because of man's sinfulness, all human relationships are tainted by the consequences of sin. In the realm of international politics, sin's effects are seen in the perpetual conflict between nations.

Fourth, human nature precludes the possibility of man creating a perfect world. The best man is capable of is minimizing the effects of sin.

Fifth, the power of nations is an important and necessary means of managing international conflict and creating a better world. In a fallen world, power is inextricably related to ethics. While God's divine Law is the standard of right and wrong, right and wrong are often, in international politics, the product of power.

Sixth, political choices in international politics are characterized by their moral ambiguity. That is, sometimes we cannot choose the best outcome, but must choose between less than ideal outcomes.

Finally, the Bible is the yardstick by which Christians must evaluate their advocacy and support of specific positions. We must measure the consequences as well as the intentions of what we advocate against Biblical norms.

These elements of a Christian understanding of international politics stand in bold contrast to the assumptions of what is often called *idealism*.[1] Idealism, or utopianism, is built upon assumptions that are secular and man-centered. Among other things, idealism rejects man's sinfulness and denies God's Lordship over man and the world. Idealism believes that man is able to overcome his "shortcomings" (i.e., sin) and build a perfect world. Idealism is not a Biblical perspective; it is not a perspective that Christians can hold. It was certainly not the view of the Reformers, Augustine, or St. Paul.

A CHRISTIAN AGENDA

Having defined the broad outline of a Christian approach to international politics, we need to define a (not the) Christian agenda of international politics. What kinds of international and foreign policy issues should Christians be concerned about? What position should Christians take on these issues?

In the aftermath of World War II and through most of the 1960s, evangelical Christians closely associated Christian faith with anti-communism. Atheistic communism, embodied in the Soviet Union with its goal of global domination, was seen as the manifestation of Satanic evil.[2] Popular radio evangelists such as Carl McIntire, John R. Rice, and Billy James Hargis continually exhorted their followers to stand fast against communism. During this period, American evangelicals (or fundamentalists, as they were then known) stressed the importance of separation from the world. They were primarily concerned with evangelism and not with political activity. Anti-communism, therefore, was seen as more of a credo than a well-thought-out theological and political position.

In the late 1960s and early 1970s, the theology and politics of influential groups of evangelicals dramatically changed. This transformation affected the way many evangelicals understood the relationship between their Christian faith and international politics. With this transformation, evangelicals began to redefine the Christian agenda of international politics. The exact nature of this redefinition is reflected in the three factors that motivated the transformation.

First, this redefinition was a *reaction against* the Fundamentalism of the 1950s and early 1960s—specifically, the close association of Christian theology with the crusade against anti-communism. Richard Pierard, a widely-read evangelical critic of 1950s Fundamentalism, referred to this union of evangelical Christianity and anti-communism as an "Unequal Yoke."[3] "Wrapping the Bible in the American flag" was considered bad enough, but worse yet was anti-communism, which was considered inconsistent with Biblical Christianity. This new perspective was profoundly important. As evangelicals of the 1950s saw anti-communism demanded by Biblical teaching, so the new evangelicals of the late 1960s and early 1970s believed that Biblical obedience demanded opposition to anti-communism ("anti-anti-communism").

Pierard argued that Christians "must not be seduced by the false prophets of anti-communism who play down the need for social justice."[4] The reason for this is simple: "The Communist vision of a better world is a clear reminder to Christians that they must redouble their efforts to achieve social justice for all men."[5] Pierard's argument that anti-communism was nothing more than a justification for unjust American values, institutions, and foreign policies was a key theme of the new evangelical movement of the late 1960s and early 1970s.

The second factor that influenced the redefinition of the evangelical agenda of international politics was a growing awareness of Christian social responsibility among evangelicals.[6] Here, too, evangelicals of the late 1960s were critical of their forebears and their preoccupation with evangelism and personal piety. The new evangelicals argued that Biblical Christianity and social responsibility go hand in hand. While this might seem obvious to many, this was a difficult issue for evangelicals earlier this century when social action was equated with the theologically-liberal "social gospel" movement. Only in the 1960s did

American evangelicalism become comfortable again with articulating a full-orbed theology—a theology teaching that social involvement went hand in hand with evangelism.[7]

The third factor redefining the evangelical agenda of international politics was simply the spirit of the times. As discussed in Chapter One, the 1960s saw a broad attack by intellectuals against traditional American values. New Left ideas about the inherent injustices of American society at home and American foreign policy abroad found a sympathetic ear among younger evangelicals who were struggling to make their Christian faith relevant to the world's problems.[8]

Jim Wallis, a major voice among the younger new evangelicals, was a militant student activist at Michigan State University during the late 1960s. When Wallis became a Christian, he did not leave his New Left politics behind. While attending an evangelical seminary in the early 1970s, Wallis and a number of his friends began to articulate a self-proclaimed "radical" approach to evangelical Christianity. What Wallis meant by "radical Christianity" was a redefinition of the Christian faith in which the political assumptions and agenda of the secular New Left were grafted onto evangelical theology. In reality, however, the political agenda defined the theology. Appropriately, the first major radical evangelical publication—started and edited by Wallis—was entitled *The Post-American.*[9]

Jim Wallis was not the only radical evangelical voice to emerge from the end of the Vietnam era. By 1973 many evangelicals, including evangelical college and seminary faculty, evangelical writers, and evangelical church leaders, accepted a redefined evangelical theology—a theology emphasizing social action within the framework of the general themes of the political Left. The culmination of this transformation was the Chicago Declaration of 1973.

This landmark statement of evangelical social responsibility was endorsed by a wide spectrum of evangelical leaders, including many not known for their radical politics. The Declaration itself, however, was radical. The purpose of the Declaration was to "call . . . evangelical Christians to demonstrate repentance in a Christian discipleship that confronts the social and political injustice of our nation" and to "challenge the misplaced trust of the nation in economic and military might—a proud trust that promotes a national pathology of war and violence which victimizes our neighbors at home and abroad." The Declaration lamented that "God requires justice, [but evangelicals] have not proclaimed or demonstrated his justice to an unjust American society."

The Declaration's focus on the injustices of American society at home and abroad clearly reflected themes that were derived directly from the secular New Left. Those who signed the Declaration, however, did not think this was so: "[We] endorse no political ideology. We proclaim no new gospel, but the gospel of the Lord Jesus Christ." In other words, the evangelicals who signed the Chicago Declaration believed that their statement was void of partisan judgments. Nowhere does the Declaration differentiate between the statement of Biblical principles and prudential judgments. The Declaration proclaims that its objectivity derives from "the gospel of the Lord Jesus Christ." The truth, however, is that the perspective articulated by the Chicago Declaration is not found in the Bible.

In hindsight, the Chicago Declaration looks very much like a product of the times in which it was written. The 1960s, Vietnam, and Watergate took their toll on the confidence that Americans had in their values and institutions and America's role in the world. The evangelicals who signed the Chicago Declaration jumped on the bandwagon and added their voices to the chorus of American intellectual, religious, and media leaders who, at the time, questioned the legitimacy of the American way of life. What distinguished the evangelicals, however, was their belief that what they were doing was demanded of them by their Christian faith. Hence, when they "challenged" the "national pathology of war and violence" they assumed they were speaking prophetically—with Biblical authority—when in fact they were mimicking ideas that were obviously extra-Biblical.

The significance of the Chicago Declaration, therefore, is not in the ideas that it expressed. Its significance is that the Declaration signaled a turning point in the way evangelicals approached the relationship of their faith and politics, including international politics. The Chicago Declaration was meant as an affirmation of evangelical social responsibility, but the Declaration tied evangelical social responsibility to the political assumptions and agenda of the secular New Left. The Chicago

Declaration contributed much to the legitimation of the radical evangelical's understanding of international politics. Specifically, the Declaration established "peace and justice" as the central component of the evangelical approach to international politics. For many evangelicals today, even those who do not consider themselves politically radical, peace and justice define the Christian foreign policy agenda.

DOING JUSTICE

According to Jim Wallis, "issues of wealth, poverty, and economic justice are central in the Bible."[10] Ronald J. Sider, another influential evangelical author, writes that "the sheer volume of biblical material that pertains to questions of hunger, justice, and the poor is astonishing."[11] In the past two decades it has become commonplace among evangelicals to argue that "doing justice" is a Biblical imperative.[12]

It is true that many Bible passages make reference to the poor and the oppressed. *Justice* is a theme that is found throughout the Scriptures, especially in the Old Testament. A sound Biblical hermeneutic, however, cannot be built upon counting the number of times a specific word is in the Bible. We need to remember that the Bible is first and foremost not just a collection of words. It is *God's Word*, God's *special* revelation to mankind.

What makes the Bible "special" revelation is that it is a true story of God's redemptive work in history. From Genesis to Revelation, the Bible lays out God's plan for the redemption of His elect through the death, resurrection, and dominion of Jesus Christ. All of the Bible, therefore, must be interpreted within this framework. Whenever we confront a Biblical passage we must ask, "Where does this passage fit into the stream of redemptive history that culminates in Jesus Christ? How is the redemptive plan of God being fulfilled in the history associated with this text?"[13] Another way of saying this is to emphasize what we should not do. That is, we violate the integrity of the Biblical witness when we take passages and attempt to make a one-to-one correspondence between the Biblical passage and current events.

A good example of this is the story of how God used Moses to deliver the Hebrew people out of Egyptian bondage. This is a story that every Christian knows. It is also a story that is very important to those who believe that "doing justice" is what Biblical Christianity is all about.[14] Ronald J. Sider writes in *Rich Christians in an Age of Hunger* that "God displayed his power at the Exodus in order to free oppressed slaves! When he called Moses at the burning bush, God's *intention* was to end suffering and injustice . . ."[15] (emphasis added). The prominence of the Exodus story in Israel's history demonstrates, Sider argues, that "the God of the Bible cares when people enslave and oppress others. At the Exodus he acted to end economic oppression and bring freedom to slaves."[16] At this point Sider adds an important caveat when he says that "the liberation of oppressed slaves was not God's only purpose in the Exodus."[17] Yet, Sider continues, "the liberation of the poor, oppressed people . . . was right at the heart of God's design."[18] "The God of the Bible wants to be known as the liberator of the oppressed," Sider concludes, and "we distort the biblical interpretation [of the Exodus] unless we see that at this pivotal point, the Lord of the universe was at work correcting oppression and liberating the poor."[19]

Sider's interpretation of the Exodus story tells us much about how he views the Bible and Christian theology. For Sider, the main point of the Exodus is to show that God's salvation is the same thing as liberation from injustice. While hedging a bit by stating that this is not "God's only purpose," Sider makes it clear that political liberation is the major purpose of God's salvific activity. This interpretation of the Exodus characterizes Sider's interpretive approach (or hermeneutic) to the entire Biblical story.[20] Just as importantly, Sider's hermeneutic is used in the service of a foreign policy agenda that is generally indistinguishable from that of the New Left.

Sider's method of Biblical interpretation gives the impression that the contemporary relevance or application of a Biblical passage (such as the Exodus story) is obvious. (In *Rich Christians*, for example, Sider selectively uses economic statistics and Biblical passages to support his critique of the United States, deftly building his case that the United States is an oppressor of the world's poor. Sider gives the impression that his critique of the United States, capitalism, and the international economic system flows directly from his Biblical exegesis. The use of putatively Biblical concepts such as "structural evil" gives a patina of theological legitimacy to Sider's analysis of contemporary events.) In fact, however, Sider's hermeneutic and his analysis of contemporary international politics are not logically connected, even though Sider gives the impression otherwise.

Sider's use of Biblical exegesis to legitimate his political sympathies typifies the approach of many influential evangelicals to international politics. "Doing justice" has become a euphemism for a Christian political agenda that is clearly left-of-center. Evangelicals who use the Biblical hermeneutic of Sider nearly always view foreign policy from the perspective of the political Left. At the same time, those Christians who embrace the New Left's political agenda claim that their understanding of foreign policy is Biblical. There is certainly an irony in this. Those evangelicals who are quick to criticize the "unequal yoking" of Christianity with anti-communism are guilty of precisely the same general type of Biblical interpretation, though in support of a radically different political agenda.

The Exodus story is a case in point. Taken out of its Biblical context, a case might be made that the Exodus story is primarily about liberation from oppression. The story's Biblical context, however, shows that God rescued the Israelites not because they were oppressed, but because they were His chosen people. There were certainly other oppressed peoples at the time of the Exodus, and God did not liberate them. God heard the voice of the Israelites precisely because they were the people of His covenant. Their rescue from Egyptian bondage was part (an important part!) of God's redemptive plan that began with God's promise to Abraham and culminated in the death and resurrection of Christ. *Only within the framework of redemptive history can the significance of the Exodus be accurately interpreted and understood.*

The Exodus story has meaning to Christians on many levels. In Hebrews 11, for example, it is used to illustrate the value of great faith. Similarly, Christians take comfort from the reality that God takes care of His people, another lesson taught by the Exodus. The Exodus story also stands as a "type" or foreshadowing of the final redemptive work of Jesus Christ. But it is particularly important to understand that God delivered the Israelites out of bondage because they were His chosen people, not merely because they were in bondage.

If we miss this point, enormous confusion results. For

example, throughout the Old Testament, from Joshua through the prophets, God commanded the Israelites to kill and to conquer. In obeying God, the Israelites engaged in activities—e.g., the killing of men, women, and children—that appear unjust to modern sensibilities. If we yank the Exodus out of context to promote a political agenda, we are also likely to promote the annihilation of opposing forces. (Even the Exodus itself resulted in the death of every firstborn Egyptian male.) And yet, such actions were utterly just because they were part of the providential unfolding of redemptive history. As described in the Bible, liberation and justice can only be interpreted within this framework.

If the Exodus is to be considered a model upon which to base our political agenda today, why then are other Old Testament stories not also models for us? At the end of his life, having fought the Philistines for the last time, David praised God in song:

> In my distress I called to the Lord; I called out to my God. From his temple he heard my voice; my cry came to his ears. . . . He rescued me from my powerful enemy, from my foes, who were too strong for me. . . . I pursued my enemies and crushed them; I did not turn back till they were destroyed. I crushed them completely, and they could not rise; they fell beneath my feet. You armed me with strength for battle; you made my adversaries bow at my feet. You made my enemies turn their backs in flight, and I destroyed my foes. They cried for help, but there was no one to save them—to the Lord, but he did not answer. I beat them as fine as the dust of the earth; I pounded and trampled them like mud in the streets.[21]

How are we to interpret David's song of praise? David's joy in the annihilation of his enemies appears cruel, God's ignoring the cries of hurting people unjust. Yet we know that God is neither cruel nor unjust. This passage, like the Exodus, must be interpreted within the framework of redemptive history. A Christian agenda for international politics cannot be discovered through wrenching Biblical passages out of context or by using selective proof-texts to support predetermined political positions.

This hermeneutical principle also relates to the way in which Biblical justice is often mentioned in the Old Testament (though rarely in the New Testament). The book of Amos, for example, is riddled with references to justice. However, if Amos demonstrates that justice is central to Christian theology, why is not holy war also central to mainstream Christian theology, since throughout the Old Testament God commands the Israelites to physically destroy their enemies? The answer, of course, is one of context. God's commands to Israel were historically specific. They were part of God's redemptive plan at that particular point in human history. They were not meant to be normative instructions to guide our actions today.

In the second place, the meaning of justice as it is used in the Bible is not self-evident. Christians who claim that "doing justice" is at the heart of the Biblical message rarely, if ever, analyze the various meanings of justice.[22] It is assumed that Biblical references to justice refer to social justice or, as it is known philosophically, distributive justice. The assumption is that when a Biblical prophet like Amos proclaims that we are to "let justice roll on like a river" he is demanding that God's people support redistributive economics (i.e., some form of socialism); that when Ezekiel declares that the wealthy "practice extortion and commit robbery, they oppress the poor and needy, and mistreat the alien" he is judging the capitalist economics and foreign policy of the United States. Those who use the Bible this way—who see it as a political manifesto of peace and justice—almost always do so in a way which justifies a left-wing political agenda. Their method of Biblical interpretation—their definition and understanding of justice—*seemingly* only allows for the solutions of the political Left.

One recent book, *Let My People Live; Faith and Struggle in Central America*, illustrates this point.[23] The six authors of the book, all evangelicals working under the auspices of the Calvin (College) Center for Christian Scholarship, ostensibly seek to objectively relate the Christian faith to contemporary Central American politics. In fact, the authors' analysis is highly critical of American foreign policy in Central America. The "gospel of anti-communism," the authors' conclude, "has become the ideology that legitimates the violence perpetuated against large segments of the population of Central America."[24] More important than the authors' political biases, however, is the way in which they suggest that their political agenda is demanded by Biblical teaching. For example, the authors write that armed Christians in Central America are

> being radicalized . . . by the leaven of biblical revelation. A new three-step hermeneutic is taking over: seeing oppression for what it is, judging it by the light of the Word as read in the context of the times, then acting upon the biblical guidelines for pastoral action. . . . They are being sensitized to the systematic injustice and institutionalized violence that devils their lives. . . . Scripture opens up new possibilities for them. Its crucial motifs such as justice, liberation, and peace, often overlooked, now speak to them in surprising ways. . . .[25]
>
> [Moreover, Central American Christians have discovered] that the biblical vision of the kingdom of God compels them to take responsible action against the evils of their society. In these actions they usually build on two basic truths of the New Testament. First, God's kingdom is a kingdom of justice. . . . Second, in Christ the kingdom has already come. Christ has risen and broken the powers of evil. "He must reign until he has put all his enemies under his feet. . . ." (I Cor. 15:25) Central Americans find such world-transforming visions throughout the Bible.[26]

It is evident that the authors of these words view social justice and political liberation as the heart of the Biblical message. It is equally clear that this approach to Biblical interpretation is used in the service of a particular political agenda. There is no acknowledgment that Biblical references to peace, justice, and liberation are part of the unfolding of redemptive history.

A reader of *Let My People Live* might not realize that the vast majority of Biblical references to justice use the concept in the sense of righteousness or virtue.[27] The most common Hebrew and Greek words for *justice* literally mean right, straight, righteous, perfect. These understandings of justice are consistent with the universal understanding of the concept as it was used in ancient times. In this universal sense, a just person is someone who is virtuous or personally righteous.

The Bible also uses the concept of justice in more particular ways—to refer, for example, to remedial justice as when a wrong is made right under the law, or to refer to commercial justice involving fair and just compensation. But the Bible does not use the term in the modern sense of social justice. For most Christians who talk about "doing justice," justice means equality of outcome. So, for example, Jim Wallis argues (unfactually) that "the people of the [Third World] are poor *because* we are rich."[28] Justice entails, therefore, economic redistribution, even the destruction of capitalism. Thus, the political agenda is defined in this way:

> The churches are faced with whether they will continue to align themselves with a world order that subordinates justice . . . to the interests of the American establishment. This choice must be made with the knowledge that such a world order is threatened by the counterviolence of those who are its victims. The consequences of a choice to align with the world order will be endless war, revolution, death and destruction. Such an outcome is inevitable unless some of those who have benefited from the American world order repudiate its basic assumptions and values, and begin to construct alternatives that will provide a new kind of leadership and direction in the wealthy nations.[29]

This "agenda for biblical people" is found nowhere in the Bible. Rather, it is derived from a predetermined political commitment as well as from a basic misunderstanding of Biblical justice. The Bible states God's expectation that the righteous person—the just person—cares about the poor and oppressed. The Bible does not teach, however, that the poor and oppressed are that way because others are rich. Nor does the Bible teach that the way to help the poor and oppressed is to support revolutionary liberation movements, socialist economics, and Marxist politics. Yet, this is often the agenda of "peace and justice" Christians.

The concept of liberation as understood by "peace and justice" Christians is similarly used to justify a politically left-of-center foreign policy agenda. According to Nicholas Wolterstorff in his acclaimed *Until Justice and Peace Embrace*, the Bible gives Christians not only a cultural mandate to "master the world," but also a "liberation mandate [quoting Isaiah] to loose the chains of injustice and untie the cords of the yoke, to set the oppressed free and break every yoke."[30] Wolterstorff's perspective on Biblical liberation, like that of Biblical justice, ignores the context of redemptive history within which these concepts are used in the Bible. Biblical liberation—as in the Exodus story and in the life of Christ—is synonymous with spiritual redemption.

It is a distortion of the Biblical message to see Christ as a political revolutionary. In His life before and after His resurrection, Christ continually reminded those around Him that His Kingdom was not of this world. Tempted by Satan to exercise political dominion over the kingdom of the world, Christ refused.[31] Touted by the soldiers at His crucifixion to save Himself, Christ refused.[32] The power of Christ was not physical or political; His was not the power of a revolutionary zealot. Rather, Christ's power—and the power of the Christian faith—is found in meekness, selflessness, and humility.[33] Biblical liberation is synonymous with God's reconciling grace in the lives of sinners, not with political revolution.

The peace side of the "peace and justice" agenda ignores the intent of redemptive history too. Wolterstorff writes that *shalom* (or Biblical peace) "is God's cause in the world and our human calling."[34] Christians who see Biblical *shalom* as defining the Christian agenda of international politics often assume that the meaning and contemporary relevance of the concept is self-evident. In particular, two implications are frequently derived from *shalom*. First, the Bible's use of *shalom* is used to justify pacifism. Second, *shalom* is used to legitimate political agendas that are more often than not ideologically leftist. Both uses of *shalom* misrepresent and distort its true Biblical meaning.

Shalom is one of several terms the Bible uses to refer to peace. The Bible speaks of three types of peace: peace with God, peace with oneself, and peace among human beings. The first two are promised to those who claim Christ as Lord. The third kind of peace, *shalom*, often means the absence of conflict. However, *shalom* is not used in the Scriptures as an expression of pacifism. The concept has a much more nuanced meaning than the word *peace* implies, meaning "completeness" or "wholeness." In this sense, *shalom* had a very special meaning to the Israelites. It represented the fulfillment of God's promises to His chosen people. *Shalom* was redemption.

At the same time, the promise of complete redemption (*shalom*) is just that: a promise. It is a gift of God, brought about, not through the work of man's hands, but by God. The peace of *shalom* is an eschatological peace which awaits the consummation of history itself.

For the Old Testament prophets, war was a manifestation of the spiritual alienation that separated God's people from their Creator. The promise of *shalom* meant the healing of that separation, a final and ultimate reconciliation of creature with Creator.[35] We misunderstand *shalom*, therefore, when we define it as simply the absence of war. A case for pacifism cannot be derived from Biblical references to *shalom*.[36]

Shalom is also used by "peace and justice" Christians to build a putatively Biblical case for "kingdom politics." The heart of this approach is the belief that in choosing to follow Christ, the Christian turns his back on the principalities and powers of this world, for the politics of the world and the politics of the Kingdom of God are completely different from one another. The essence of the politics of God's Kingdom is *shalom*, defined in terms of perfect justice.[37] Indeed, peace and justice are at the heart of the Christian message. Hence, in engaging the issues of international politics the Christian can settle for nothing less than complete justice. Without justice, there is no true *shalom*. The role of the Church in international affairs, therefore, is unique: it is to witness to the politics of the Kingdom. *Shalom* —peace with justice—is the defining criterion of a Christian approach to international politics, they claim.

In practical terms, "kingdom politics" equates the principalities and powers of darkness with earthly nations. Consequently, Christians must stand against the injustices that are an inherent part of earthly political systems. Stanley Hauerwas, a Duke University theologian, writes that the most important demand of the Christian faith as it relates to international politics is for Christians "to live truthfully between the times. Only by being such a people will [Christians] be able to resist the false choices—such as choosing between America and the Soviet Union—that would have us take sides in a manner that divides Christians from each other and their true Lord."[38]

What Hauerwas argues is that no earthly political system or ideology meets the minimal requirements of Biblical *shalom*, the essence of God's Kingdom. Liberal democracy and Marxism, for example, are equally unacceptable according to Biblical standards; both perpetuate unjust values and structures. The only Biblical politics is found in what Hauerwas has called the "peaceable kingdom," or the ethical community of *shalom*.[39] For Hauerwas and the evangelical Christians who hold to this theology, the Bible is interpreted as an account of political liberation from earthly injustice. Biblical redemption is equated with political liberation from injustices perpetuated by the principalities and powers of the world.

"Kingdom politics" is the politics of most evangelicals who believe that "peace and justice" defines the Christian agenda of international politics. It is an appealing approach because of its claim to Biblical distinctiveness. More often than not, however, "kingdom politics" is also used in the service of a left-wing political agenda. This is not always the case; however, it is generally true that the adherents of "kingdom politics" share a political agenda similar to that of the secular Left.

Clark Pinnock, a well-known evangelical theologian, was closely associated with radical evangelicalism during the late 1960s and through most of the 1970s. An editor of Jim Wallis's *Sojourners* magazine, he was an outspoken critic of the United States, capitalism, and Western society and culture—all in the name of Biblical "peace and justice." In an autobiographical account, Pinnock described the attraction of "kingdom politics": "It was Christ-centered and biblicist and so appealed to our evangelical instincts, but it was radical and subversive of every status quo and so confirmed the cultural alienation that we felt."[40] Pinnock recounts that "When it dawned on us, we had the feeling of a second conversion."[41]

Pinnock, who now opposes "kingdom politics," understands the appeal of its implicitly radical political agenda. Since those who advocate this theology are generally Americans, they tend to identify the principalities and powers of darkness with American values and institutions. On the other hand, political forces opposed to American values and institutions tend to be uncritically accepted as representing the values of Biblical *shalom*. This certainly accounts for the sympathetic way in which revolutionary movements in the Third World have been perceived by "peace and justice" evangelicals. In Nicaragua, El

Salvador, South Africa, even Cuba, left-wing (even Marxist) movements and governments are often held in high esteem as examples of peace and justice in the making. This preferential option for Socialist, even Marxist, politics is built into the logic of "kingdom politics." It is certainly not the product of a prudent study of history and the realities of contemporary international politics.

Relatedly, "kingdom politics" posits a moral equivalence between all the principalities and powers of the world. All nations (with the exception of those regimes seeking to build communities of *shalom*, such as the Sandinistas in Nicaragua) are viewed as intrinsically evil. There is no basic difference, for example, between democracies like the United States and Communist nations like the Soviet Union. "A totalitarian spirit fuels the engines of both Wall Street and the Kremlin," writes Jim Wallis.[42] The United States, like the Soviet Union, is a "brutal" nation intent on expanding American "profit and power" in the world at the expense of the poor and the oppressed in the Third World.[43]

For Christians who believe this, tyranny is not the result of the values and institutions of political systems, but is posited to be an inherent quality of principalities and powers. Relative differences between political systems are considered unimportant. Moreover, the fact that leftist revolutionary movements and governments are believed to somehow transcend the principalities and powers of darkness demonstrates that "kingdom politics" is driven more by ideological bias than Biblical theology. Daniel Ortega, the leader of Sandinista Nicaragua, talks about building peace and justice in Nicaragua, but this does not mean the Sandinistas are interested in peace and justice. Similarly, the African National Congress says it desires peace and justice in South Africa, but this does not mean that an ANC-ruled South Africa would be characterized by peace and justice.

"Kingdom politics" establishes an unachievable criterion in the world in which we live. The reality is that *no* earthly nation, *no* earthly political system can be equated with God's Kingdom; no nation or political system can meet the perfection of Biblical *shalom*. The Biblical vision of *shalom* is just that—a vision of what will be when Christ returns to establish the Kingdom of God in all its fullness and glory. In the meantime, the effects of sin as they manifest themselves in earthly injustice and oppression—i.e., political and economic tyranny—are most effectively dealt with by political means.

Perfect peace and perfect justice will never reign on this earth before Christ's return. Injustice and oppression, however, can be overcome—albeit to an imperfect degree. Christians need to realize that injustice and oppression are the products of the *misuse* of power, not of power itself. Tyranny is the *direct* product of specific political values and institutions.

The freedom and the prosperity that citizens of Western nations enjoy are not the result of random chance. Similarly, the injustices that millions of the world's citizens continue to suffer are not the result of happenstance. Why is it that Western European nations are relatively just and prosperous societies and Eastern European nations are relatively unjust and unprosperous? Why is it that the citizens of Taiwan live in a society that, though far from perfect, is relatively just, while the citizens of Tanzania, on the African continent, live in a society that is far more unjust? Why is it the citizens of South Korea have more than enough food to eat, are protected by the rule of law, and have the right to control the destiny of their nation, while the citizens of Vietnam do not have enough food to eat, have no expectations of having their human rights protected by the rule of law, and have absolutely no say in the destiny of their nation?

These are important questions because they cut to the heart of the relationship of the Christian faith to international politics. They also cut to the heart of peace and justice. Taiwan, South Korea, and the nations of the West are not perfect societies. Indeed, even among these nations there is a continuum of justice—France, for example, being a more just society than South Korea. Having said this, the important point is that the differences between Taiwan and Tanzania, South Korea and Vietnam, and England and Romania are of utmost significance. In words that are as relevant today as when they were written, Reinhold Niebuhr reminds us that

> It is sheer moral perversity to equate the inconsistencies of a democratic civilization with the brutalities which modern tyrannical states practice. If we cannot make a distinction here, there are no historical distinctions which have any

value. All the distinctions upon which the fate of civilization have turned in the history of mankind have been such relative distinctions. [To fail to make such distinctions] invariably means that a morally perverse preference is given to tyranny.[44]

FAITH AND FREEDOM

Tyranny is a consequence of the choices nations make about how to order their societies. Nowhere does the Bible contradict this fact. The Bible does not teach that either the institution of government or the exercise of political power is evil. There is no Biblical dichotomy between obedience to Christ and obedience to Caesar—as long as we remember what belongs to whom.

The sources of tyranny are not found in principalities and powers. Specifically, tyranny is a direct consequence of man's denial of his transcendent Creator and Sustainer—God. Governments that tyrannize are governments which attempt to usurp God's sovereignty by making themselves absolute. It is an indisputable fact that the values and institutions of democratic government create societies which are far more just than societies governed by the values and institutions of nondemocratic government. The experience of human history leads to the inescapable conclusion that earthly peace and justice are the product of political and economic freedom. And freedom is a by-product of faith in God.

Faith and freedom—these are the foundations of a Christian understanding of international politics. Without freedom grounded in faith, tyranny will inevitably triumph. Therefore, freedom and faith must be at the top of a Christian agenda of international politics.

PART THREE

TYRANNY, FREEDOM, AND CHRISTIANITY

SIX

TYRANNY AND THE MODERN CRISIS OF FAITH

On a Fall day in 1948, Whittaker Chambers walked to the pumpkin patch on his Maryland farm and placed a small container of microfilm inside one of the pumpkins. The hidden microfilm would later prove decisive in vindicating Chambers and his accusation that former State Department official Alger Hiss was a Communist spy. A little more than a year later, in January 1950, Hiss was convicted of perjury for denying Chambers's charges. Thus ended one of the most celebrated political trials in American history. Hiss served nearly four years of his five-year sentence, but since his release from prison almost forty years ago has maintained his innocence. While most credible scholarship sustains the guilty verdict against Hiss,[1] the drama of the case continues to stir interest in two men who, perhaps more than any others, symbolize for Americans the post-World War Two struggle between freedom and tyranny.

The life of Whittaker Chambers reads like a novel. Born in 1901 to an emotionally-troubled upscale Long Island family, Chambers briefly attended Columbia University in the early 1920s. After dropping out of college, Chambers traveled to Europe, hoping to find in Soviet Russia the blueprint for the making of a better world. Chambers never made it to Russia, however. Instead, he stayed in Europe where, like many other intellectually-gifted young people of his day, he was attracted to communism. Upon his return to the United States, Chambers joined the American Communist Party. For the next decade and a half, Chambers lived two lives: one as a respected family man and intellectual, the other as a covert espionage agent for the Soviet Union. Then in 1937, aware of Stalin's campaign of terror, Chambers started his journey away from communism. "I began, like Lazarus," Chambers later recalled, "the impossible return."[2]

By 1938 Chambers's break with the American Communist Party was complete. He was summoned to Moscow to explain his defection, but went into hiding, fearing that the Soviet authorities had ordered his execution. For the next ten years Chambers worked as an editor for *Time* magazine, where his articles reflected his new distaste for communism. 1948 was another turning point in Chambers's life, for in that year he was called to testify before Congress about Soviet infiltration of the United States government. Following the two-year ordeal of the Hiss trial, Chambers felt the need to tell the intimate details of his lifestory. The result was *Witness*, a book that became an immediate best-seller. Sadly, the Hiss case and Chambers's subsequent personal witness against communism in his autobiography took its toll on Chambers's emotional and physical health, and in 1961 Whittaker Chambers died of a heart attack.

Witness is a remarkable account of a remarkable life. But Chambers's autobiography is more than a tale of one man's experience with communism and his subsequent disillusionment. More significantly, *Witness* stands as a classic statement of the crisis that confronts our contemporary world—a world that is no longer tethered to a belief in God. In rejecting communism, Chambers came to the realization that tyranny is the inevitable by-product of the denial of God. In spite of communism's claims to shape a more just and equitable world, its atheistic assumptions preclude the one thing that can hold in check the pretensions of human power—God. Chambers understood, in a way few others have, that the political struggle between freedom and tyranny has religious roots. Describing his conversion to Christianity at the time that he broke with communism, Chambers wrote that the rags that fell from me were not only communism. What fell was the whole web of the materialist modern mind—the luminous shroud which it has spun about the spirit of man, paralyzing in the name of rationalism the instinct of his soul for God, denying in the name of knowledge the reality of the soul and its birthright in that mystery on which mere knowledge falters and shatters at every step. . . . If I had rejected only communism, I should have changed my faith; I would not have changed the force that made it possible. I should have remained within that modern intellectual mood which gives birth to communism, and denies the soul in the name of the mind, and the soul's salvation in suffering in the name of man's salvation here and now. What I sensed without being able to phrase it was what has since been phrased with the simplicity of an axiom: "Man cannot organize the world for himself without God; without God man can only organize the world for himself *against* man." The gas ovens of Buchenwald and the Communist execution cellars exist first within our minds.[3]

Chambers saw the conflict between the United States and the Soviet Union—the conflict that has defined international politics for a half a century—as "a critical conflict of faiths."[4]

[F]aith is the central problem of this age. The Western world does not know it, but it already possesses the answer to this problem—but only provided that its faith in God and the freedom He enjoins is as great as communism's faith in Man.[5]

Communism is the "great alternative faith of mankind."[6] It is a religious faith that inspires men to strive for great things. But what distinguishes it from other religious visions is that it is a "vision of Man without God. . . . [It] restores man to his sovereignty by the simple method of denying God."[7]

THE DEATH OF GOD AND TYRANNY

Whittaker Chambers's witness of the crisis of our time has been all but forgotten. Yet, his diagnosis of that which troubles our world is as accurate today as it was in 1952. Chambers understood that tyranny flows from the denial of God, just as freedom flows from a belief in God. In making this connection, Chambers realized that the political crises of the twentieth century are the reflection of a religious crisis. Through his life and writings, Chambers powerfully described the timeless connection between tyranny and man's loss of faith in God.

The twentieth century has been the most brutal in all of human history. Wars of various kinds have claimed over 100 million lives, and tyrannies have killed more men, women, and children this century than all the bombs and bullets of war. What is particularly striking and novel about this is not man's brutality toward other human beings—that has been a reality throughout history—but rather that this brutality has been carried out in the name of remaking mankind and human society. Adolf Hitler, Josef Stalin, and Mao Zedong were personally responsible for the deaths of over fifty million of their own citizens.[8] In each case, the millions who were slaughtered were sacrificed because the secular ideological visions of National Socialism (Nazism) and Marxism demanded it.

Today it is common to hear people argue that times have changed: National Socialism died with Hitler in the bunkers of Berlin, and Marxism-Leninism seems to be experiencing its final death-throes in Moscow and Eastern Europe; totalitarian ideologies are a thing of the past. The reforms of Gorbachev's Soviet Union and in the capitals of Eastern Europe appear to herald the end of brutal totalitarianism and the birth of a more benign, global politics of pragmatism. We do not know the final outcome of these reform efforts. What we do know is that recent global events have not changed man's sinful nature or man's basic yearning for meaning. We might call the latter man's desire to make sense out of life. This desire is universal. It is found among rich and poor, educated and uneducated, among all nationalities and ethnic groups. Moreover, it is an innate part of what we are as human beings. The human desire to know who we are, how we got here, whether there is meaning to life, and where history is going are all reflections of the spiritual dimension of human nature. And this spiritual dimension has a direct impact on international politics.

From the early years after Christ until the seventeenth century, theism, or the belief in God, was the dominant worldview in the West. While not every person was an orthodox believer, the reality of God's existence framed everyone's experience. God, in the words of historian James Turner Johnson, "provided the axiom from which followed all comprehension of man, nature, and the cosmos."[9] Belief in God as interpreted through Christian theology answered the fundamental questions about life: God created the world, God is the sovereign Lord of history, Christ will return to establish His Kingdom. In short, belief in God gave meaning to human life.

By the seventeenth century, something literally world-changing began to take place. Namely, for the first time in over 1,000 years people in the West began to question the existence of God. As a result, in Johnson's words, "the center fell out of Western intellectual life."[10] By the 1800s theism was no longer the dominant worldview. To be sure, individual people still believed in God (as they do today), but modern intellectual thought dispensed with God. Christian theism no longer provided viable answers to man's religious yearning. The dominant worldview was now naturalism, the core premise of which is that God does not exist.

By the end of the 1800s, Western mankind was spiritually adrift.[11] This was even evident to Friedrich Nietzsche, the influential nineteenth-century atheist (and the father of philosophic nihilism), who proclaimed that "the greatest event of recent time—'God is Dead,' that the belief in the Christian God is no longer tenable—is beginning to cast its first shadows over Europe."[12] God may have died in the minds of the Western intellectuals, but the human desire for meaning did not. Christian theism could provide meaning to life; atheistic naturalism could not.

The result, with momentous and brutal consequences for hundreds of millions, has been a religious vacuum. The history of the past 100 years, indeed much of the history of international politics for the past century, is the history of how human beings have attempted, through God-denying ideologies, to fill that vacuum.[13] Since the end of the First World War, international politics has been driven by a clash between religious visions.[14] Specifically, National Socialism and Marxism have tried to fill the religious vacuum left by the demise of Christian theism. Both have left an indelible imprint on the politics and the history of our age.

TOTALITARIAN RELIGIONS

From the beginning of history, men have envisioned creating a better world. Men have often imprisoned, tortured, and killed other human beings to satisfy their own designs. Visions of utopia and the practice of tyranny are nothing new. Karl Marx was not the first European to condemn the rich and the powerful. Adolf Hitler was not the first tyrant to execute his enemies. Yet, more than any other men Marx and Hitler have defined the twentieth century. Why? How did a grossly irresponsible, second-rate scholar who rarely took a bath and never held a job, and a paranoid neurotic who had aspirations of being a great architect but had little ability change the world?[15]

The answer to this question is both complex and simple. It is complex because Hitler's and Marx's rise to prominence took place in the context of a specific historical environment. Hitler, for example, rose to power after Germany's humiliating defeat in World War I. Marx's influence grew in a nineteenth-century Europe that was experiencing economic and political uncertainty associated with industrialization and the breakdown of old non-democratic political institutions. In other words, nationalism and the rise of mass democracy nurtured the soil in which the ideas of Hitler and Marx were planted.

But by themselves these historical factors do not explain the impact these men had on the history of modern times. The answer is found elsewhere—in the ideas that these men articulated. Very simply, National Socialism and Marxism have had such a tremendous appeal because they express a religious vision. They are secular religions.

The term *communism* was used by the French philosopher Rousseau nearly a century before Karl Marx began to write. Marx was not the first Socialist; socialism as an economic idea was popular in Europe before Marx's birth in 1818. Marx's appeal, therefore, cannot be explained because of his putative concern for the poor and downcast of society. What Marx did do was to develop a worldview that provides answers to all of man's most basic questions about life and history. Marx's worldview fell on fertile soil since, as noted before, Christian theism was by the nineteenth century no longer a viable worldview for those who influenced the shape and direction of Western culture. Whereas Biblical Christianity had once provided satisfactory answers to man's quest for meaning, now Marxism provided such meaning. Marxism filled the spiritual vacuum left by the demise of the influence of Christianity on Western intellectual thought.

Marxism has all the attributes of a religion. What Karl Marx did was to create an all-encompassing worldview which explains man and his destiny. The core idea of Marx's thought is the concept of dialectical materialism. As a naturalist, Marx denied that there was a God or a spiritual dimension to reality; the only reality is the material world of material objects and material relationships. Moreover, reality (i.e., history) is shaped by the constant struggle (or dialectic) between material forces. The fundamental conflict of history is between economic classes. Marx believed that economic relationships condition all of life. In other words, everything in life—whether it be religion, government, art, education, or the family—reflects the values of the dominant economic class. It is in this context that Marx said religion is the opiate of the people. What he meant was that traditional religion is used by the dominant economic class to oppress the masses of people. Similarly, our notions of the ideal family, of morality, of government—everything, even the music we listen to—are shaped by economic relationships.

Dialectical materialism, therefore, is shorthand for referring to the ongoing conflict that exists between economic classes. This idea might seem abstract and of little relevance to the real world, but Marx believed that dialectical materialism explains *everything* about man and history.[16] For example, Marx believed that man's personal anxieties—what he called alienation—are the direct result of his exploitation by the owners of capital. He also wrote that history is inexorably moving toward its final showdown when the workers of the world—the proletariat—will overthrow the capitalists and establish a classless society. At this final stage in history, all of man's problems will end.

There are many striking parallels between Marxism (viewed as a systematic worldview) and Christianity. At root, Marxism and Christianity are fundamentally antithetical to one another. Marxism is atheistic, while Christianity affirms the existence of a sovereign, transcendent Creator and Sustainer. But in terms of the functions they perform, Marxism and Christianity are remarkably similar.

The redemptive story of Christianity begins with the perfect creation of man. Man's perfection is shortly spoiled, however, by his disobedience against God. This disobedience is called sin. Sin distorts every dimension of man's life, so that man's personal life and his relationship to other people is deformed. However, God provides a way, through Jesus Christ, for the effects of sin to be healed. Furthermore, one day Christ will return and establish His Kingdom; man will be restored to his original state of perfection. Central to Biblical Christianity are the ideas of the Fall, human sin, redemption, and a promised future state of perfection.

The Marxist worldview revolved around similar themes, though packaged in a naturalized shell. According to Marxism, man once existed in a primitive state, where man lived in happiness. This primitive state of happiness was shattered by the rise of economic classes where one class sought to oppress and exploit another for its own advantage. All of man's problems, personal as well as interpersonal, are the result of this class exploitation. Poverty, war, and man's "spiritual" and psychological problems are caused by the oppressor class exploiting the oppressed. Salvation for the masses, however, is imminent in the form of the proletariat class, the redemptive class of history. Unlike other classes in history, the proletariat (or working class) has the necessary power and sensitivity to rise up, overthrow oppressors, and create a classless society. This is the final stage of history—communism—where all of man's problems will vanish.

In sum: Marxism replaces human sin with class conflict, the redemptive work of Christ with the revolution of the proletariat, and the Heavenly Kingdom with a classless earthly utopia. There are two other important parallels between Christianity and Marxism. Christianity affirms that God is actively working in history and will one day bring about the restoration of all things through the establishment of His Kingdom. History is moving inexorably—i.e., apart from what man does—toward its culmination. Likewise, Marxism posits that history (through the dialectic conflict of economic classes) is inexorably moving toward its culmination, not in the form of the Kingdom of God, but in the form of a classless society. Thus, there is an historical inevitability to both Christianity and Marxism.[17]

In addition, both have an evangelistic component. For the Christian, studying the Bible or theology is not enough. Biblical Christianity demands discipleship—living the Christian life and spreading the Good News of Christ's salvation to others. Marxism too emphasizes the importance of thinking and acting. As the Christian is commanded to work for God's Kingdom, so Marxism calls upon the Marxist believer to help history along by working for the final triumph of communism.

In the 100 years since Karl Marx's death, his ideas have been claimed by true believers in every corner of the earth. The appeal of Marxism has transcended nationality, ethnicity, socio-economic status, and educational background. It is arguable that Marxism has had more of an impact on more people *in a shorter period of time* than any other worldview in the history of mankind. The reason for this is simple: Marxism is a powerful religious vision in a secular age. Under Hitler, National Socialism was also a powerful religious vision, and the religious similarities between it and Marxism—particularly Marxism as embodied in the Soviet Union, at least until Gorbachev—cannot be underestimated. Both believed they stood at a pivotal moment in history; both believed they were uniquely situated to bring about the inevitable climax of history; both sought to create a "new man" and "new society" (through, respectively, biological breeding and the destruction of economic classes); both justified their brutal policies in terms of what was best for "the people."

The fundamental difference between National Socialism and Marxism, and the reason the former was so short-lived, has to do with the particularism of National Socialism. National Socialism was a unique expression of nationalism (i.e., German) directed against all other nationalities. The heart and soul of Nazism was racism. The appeal of National Socialism was indeed religious; but it was a religion in which only the German peoples could be elect.[18]

In contrast, Marxism has endured because of its universalistic message. Unlike either fascism or National Socialism, Marxism does not define itself negatively as a reaction against a race or another nationality. Marxism promises a better world for *everyone*. Marxism has experienced numerous modifications in the past century, but its compelling religious vision remains the same.[19] Herein lies both Marxism's appeal as well as its claim to legitimacy.

In theory, Marxism appears humane and decent.[20] When actually wed to the power of the state, however, the reality is very different, for the history of Marxism is one of unprecedented brutality. To the millions murdered by Stalin and Mao must be added the terrible cost in human life exacted by Pol Pot in Cambodia, Castro in Cuba, and Kim Il Sung in North Korea. Even this list does not include the repression, human degradation, and atrocities associated with Marxism in Eastern Europe, Ethiopia, Angola, Mozambique, and elsewhere throughout the world.

To be sure, Marxist regimes are not the only ones to terrorize their citizens. But what needs to be emphasized is that there is a consistency about the brutality of Marxist governments. Too often the *actual* shortcomings of non-Marxist governments are compared unfavorably to the *vision* or ideal of Marxism. This is an unfair comparison. The only viable comparison is between the actual practice of both Marxist and non-Marxist governments. Using this standard, the evidence is overwhelming that there is not a single Marxist government which has been able to fulfill the promise of the Marxist vision.

Sadly, it is the vision, not the reality, that draws people to Marxism. This is understandable in light of what we have been discussing. Marxism offers a religious vision that is terribly seductive to a secular, naturalistic world. It is this vision which excites people. The excesses that are an integral aspect of the outworking of Marxism in practice are either dismissed as aberrations or are excused as being necessary for the achievement of the Communist utopia. What apologists for Marxism fail to acknowledge—even after the overwhelming evidence that this century provides—is that tyranny is inherent in the Marxist worldview.

The fact that Marxist regimes kill, imprison, and otherwise violate the basic human dignity of their citizens is not in and of itself unusual. What is historically unique about Marxist political systems is the scale of their brutalities and the claim that Marxism makes over the individual and society. Indeed, it is this claim—rooted in the very logic of the Marxist worldview—that produces the tyranny of Marxism. Marxist-Leninist political systems differ in a fundamental way from other political systems by virtue of their objective of remaking man and society. This objective is central to the religious dimension of the Marxist worldview. Moreover, it can only be carried out if every aspect of human life and society is controlled. It is in this sense that Marxist political systems are by definition totalitarian.

There is a basic and important distinction between Marxist political systems and other unjust non-Marxist authoritarian governments. Authoritarian dictators such as Chile's Pinochet or Panama's Noriega are committed to crushing those who pose a threat to their dictatorial rule. The goal of the authoritarian leader is simply to maintain power. As a result, there is not necessarily an attempt to control religion, education, art, and other areas of personal and social life.

In contrast, Marxism is an eschatological worldview in the sense that a bedrock promise of Marxism is: communism will inevitably triumph throughout the world. Marxist regimes are not content to simply maintain power. The consolidation of a Marxist regime is not only an end in itself, but is also a vehicle for extending the Marxist revolution to other nations. In addition, creating "the new man" requires that Marxist political systems control *every* aspect of individual and social life. The Communist Party—through the apparatus of the state—absorbs every individual and social activity, obliterating the distinction between state, family, school, art, labor union, and education. (See Figures One and Two.)

STRUCTURE OF NON-MARXIST SOCIETY

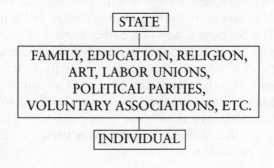

FIGURE 1

STRUCTURE OF MARXIST SOCIETY

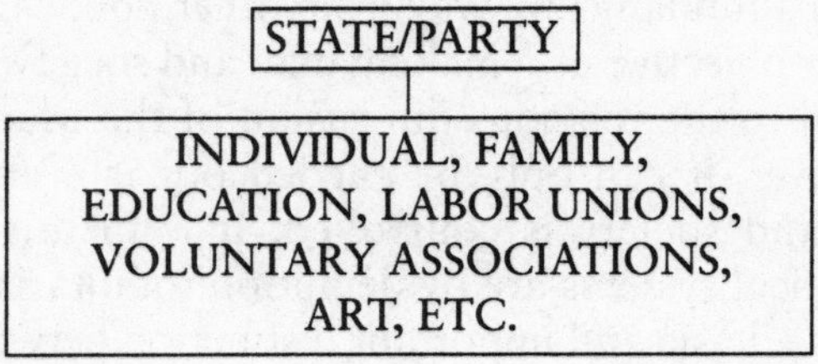

```
STATE/PARTY
```
```
INDIVIDUAL, FAMILY,
EDUCATION, LABOR UNIONS,
VOLUNTARY ASSOCIATIONS,
ART, ETC.
```

FIGURE 2

The tentacles of Communist Party control extend from the top of Marxist society to the very bottom. No aspect of life is left untouched.[21] The state, the media, schools, artistic expression, the workplace—all are controlled by the Party to serve the Party. As a coherent worldview, Marxism necessitates this kind of social organization. What this means in practical terms is that a small minority of people in the Communist Party hierarchy control the lives and destiny of the vast majority of citizens. Every area of life belongs to the state, and everything the individual does must serve the interests of the Communist Party through the state. The interests of the Party, in turn, are defined according to the Marxist worldview with all of its assumptions about reality and history.

Everywhere a Marxist regime has been established, this pattern has been repeated. The state absorbs all spheres of social life, and individuality is destroyed. The logic of the Marxist system dictates that the state is ultimate; nothing exists outside or above it. The Communist Party, embodied in the state, is accountable to no one except itself. The secular religion of Marxism demands total control of mankind in order to remake mankind. The Marxist vision of a better world has proved to be a cruel illusion. In spite of the hope that Marxism can exist with a human face, history is unambiguous in its judgment that Marxism delivers only totalitarian tyranny. The countless tens of millions of human beings who have been sacrificed in order to make the "new Marxist man" bear testimony to this fact. They also remind us that political tyranny is a product of modern, God-denying naturalism.

BUT HAVEN'T THINGS CHANGED?

The recent and often spectacular changes taking place in many Marxist countries raise the inevitable question of whether we are witnessing the death of Marxism. In China, for ten years before the crackdown of the Spring of 1989, the Communist rulers encouraged the slow but steady liberalization of Chinese life. Everything from clothing styles to academic life to economic decision-making was affected. While the events of Tiananmen Square brought about a sudden, deadly halt to Chinese Communist reform, there is good reason to believe (and to hope) that this period of retrenchment represents but a temporary setback for freedom.

A more pragmatic, less ideological Marxism is perhaps most evident in the fatherland of Marxism, Soviet Russia. The ideological zealotry that has characterized all Soviet history is noticeably missing in Mikhail Gorbachev's Russia. Not only has Gorbachev ignored ideological considerations as he has pursued his reforms, but he has also explicitly rejected such hoary Marxist axioms as the inevitability of conflict between the capitalist and Communist worlds. While the Chinese have been cautious in embracing reform, cognizant of the implications for Marxist orthodoxy, Gorbachev appears willing to jettison many Marxist shibboleths in favor of, to use Gorbachev's words, "new thinking."

The major reforms occurring in the Soviet Union represent an admission that Marxism has failed. The failures, exacted in the lives of hundreds of millions of human lives, have been candidly admitted by the Communist Party leaders in Moscow and Beijing.[22] In addition to the failures of Marxism in these leading Communist nations, Marxism's balance sheet in the rest of the world has been dismal as well. In Eastern Europe, Hungary, and Poland, are drifting away from both the Soviet Union and Marxism.[23] In the Third World, regardless of the criteria that are used, the Marxist experience of nations such as Ethiopia, Mozambique, and Cuba has been a nightmare. Castro's Cuba survives only because of the largesse of the Soviet Union (over eight billion dollars a year), while both Ethiopia and Mozambique are basket cases.[24] In short, the vision of Marxism has been shattered by its real-world manifestations. It would appear that Marxism is exhausted.[25]

Surveying the contemporary world, this is the conclusion that many have drawn. Usually this conclusion is fused with an optimistic assessment that growing pragmatism in much of the Marxist world will bring about a general decline in the importance of ideology and with it a commensurate reduction of global tensions. In this equation, pragmatism is associated with reasonableness. In other words, a more pragmatic Soviet Union will be a more reasonable Soviet Union—a less tyrannical nation. The same equation is posited for other Marxist countries as well. Judging from the reaction of many observers in the West, it appears that they expect the exhaustion of Marxism to bring about a revolution in international politics. Perhaps, it is thought, human beings have finally learned what it takes to bring peace and justice to all citizens of the world. Is this a wise reading of what has taken place and will likely occur in the future? There are good reasons not to think so.

The reforms taking place within Marxist nations must not be mistaken for a revolution in human nature. The immutability of human nature apart from the supernatural work of God is the great constant of international politics. To the extent that reforms within the Communist world bring about real change for the better, they should be welcomed and encouraged. We should not delude ourselves, however, into believing that the central problem of international politics has disappeared. The problem of modern tyranny remains rooted in a crisis of faith. Marxism *may* no longer be the primary source of tyranny in the world and therefore may no longer be the primary challenge to free societies. But modern man's craving for meaning, for utopia, has not disappeared.

This problem is sufficiently defined by Paul Johnson when he states: "We live, we shall always live, in an imperfect world, and the human spirit, with its strong element of idealism, will always be tempted to devise means to perfect it."[26] Unlike Christianity which understands that God's Kingdom is not of this world, modern secular man craves for utopia on earth:

[W]e have to recognize that a large proportion of mankind, and more to the point a majority of the intelligentsia, do not accept the Christian vision of another world—or any similar religious alternative—and therefore will continue to feel the itch to Utopianize on earth. Such restless spirits will always be numerous, active, ingenious and persistent to the point of fanaticism. . . . They seek a light which reveals the secrets of perfection in the here-and-now, and if the light of Marxism-Leninism is currently seen to be failing them, they will turn to other sources of illumination and possibly even more dangerous ones.[27]

Man abhors a spiritual vacuum because he is a spiritual being, created in God's image. If Marxism no longer provides a viable framework of spiritual meaning, then man will search elsewhere. And unrestrained by a sense of sin and an awareness that all men and all human institutions stand under the judgment of a transcendent Creator, secular man's blueprints for utopia will inevitably produce tyranny. The Marxist experience in utopia-building provides incontrovertible proof of this.

THE SOURCES OF CONTEMPORARY TYRANNY

*I*n coming years, the primary challenge to peace and freedom in the world will remain rooted in secular man's quest for meaning and utopian perfection. Of all the changes that have revolutionized the modern world, none is more important—or neglected in the study of international politics—than the decline of Christianity and the rise of secular, naturalistic worldviews. Throughout this century, Marxism has been the dominant manifestation of naturalist man's quest for meaning.

On the eve of a new century, with Marxism in a state of disintegration, new utopian blueprints for remaking man and society are emerging and are likely to have a major impact on international politics well into the twenty-first century. While different in important respects, each is a response to modern man's quest for meaning, and each views the power of the state as the primary means by which to forge a utopian future. Therefore, each contains within it the seeds of tyranny.

THE ALL-POWERFUL SECULAR STATE

Intellectual historian Robert Nisbet points out that "the single most decisive influence on Western social organization has been

the rise and the development of the centralized territorial state."[1]
What Nisbet means is that prior to the eighteenth century—usually cited as the beginning of modernity—society was organized
around individual family and religious ties. The declining
influence of Christianity and a growing secularization led to the
breakdown of these ties and resulted in a new form of social
organization centered around the expanding influence of the centralized state. The ever-growing power of the state has been one
of the salient characteristics of the past 200 years.

The state has become the dominant force in modern societies.[2] Even in non-Marxist societies, the trend has been toward
increasing government encroachment in all areas of life, blurring
the distinction between state, society, and the individual. Those
spheres of human life that are considered legitimate for the government to influence and direct have expanded, so that the reach
of government now extends beyond the minimal tasks of
providing protection, order, and justice, to education, voluntary
associations, even religion. The public realm—regulated by
government—is expanding, while that which is not touched by
government—the private realm—is getting smaller and smaller.
In short, the autonomy of the individual and society is being
slowly swallowed up by the claims of the all-powerful state.

As we have seen, the Marxist worldview provides an explicit rationale and legitimation for the total control of the state over
all areas of human life. But Marxism is not the only modern
worldview to justify the all-powerful state. Marxism is simply
one response to the alleged "death of God." The expanding
power of the state is closely associated with the decline of the
influence of Christian theism.

For centuries human beings lived in small family-based tribal communities. These tribal communities were part of larger
political empires or kingdoms. Most people, however, did not
have direct contact with the political institutions of these empires
and kingdoms. People lived their lives virtually untouched by
alien ideas or institutions, including government. During the
Middle Ages, feudalism became the dominant form of social
organization in the West. Under feudalism, society was organized
vertically, with the masses of people dependent on the feudal lord
or king for their well-being. But the feudal relationship was personal in nature: the vassal—or common person—would pledge

his loyalty to the feudal lord in return for land and protection. The idea of a powerful, centralized state touching the daily lives of the average person was still unknown.

From the tenth century onward, Europe was united under the rule of the Holy Roman Emperor. But his domain—the Holy Roman Empire—was really a fiction, since it was neither holy, nor Roman, nor a real empire. Nonetheless, for several hundred years the dream of a universal Christian empire drawing all peoples of the world together was a powerful one. By the time of the Reformation in the sixteenth century, political life in Europe was characterized by decentralization, weak government, and a general belief that all Europeans lived in a Christian empire with claims to universality. The political life of Europe and the course of history began to change after the Reformation. The rise of commerce and the emergence of towns eroded the feudal organization of European life. Growing conflict between the Pope and political authorities shattered the myth of a universal Christian empire. And the Reformation challenged previous notions of spiritual and secular authority.

The sixteenth century was a time of great turmoil in European life. It was at this time and in this historical context that the modern nation-state emerged, and with it the foundation of modern tyranny. The writings of three men, in particular, paved the way for the growth of state power. Their writings have had an enormous impact on modern life, including modern international politics. Niccolo Machiavelli (1469-1527) is probably the most well-known of the three by virtue of his giving birth to the idea of being "Machiavellian." In our popular understanding, to say that someone is Machiavellian is usually not meant as a compliment, implying that the person is sinister and cunning. Machiavelli, however, was a serious student of diplomacy and political philosophy. He was also a secularist who believed that Christianity, like all religions, was a human invention. [3] In his most famous book, *The Prince*, Machiavelli wrote that

There is so great a distance between how one lives and how one ought to live that he who rejects what people do in favor of what one ought to do, brings about his ruin rather than his preservation; for a man who wishes to do in every matter what is good, will be ruined among so many who are not good. Hence it is necessary for a prince who wishes to maintain himself, to learn to be able not to be good, or to use goodness and abstain from using it according to the commands of circumstances.

From passages like this one, the popular notion of "Machiavellian" behavior emerges. But the purpose of *The Prince* is not to tell political rulers to act immorally—this is a misreading of Machiavelli and a misunderstanding of the significance of his contribution to modern international politics. At the heart of Machiavelli's political philosophy is an assumption that changed the course of history; namely, that the political ruler (or prince) is accountable to no one but himself. In other words, the prince is *not* accountable to the Pope, to the Holy Roman Emperor, or the institutional Church. The prince must rule, said Machiavelli, by "reason of state"; he is bound by no higher authority than the interests of the state.

Machiavelli's "reason of state" would revolutionize the modern understanding of international politics. Starting from a God-denying premise, Machiavelli removed the state from under the judgment of a transcendent Creator. To Machiavelli, the state is a purely secular entity responsible only to itself; the state's reason for being is to serve itself. Shocking as this was in the sixteenth century, Machiavelli's conception of the state eventually became accepted as an accurate description of the modern nation-state. Machiavelli's writing marked the beginning of the *secular* state as a central force in the modern world.

Machiavelli's ideas about the secular state were developed further and were given concrete legal status in the writing of sixteenth-century French lawyer Jean Bodin (1530-1596). Writing at a time of turmoil associated with the breakdown of old social structures such as feudalism, Bodin searched for a formula that would bring cohesion to French life. He found the answer in the concept of sovereignty. "Sovereignty," he wrote, "is the most high, absolute and perpetual power over the subjects and citizens in a Commonweale." In other words, the essence of the state is its sovereignty or its absolute power. In practical terms, Bodin's concept of sovereignty implied that no authority existed above the king. Furthermore, sovereignty was a legal concept in the sense that the king was legally entitled to it.

Bodin's formulation of the concept of sovereignty provided the justification for the all-powerful monarch, and in doing so provided a mechanism for forging political unity. In the historical context in which he developed the idea, Bodin's idea had the effect of controlling the centrifugal forces that were pulling six-teenth-century European society apart. Bodin's doctrine of sovereignty established the primacy of the king as the final source of social authority. The doctrine silenced all other claims—including those of the Church—to temporal authority.

Bodin's original concept of sovereignty referred to the per-sonal attributes of a ruler. That is, it was the king who was sovereign. Moreover, Bodin had a keen appreciation for the dis-tinction between state and society. Bodin's understanding of sovereignty did not imply that the state should swallow up all of society. No higher authority existed above the king, but the supreme authority of the king (i.e, his sovereignty) was limited to the legitimate functions of the state. Bodin maintained that the state, society, and the individual were autonomous spheres whose integrity needs to be respected by the other spheres.

Jean Bodin did not, therefore, develop a justification for a totalitarian state. What Bodin did do was to build on the foun-dation laid by Machiavelli. Bodin took the idea of "reason of state" and originated the legal concept of political sovereignty. Within a short period of time, sovereignty became an attribute of the state itself. By the mid-seventeenth century, the doctrine of state sovereignty defined the legal status of the new territorial nation-states of Europe.[4] No longer simply a philosophical idea, that which defined the state was its sovereignty. By definition, no authority existed above the state. Bodin's doctrine of sovereignty resulted in a quantum leap in the power of the state.

It was the eighteenth-century French philosopher Jean-Jacques Rousseau (1712-1778) who would take the idea of state sovereignty to its most extreme form. Of all political thinkers from Machiavelli onward, Rousseau is the most important. Rousseau's ideas about the state have had a profound impact on the modern world. His ideas represent the blueprint that have guided totalitarian projects from Stalin to Castro, and his under-standing of the state has subtly influenced the way all modern nations—including nontotalitarian ones—view the nature of the state.

Rousseau believed that while man is born free, he is corrupted by society. Man's happiness can only be attained when the individual, through what Rousseau called a "social contract," subordinates his will to that of the collective will, embodied in the state. Complete obedience and subservience to the state—what Rousseau called "the general will"—is the prerequisite to freedom. The significance of this understanding of the state cannot be understated. In the words of Robert Nisbet:

> It would be difficult to find anywhere in the history of politics a more powerful and potentially revolutionary doctrine than Rousseau's theory of the general will. . . . Its mission is to effectuate the independence of the individual from society by securing the individual's dependence upon itself. The state is the means by which the individual can be freed from the restrictive tyrannies that compose society. . . . Power is freedom and freedom is power. . . . There is no necessity, once the state is created, for carving out autonomous spheres of right and liberty for individuals and associations. Because the individual is himself a member of the larger association, despotism is impossible. By accepting the power of the state one is but participating in the general will.[5]

Rousseau obliterated the distinction between state and society. Everything—the family, education, religion, etc.—is within the state. Put differently, nothing exists outside of the state. [6] In placing a claim upon man's total being, the state becomes, Nisbet observes, "the means of freeing man from the spiritual uncertainties and hypocrisies of traditional society. It is a spiritual refuge even as the Church was a refuge from life's uncertainties in earlier ages. . . ."[7]

In the writings of Machiavelli, Bodin, and Rousseau, we see the development of a philosophical framework for the modern, all-powerful, secular state. Over the course of the past two centuries, the evolution of the state has taken numerous twists and turns. Some nation-states, such as those of North America and Western Europe, have consciously limited the power of the state through constitutional and institutional means (e.g., separation of powers). Others, such as the Marxist-Leninist nation-states, have made total state power the cornerstone of their political systems.

The common denominator of all modern nation-states, regardless of their political systems, has been a steady growth in their power, resulting in a expansion of those areas of individual and associative life that the state claims as its own. This trend is obviously more evident in monistic (i.e., totalitarian) political systems, but it is apparent in more pluralistic (i.e., democratic) political systems as well. In other words, those areas of life that are considered the "legitimate" domain of public or state domination are expanding, while those areas that remain untouched by the tentacles of the state are diminishing.

To be sure, the reasons for this trend are numerous. Many of them, like the impact of communications technology, are embedded in the nature of modernity itself. Central to the swelling power of the state, however, is a religious factor—that is, the supposed "death of God" and the secularization of modern thought. Modern man no longer has a sense of a transcendent Creator and Sustainer, and as a consequence there is nothing left to restrain the sovereign claims of the state. There are no barriers to the man-centered quest for an earthly utopia.

Philosophers such as Machiavelli, Bodin, and Rousseau are not the only ones responsible for the secularization of modern life. But their writings—grounded in secular, naturalistic assumptions—serve to justify the state's claim to ultimacy. Marx and Hitler are not their only progeny. The fact that Marxism appears on the wane suggests only that one manifestation of the modern crisis of faith has exhausted itself. There is no evidence that the trend of growing state power shows signs of reversal. Indeed, such a reversal is unlikely until modern man acknowledges his dependence on a power greater than that of the state.

In the meantime, the danger of tyranny grows, often embryonically, in every modern nation-state. The challenge to peace, justice, and freedom may have changed forms, but the challenge nonetheless remains. Among the Western nations, the threat of tyranny is likely to emerge in non-Marxist utopian movements that are ostensibly anti-ideological, but that in fact assume all man's problems can be solved by a benevolent state.[8]

A contemporary example of this phenomenon is the Green movement in West Germany. The Greens emerged in the 1970s as an environmental protest movement. By the end of the decade, their agenda included positions on everything from nuclear weapons, capitalism, NATO, and anti-communism. In 1980 the movement became a formal political party (*Die Grunen*) and has since seen a steady increase in its popularity and influence. The Green Party defines itself as an "anti-antiparty." Its agenda is certainly unorthodox, but it is anything but nonideological. In spite of their avowed neutrality, the Greens' antipathy toward democratic capitalism plays directly into the hands of the enemies of freedom. Just as importantly, the Greens' agenda is part of a systematic worldview for forging an earthly utopia void of the material and spiritual pollutants of democratic capitalism. The state is the means of accomplishing this objective. If the Greens were to capture control of West German politics—a scenario that is not impossible—the power of the state would increase dramatically.

The Green movement represents one contemporary expression of secular man's unending quest for utopia. However, it is illustrative of the global trend of expanding state power. To the extent that the power of the state continues to grow and continues to attach itself to secular ideologies, the likelihood of tyranny increases as well. For this reason, growing state power must be taken seriously when discussing contemporary international politics. The continuing seduction of secular schemes for building an earthly utopia, however, is not the only source of contemporary tyranny. Ironically, the threat of tyranny is also expanding in the form of a traditional religious movement—Islam.

THE ISLAMIC REVIVAL

Most textbooks of modern international relations ignore discussions of traditional religious belief, viewing it as peripheral to the day-to-day interaction of nation-states. While this might be true in the context of certain international relationships, it ignores the decisive role that such belief plays in influencing Islamic nations and nations with large Islamic populations. Not too many years ago, Islam was generally little understood in the West. To most, Islam was something associated with strange-looking people right out of the pages of the *Arabian Nights*. This began to change in the late 1960s when the West was rudely awakened out of its ignorance by oil shortages and the Iranian hostage crisis. The dynamics of global interdependence and television images have contributed to the West's rediscovery of Islam.

It is instructive, however, that many in the West still equate Islam with the Arab world.[9] This misconception suggests that in spite of a growing awareness of Islam, the West's understanding of it is still incomplete and distorted. This is unfortunate because Islam represents one of the most important forces in contemporary international politics, and its influence is expanding dramatically. The influence of Islam derives in part from the size of its following. There are nearly one billion Muslims in the world. Put in perspective, one out of five people in the world are Muslim.[10] Most Muslims (75 percent) are located *outside* the Arab world. The nations with the largest Muslim population are Indonesia, Pakistan, and Bangladesh, although large numbers of Muslims are found throughout Africa and South Asia, including such nations as the Philippines and Nigeria.

What makes Islam a factor in international politics is the nature of the religion and its relationship to the politics of those nations with which it is associated. Islam was born in the seventh century after Christ on the Arabian peninsula. Mohammed, its founder, claims to have received a series of visions from God (Allah). Allah told Mohammed that he was to be his prophet on the earth, prophesying of Allah's control over the destiny of mankind. Moreover, Mohammed was to proclaim that all people must acknowledge Allah as the one true God and must submit to his laws. The laws of Allah are contained in the Muslim holy book, the Koran, which according to tradition represents Allah's revelations to Mohammed. Mohammed's status as Allah's prophet was not at first appreciated by his fellow-Arabians; Mohammed had to flee Mecca in 622 in order to save his life. In 630 he triumphantly returned as the revered prophet of Islam.

Following Mohammed's death in 632, Islam spread rapidly throughout what we today call the Middle East into Northern Africa, present-day Turkey, and Spain. Only their defeat by the French king Charles Martel in 732 prevented the Muslim conquest of Europe. In the years after its initial expansion, Islam became closely associated with the spread of the Ottoman Empire, established in the fifteenth century. The Ottoman Turks extended their influence and that of Islam throughout the Middle East and the Balkan nations of Eastern Europe, right up to the doorstep of Western Europe. During the period of Ottoman rule, which lasted until the early twentieth century, Islam matured and left its distinctive imprint on the social and political life of those nations with whom it came in contact.

Central to Islamic belief is the idea of the *umma*, or the universal Islamic community. The concept of *umma* implies a unity of all Muslims regardless of their ethnic or national backgrounds.[11] Implicit in this notion of unity is the Islamic understanding that all Muslims should be united politically and theologically. There is no idea of the separation of church and state. According to Islam, the principal function of the state is to enable individual Muslims to lead good Muslim lives. According to Bernard Lewis, one of the foremost students of Islam,

> The worth of the state, and the good and evil deeds of statesmen, are measured by the extent to which this purpose is accomplished. The basic rule for Muslim social and political life, commonly formulated as to "enjoin good and forbid evil," is thus a shared responsibility of the ruler and the subject, or in modern terms, of the state and the individual. In principle, the Holy Law, in politics and in other matters, is based on revelation.[12]

In other words, Islam allows no "space" between the church and the state. The secular and the sacred are one and the same. The state exists to serve Islam; government is part of the sacred. Unlike the Western understanding of democracy, in Islam there is no justification for the limited state. Islam is all-consuming in its demands on the individual and society. While the Western concept of "theocracy" does not precisely describe Islamic political thought, since there is no church or priesthood in Islam, Islam believes that God alone makes the law governing all of life. Lewis describes how this relates to politics:

> In the traditional Muslim view, the state does not create the law, but is itself created and maintained by the law, which comes from God and is interpreted and administered by those skilled in these tasks. The ruler's duty is to defend and uphold, to maintain and enforce, the law, by which he himself is bound no less than the humblest of his subjects. For these purposes he may make rules and regulations, to clarify

and apply the law. He may in no way abrogate or amend the law, nor may he add to it.[13]

It is this understanding of the state coupled with the idea of the Islamic *umma* that makes Islam an important actor in contemporary international politics. At the same time, these same factors pose a *potential* threat to global peace, justice, and freedom.

It needs to be emphasized that Islam is not in and of itself tyrannical. There are millions of Muslims throughout the world whose practice of Islam is conducted apart from any political agenda. However, since the collapse of the Ottoman Empire and the end of colonialism, those nations with large Muslim populations have struggled to relate their faith to the modern world of secular nation-states.[14] The reason for this struggle is that in most Muslim societies, identity and loyalty have been religious and not national in nature. The modern (and Western) idea that the nation is worthy of individual loyalty is alien in most Muslim societies.[15] The power of nationalism is still alive and well, as is evidenced by nationalistic movements in such places as Canada, Great Britain, Spain, and the Soviet Union. The quest for national self-determination is likewise a driving force among the ex-colonial nations of the Third World. It is against the backdrop of this fact of contemporary international life that Islam stands out.

There are those within the Muslim world for whom modern nationalism is acceptable. These Muslims have adapted the traditional teachings of Islam to "fit" the modern realities of the international system. Accommodating themselves to nationalism and the world of nation-states, these Muslims (mostly intellectuals) argue that there is nothing inconsistent between the modern world of nation-states and the unity of the Muslim world. For them, *umma* is defined spiritually, not politically.[16] Those Muslims who hold to this view arguably represent the majority of Muslims worldwide. However, recent years have seen a remarkable Islamic revival that stands opposed to the modern international order. For these Muslims, the quest for *umma* is as much political as it is spiritual.

The Islamic revolution ignited by the late Ayatollah Khomeini is the most visible evidence of contemporary Islamic fundamentalism. This involves a search for the fundamentals of the Islamic faith, a militantly Islamic government, a revolt against modernity (including the nation-state system), and a determination to forge a literal political-spiritual unity of all Muslims throughout the world. The power of Islamic fundamentalism is illustrated in the relative ease with which it triumphed in Iran. Before the revolution of 1979, Iran was one of the most modern societies in the Middle East, with a highly educated population. And yet, contrary to all expectations, the Iranian people overwhelmingly turned their back on modernization and nationalism in favor of a rebirth of a radically traditional Islamic society.[17]

Though the best-known and most militant expression of Islamic fundamentalism, the Iranian revolution represents the tip of the Islamic fundamentalist iceberg. The Islamic revival is in fact a worldwide phenomenon. As noted earlier, Islam is found throughout the world.[18] And everywhere Muslims are found, Islamic fundamentalism is growing. R. Hrair Dekmejian, an American scholar of Islam, observes that not only is Islamic fundamentalism found in every Muslim community, but it is intensifying as well.[19] The reasons for this intensification are many, including the loss of the holy city of Jerusalem to the Israelis in 1967 and a general sense of inferiority toward the Western industrialized nations of Europe and North America.[20]

Among the factors explaining the recent Islamic revival, however, none is more important than the modern crisis of faith we have been discussing. We have seen that modernity has resulted in secularization. In the West this secularization has manifested itself in the growth of secular utopian ideologies that perform the functions of traditional religion. Ironically, in many parts of the Third World—but not exclusively there—this secularization has initiated a backlash against the secularism of the modern world. In this sense, the Islamic revival is the product of a quest for answers that modern secularism cannot provide. For growing millions, Islam provides a common worldview that makes sense out of the modern world.[21]

This spiritual quest connects with international politics in the same way that Marxism does. While Islam is a traditional religion, Islamic fundamentalism does not make a distinction between the secular and sacred. Hence, the Muslim fundamentalist wants to create a Islamic spiritual order, but that spiritual order also demands the creation of an Islamic political order. In the words of James Piscatori, "both [Marxism and Islam] are ideologies that seek to create political orders, and in this sense are similar."[22] Islamic fundamentalism believes—as does Marxism—in the inevitability of its worldwide triumph. Moreover, Islamic fundamentalists—like Marxists—believe they have a responsibility to help history along.

In this regard, the idea of *jihad*, or holy war, is central to Islamic fundamentalism and has profound implications for contemporary international politics.[23] According to traditional Islamic teaching, the *jihad* is an obligation of all Muslims. Islam is universalistic in the sense that the Koran teaches Islam is for all mankind. It is the duty of Islamic believers, therefore, to convert the unbelievers and if that fails, to subjugate them by force. Until Islam triumphs over all the earth, the world remains divided between Islam and all others. Between the two, writes Bernard Lewis, "there is a morally necessary, legally and religiously obligatory state of war, until the final and inevitable triumph of Islam over unbelief."[24]

The impact of Islamic fundamentalism on international politics is already evident in many parts of the world. In the politics of the Middle East, Islam is a major factor stoking the ongoing Arab *jihad* against the state of Israel. Elsewhere in the Middle East, tensions between fundamentalist Shi'ites and more moderate Sunnis threaten to tear apart countries such as Saudi Arabia, Iraq, and Egypt. Lebanon's degeneration into anarchy is in large measure the result of Shi'ite extremism. Islamic fundamentalism is similarly a major factor in the politics of such relatively stable countries as India and Pakistan.

One of the major problems facing Soviet President Mikhail Gorbachev is the Soviet Union's large Islamic population, numbering nearly sixty million.[25] In southern Republics like Uzbek and Azerbajaijan, Muslims represent the vast majority of the population. The collision of the openness associated with *glasnost* and a growing fundamentalism among the Islamic population has created major political problems for the Soviet Communist Party. Put in perspective, approximately 20 percent of the total Soviet population belongs to the potentially hostile House of Islam. Indeed, the Gorbachev years have been marked by intensifying demands for autonomy among Soviet Muslims, particularly in those Republics with large Islamic populations bordering on the Middle Eastern Islamic nations of Turkey, Iran, Afghanistan, and Pakistan, The Soviet Union's failed ten-year war against the Islamic holy warriors or *mujahadeen* of Afghanistan has only strengthened the sense of *umma* among the Islamic believers of Russia.

The common wisdom of our day says that traditional expressions of religious belief cannot stand against the secular onslaughts of the modern world. While this seems to be true in the old Christian nations of the West, in much of the non-Western world traditional religious belief, in the form of Islamic fundamentalism, is on the rise. Because of its nature, Islam will likely continue to be a major force in international politics for years to come. What is particularly disturbing about this is that militant Islamic fundamentalism—the type of Islam that is gaining ground throughout the world—is inhospitable to the idea of freedom. As a result, the spread of militant Islam will inevitably bring tyranny in its wake.

REBORN MARXISM

A survey of the sources of modern tyranny would be incomplete without discussing the possibility of a rebirth of a reinvigorated Marxism. While the Marxist vision for remaking mankind has lost much of its luster in places such as the Soviet Union and China, the Marxist worldview remains a compelling one to many modern intellectuals. This is especially true in the Third World nations where orthodox Marxism has been incorporated into new movements such as liberation theology. The fact that Marxist-Leninist ideas are still popular among revolutionary movements in Central America and Africa demonstrates that rumors of Marxism's funeral are premature. The dream of Marxism with a human face lives on. Moreover, there is another possibility that cannot be discounted. Should the forces of reform fail in the Soviet Union, a return to brutal Stalinist repression and international expansion is not unthinkable.

In the final analysis, Marxism is a powerfully seductive worldview that will be a factor in international politics for years to come. However, we have seen that Marxism is not the only source of tyranny in our world. Modern tyranny, the product of a crisis of faith, will continue its march until man realizes his dependence on his Creator. This realization is the necessary first step in fighting modern tyranny. The second step is to understand that man's claim on God's creation is limited. Ultimately, as we shall now see, it is freedom that is the antidote to tyranny.

CHRISTIANITY AND DEMOCRACY

*A*s we have seen, the roots of tyranny are found in man's denial of God's transcendence. Because they begin from a God-denying premise, secular political ideologies are unrestrained in their appetite for controlling mankind. Most of the political horrors of this century are the direct consequence of man's unfettered desire for political control. The fact that this control is often exercised in the putative "interests of the people" does not mask the fact that God-denying ideologies are inherently tyrannical.

We have also seen that the Christian faith demands that we be concerned about the world. The Biblical injunction that we love our neighbor means that we cannot ignore modern tyranny.[1] A Christian approach to international politics does not allow the separation of politics from morality. All politics, including international politics, is a moral enterprise. The issue of how people live their lives and how they are treated by other human beings intersects with the Christian's cultural mandate to care for God's creation. For this reason, we should pay close attention to the fact that democratic government is a powerful antidote to modern tyranny.

NURTURING THE DEMOCRATIC IDEA

Democracy is a revolutionary idea. Throughout the long centuries of history, the twin tyrannies of oppression and poverty have been a normal part of the human experience. Just 300 years ago famines ravaged the world every generation, plagues were a regular occurrence, life expectancy in many countries was below thirty, there were no effective medicines, most people were illiterate, infant mortality rates exceeded 50 percent, and the average person spent most, if not all, that he had to provide food and shelter for himself and his family.[2] Moreover, nearly all individuals lived their lives unprotected from the capricious acts of despotic rulers. Respect for the dignity and inviolability of human beings was—with the exception of England, and there only partially—institutionalized nowhere. The rule of law was arbitrary and often nonexistent. The concept of human rights was virtually unknown.

It was against the backdrop of these hoary realities that the founders of the American government understood their endeavors as constituting "a new order of the ages." The idea that all men are created equal and that the institutions of government should be constructed upon this premise was world-changing in its implications. "We the people"—the first three words of the American Constitution—represented a revolution without precedent.

Though the United States gave birth to the democratic spirit in the modern world, the democratic idea was actually nurtured for several hundred years before the American Revolution of 1776.[3] The breakdown of European feudalism contributed to the demise of a hierarchal social order in which the masses of people were dependent on a relatively small privileged class for their economic and physical security. The subsequent rise of cities populated by a new merchant class led the latter to demand political power commensurate with their growing economic power. Even the Protestant Reformation of the sixteenth century contributed to the nourishment of the democratic idea through its assault against centralized authority and its affirmation of the sanctity of the individual conscience. Finally, the Enlightenment made its own contribution to democracy through the work of philosophical giants such as John Locke and Montesquieu—with whom the American Founders were thoroughly acquainted.[4]

THE NATURE OF DEMOCRACY

The American Founding Fathers, therefore, inherited a democratic legacy that was centuries old. Yet while the idea was old, it was untried. The American experience with eighteenth-century British tyranny unleashed the democratic spirit and resulted in a new kind of government—in Lincoln's memorable words, "government of the people, by the people, for the people." The American Founding Fathers understood, however, that true democracy is more then self-interested individualism exercised by an unrestrained mass citizenry.[5] American democracy is built on four assumptions, each essential to the success of the democratic experiment.

The first assumption is that human rights are inalienable and prior. This simply means that human beings are—to use Jefferson's words—*endowed* with certain rights. These rights exist by virtue of our humanity; they are God-given. Human rights do not derive from the state; rather, they exist prior to the state. The purpose of the state, therefore, is to protect man's inalienable rights of life, liberty, and property.

The second assumption of American democracy is that all human beings are morally, politically, and legally equal.

The third assumption is that man and government stand under God's transcendent judgment. Because of this, the pretensions of man and government are necessarily limited.

Finally, liberty must be tempered by virtue, and self-interest by sympathy toward others.

On these assumptions the Framers of American democracy built an edifice of democratic institutions, including representative government, the separation of powers, federalism, and a limitation on the power of government through a Bill of Rights. In the two centuries since the American Revolution, these institutional structures still define democratic government.

While the theory of democratic government may seem complicated, the heart of democracy is found in its provision for the expression of the will of the people *and* in its delimitation of the power of the government.[6] That is, democratic theory can be reduced to these two principles: representative government and limited government. These principles contrast sharply with tyrannical forms of government. In the first instance, tyrannies are never broadly representative. A myth of modern tyranny is that it reflects the wishes of the people. The fact of the matter is that all of the totalitarian revolutions of this century, whether Fascist or Marxist-Leninist, have been revolutions "from above"—that is, revolutions led by a relatively small group of true believers who are usually well-educated and come from more privileged economic backgrounds. Marxist rhetoric notwithstanding, there are *no* historical examples of a spontaneous Marxist revolution led by the masses of workers or peasants.

In the second instance of contrast with modern tyranny, democratic government, by virtue of being limited government, is inherently anti-utopian. The American Founding Fathers were certainly influenced by the optimism of the secular Enlightenment, but they were equally influenced by the record of history and the teachings of Judeo-Christian religion. The latter influences led James Madison to remind his countrymen that the American government (like all government) is a government of men and not of angels. Madison knew, as did all of the American Framers, that man's appetite for power is insatiable unless checked. Since tyranny results from the concentration of state power, the way to prevent tyranny is to ensure that the power of the state is always limited. This is accomplished institutionally through clearly defined constitutional procedures. But it involves more than words and institutions. It also involves a common understanding that the state is not ultimate—that like all human endeavors, it too stands under God's transcendent judgment.

THE CHRISTIAN FOUNDATIONS OF DEMOCRACY

Democracy works as an antidote to tyranny precisely because it protects human liberty against the pretensions of state power. Democracy, in turn, is only possible when it acknowledges that God exists and that all government exists under His sovereign rule. This is an important point. As we have seen, the essence of democratic government—that which distinguishes it historically from all other forms of government—is that it is limited government.

How does democracy guarantee that the state's claims will be limited? One might answer: Through a constitution that establishes what the government can and cannot do. The problem with this is that constitutions by themselves do not provide an *absolute* check on the pretensions of state power. In other words, while a constitution is a necessary prerequisite for democracy, it is not sufficient—at least not in the long term. The only absolute restraint on state power is a belief in something bigger and more powerful than the state itself. Democracy, therefore, is possible *and* sustainable only when grounded in a God-centered worldview.[7] There is a direct relationship between Biblical faith and democratic government, between Judeo-Christianity and human liberty.

Nowhere does the Bible talk about, let alone endorse, democracy. We cannot point to specific Biblical passages to support our contention that there exists an important relationship between Christianity and democracy. However, history and God-created human wisdom demonstrate that such a relationship does exist, at two levels. On the first level, Judeo-Christian faith nourishes those individual and community values that are absolutely essential to the success of democratic government. Human liberty will inevitably become individually and socially destructive unless tempered by a sense of responsibility. Man's sin, particularly his selfishness, makes free, democratic government problematic. The only way democracy can work, therefore, is if man's sinful instincts are restrained.

Christianity is essential to democracy because it embodies values of charity, fair play, honesty, integrity, and moderation that temper man's selfish inclinations.[8] The American Founding Fathers were acutely aware of this reality. In his Farewell Address, George Washington stated that

> of all the dispositions and habits which lead to political prosperity, religion and morality are indispensable supports. Let it simply be asked where is the security for property . . . [respect for] life [without religion]? And let us with caution indulge the supposition that morality can be maintained without religion. Reason and experience both forbid us to expect that national morality can prevail in exclusion of religious principle.

Thirty years later, in 1831, a young Frenchmen by the name of Alexis de Tocqueville traveled throughout the United States seeking to discover why democracy was successful in America. In his classic account of his travels, *Democracy in America* (1835), Tocqueville argued that the first principle of American democracy—that which explains its triumph—involves the "habits of the heart" of the American people. Very simply, the "habits of the heart" are the values, morals, and customs of the American people which act like a glue holding together American life. Just as importantly, de Tocqueville recognized that in America the "habits of the heart" were the product of Judeo-Christian religion. "In the United States," de Tocqueville wrote, "religion exercises but little influence upon the laws and upon the details of public opinion; but it directs the customs of the community and, by regulating domestic life, it regulates the state."

In other words, religion's influence over American democracy does not come from religion dominating or controlling the state, but from the pervasive influence that religious values exercise over all areas of American life. It was this observation that led de Tocqueville to conclude that American religion—not the American Constitution, its laws, or its leaders—is "the first of their political institutions."

The relationship that de Tocqueville discerned between democracy, "habits of the heart," and religion is as necessary today as it was during his time. Recently Richard John Neuhaus perceptively alerted our generation to the dangers of a "naked public square" where religiously-informed values are excluded from public life.[9] Democracy will flourish and endure only when planted in the soil of a common set of shared values. The state and secular ideologies, for all of their good intentions, cannot create a genuine community of responsibility. There is no way to legislate a sense of duty toward other human beings. Ultimately a commitment to others is nourished in the soul and expressed through individual "habits of the heart."

There is a second way Christianity and democracy are linked: Christians have a stake in democratic government. Again, it must be stressed that the Bible does not make such a connection. The Bible is not a political science textbook. The Bible, however, does lay down general principles by which we are to live, and these principles often make contact with politics. When we talk about democracy—or any other kind of political system—we are inevitably discussing how people *ought* to live their lives. To the extent that Christians are concerned about Biblically-grounded principles in the context of international politics, we must be concerned with political systems. The moral component of politics cannot be discussed apart from a consideration of the political values and institutions by which nations govern themselves.

No political system, including democracy, is the Kingdom of God. Indeed, all political orderings short of the consummation of God's Kingdom are flawed. Nevertheless, history provides proof that democracy is best able to provide an environment in which the Biblical principles of peace, justice, and freedom can be achieved.[10] This is an empirical observation, a fact of contemporary political life. There is a close (though not perfect) correlation between democracy and respect for the inalienable rights and dignity of human beings.

Christians also have a stake in democracy because it is a Biblical alternative to totalitarianism. Of all the political systems man has lived under, democracy is the most consistent with Biblical principles. Specifically, there are two aspects of democracy which coalesce with Biblical teaching.

First, the heart of democratic government is its limited nature. The institutions of democratic government delimit the legitimate boundaries of governmental activity and control. In a democracy, government's responsibilities are plainly spelled out; the government does not and cannot lay claim to more than belongs to it.

Another way of looking at this is in terms of what is public and what is private. In a democracy, that which falls under the private realm must always be larger than that which falls under the public realm. Using the distinction discussed previously, a democracy respects the autonomy of the individual and individual associations, whether these be the family, schools, the workplace, or whatever. These are private "spaces" that remain protected from the reach of the state or government. By contrast, tyrannical governments often blur or completely absorb these private "spaces," making every human activity a public concern. It is in this sense that we refer to democratic government as pluralistic government. Democratic government allows for a diversity—a pluralism—of human expressions and activities which are a reflection of individual freedoms. In a democracy the state has its job to do, but that job is always limited.

By limiting the power and authority of the state, democratic government acknowledges that the state is not ultimate. This is very important to Christians who believe that it is God, not man or his institutions, who is ultimately sovereign. The Bible teaches that all authority finally belongs to God,[11] and democratic government recognizes this Biblical truth. This recognition is implicit in all democratic government by virtue of its being a limited government. But it is also explicitly recognized in the United States, where the affirmation "one nation *under* God" is a national creed.

The second aspect of democracy that reflects Biblical teaching follows directly from the limited nature of democratic government. Democracy respects the teaching of the First Commandment that human beings should have no other gods before the sovereign Creator and Sustainer of the universe. Whether individual citizens of a democracy acknowledge God's sovereignty is not the point here. What is important is that, unlike nondemocratic governments, democracies recognize that all human ambitions, institutions, and activities are circumscribed. This reality provides the justification for individual freedom and liberty. Democracies cherish and protect individual liberty precisely because they recognize that human nature is flawed and thus prone to abuse power. The only way to protect human beings from the misuse of power is to limit the power that human beings can exercise over each other. This is why in a democracy limited government and individual freedom are inextricably linked.

Central to individual freedom and democracy itself is religious liberty. It is not happenstance that the first freedom mentioned in the American Bill of Rights is freedom of religion. The Framers of American democracy realized that freedom of religion was basic to all other freedoms and therefore was the bedrock of democracy. In the words of the Williamsburg Charter:

> The right to freedom of conscience is premised not upon science, nor upon utility, nor upon pride of species. Rather it is premised upon the inviolable dignity of the human person. It is the foundation of, and is integrally related to, all other rights and freedoms. . . .[12]

In other words, freedom of religion is important because it implies that each human being is sacred. Democracy assumes that no person or human institution can violate that which defines the essence of our God-created nature—the individual conscience. The inviolability of the conscience is *the* foundational right from which all others flow. Peter Berger observes that the political system "which recognizes religious liberty as a fundamental human right thereby recognizes (knowingly or unknowingly) the limits of political power."[13]

Implying as it does something bigger than the state, something more important than human pretensions, religious belief represents an ever-present threat to the tyrant.[14] Because of this, religion is most effective as a sustainer of freedom and democracy when it remains a witness to its transcendent source. To again quote Berger:

> [R]eligious institutions serve their most important secular purpose precisely when they are least secular in their activities. Society, under certain circumstances, can easily dispense with church-operated soup kitchens or universities. But society can ill afford to lose the reminders of transcendence that the Church provides every time it worships God.[15]

Democracy, therefore, reflects the principles of Biblical faith by respecting the God-created dignity—the inviolability—of every individual and by continually reminding mankind that human power is less than ultimate.

CHRISTIANITY, DEMOCRACY, AND INTERNATIONAL POLITICS

In summary, there is an important link between Christianity and democracy. The assumptions upon which democracy is built reflect Biblical principles. Moreover, there is an interrelationship between the Christian faith and democratic government. Namely, democracy cannot be nurtured and sustained apart from religious values, while democracy does ensure the freedom to practice and proselytize one's religious beliefs. These ties between Christianity and democracy are all-important but not exhaustive.

There is another equally important connection: Christians have a stake in democracy because freedom serves as a powerful antidote to tyranny. Democratic government works. Of course, democracy is far from perfect, because it is practiced by imperfect men. But the genius of democracy is that it takes into account man's sinful nature. In the famous formulation of Reinhold Niebuhr, "[M]an's capacity for justice makes democracy possible; but man's inclination to injustice makes democracy necessary."

While not the Kingdom of God, democracy represents, as Richard Neuhaus so eloquently argues, both a gift and a task.[16] Democracy represents a revolutionary remedy to the ancient scourges of injustice, war, and poverty. Apart from obvious shortcomings, the achievements of the world's established democracies are remarkable. Theirs is a story of freedom, respect for the dignity of each human being, prosperity, and peace.

At precisely this point the Christian faith, democracy, and international politics connect. A Biblically faithful, responsible Christian approach to international politics must start with a sensitivity to the evils of tyranny and an appreciation of the achievements of democratic government. God, through His grace, has given mankind the gift of freedom. It is our Christian responsibility to act as stewards of this gift.

PEACE, JUSTICE, AND FREEDOM

*B*ecause it is an antidote to tyranny, the future of democracy should be a major concern to Christians. Freedom must be at the top of a Christian agenda of international politics. The great international issues of our time—war and peace, wealth and poverty, justice and injustice—cannot be responsibly or effectively addressed independent of a consideration of freedom. Since democracy celebrates and protects freedom, faithfulness to Biblical Christianity requires us to support what might best be called the democratic project.

OBSTACLES TO DEMOCRACY

To argue this is not to suggest that the problems of international politics can be easily solved by crusading for the establishment of a reign of democracy throughout the world. Politics, because it involves fallen human beings, is much more difficult and complicated than that. While the evidence supporting the value of democracy is incontrovertible, the obstacles confronting the success of the democratic project should not be underestimated.

In the first place, while the majority of governments in the world claim to be democratic, only a minority truly are. Less than 20 percent of the world's population lives under a stable democratic government.[1] Put differently, at least eight out of ten people in the world live under some form of tyranny or unstable democracy. Even in the midst of the present "global spring," democracy is rare and its future uncertain. This tension between the global march of democracy and those seeking to extinguish it was evident in China during the Spring and Summer of 1989. The world watched incredulously as millions of Chinese peacefully demonstrated for freedom, only to have their democratic dreams brutally smashed by a Communist government determined to maintain totalitarian control at any cost.

A second impediment to the democratic project has to do with the nature of democracy. Unlike communism, democracy does not have a central authority to define its orthodoxy, nor does it have a generally accepted definition. Communists accept the writings of Marx and Lenin (and others) as authoritative while affirming specific assumptions—e.g., dialectical materialism, the class struggle, etc.—that represent a universally-identifiable Communist orthodoxy. This authority structure and systematically-defined unity of belief energizes the utopian quality of communism. To its detriment, democracy has none of this.

Jacques Barzun captures the problem when he writes that "[c]ompared with a scripture and prophecy, the concrete plans and varied means of the writers on democracy present a spectacle of pettifogging and confusion."[2] Democracy's historical record of success is compelling. The problem, notes Barzun, is that "[d]emocracy has no theory to cover the working of its many brands of machinery whereas its antagonists use a single, well-publicized theory to . . . conceal the workings of one rather uniform machine, the police state."[3] Democracy, therefore, is a fluid idea, allowing for a multitude of fraudulent impersonators.

There are additional obstacles which democracy faces, corollaries of those we have just mentioned. Democracy is not easily planted. While democracy is valued in the rhetoric of people throughout the world, few nations have been successful in establishing genuine, stable democratic governments. There are many reasons for this. In some cases, such as in Marxist Nicaragua, the ruling elites give lip-service to democracy, but their use of the language of democracy is really a calculated tool for the establishment of a one-party Communist dictatorship. In other cases, there is a sincere attempt on the part of large segments of the population to establish a democracy, but the anti-democratic traditions of the country are so strong that the success of democracy is always problematic. Once again, the past twenty years of Chinese history provides a powerful illustration of this.

The entire twentieth-century history of Latin America provides an excellent illustration of this situation. Despite the sincere attempt on the part of many Latin Americans to establish democratic governments, democracy has always been fragile in that part of the world. There are prominent exceptions, such as Costa Rica and Venezuela. However, tenuous democratic governments like those found in Brazil and Argentina are the Latin American norm. The tremendous counterpressures working for and against real democracy in Latin America were particularly evident in Panama in 1989. Time and again the wishes of the vast majority of the Panamanian people were frustrated by the brutal tactics of a traditional Latin American military dictator, Manuel Antonio Noriega. Similarly, in Nicaragua the democratic aspirations of the Nicaraguan people have been dashed by the less traditional but equally repressive dictatorship of the Sandinista Party, led by Daniel Ortega.

As the history of Latin America illustrates, the forces working against democracy are many, and are determined to defeat it. But not all the forces working against democracy are the product of overt opposition. Democracy is more than institutions; more importantly, it involves a particular set of values in order to be successful. Earlier we defined these values, using de Tocqueville's phrase, "habits of the heart." In other words, the institutions of democracy *by themselves* do not make a democracy. The institutions of democracy are necessary to build a democracy, but they are not sufficient.

In this very important sense, democracy is *not* an ideology. An ideology is an all-encompassing worldview that can be expropriated for political purposes by simply imposing an institutional edifice derived from a clearly spelled-out intellectual dogma. This is exactly what Marxist-Leninist regimes have done throughout the world. In Cuba, Ethiopia, Vietnam—indeed, everywhere that Marxist-Leninist regimes have been established—Communist revolutionary elites have imposed institutions of social control acquired from the formal axioms of Marxism-Leninism. In this sense we can say that tyrannical forms of government are much easier to establish than democratic forms of government.

Again, democracy requires more than institutions. Democracy cannot be wished into existence any more than it can be imposed by a well-intentioned elite. Democracy is nurtured and sustained in the habits of the hearts *of an entire citizenry.* If it is not, democracy will fail or will be a sham. The implications of this conclusion for the global democratic project are sobering: democracy will not blossom just anywhere.

In the previous chapter we noted that democracy and Judeo-Christianity are inextricably related. In a nutshell, Judeo-Christianity nourished the soil in which democracy has grown and matured. It is not coincidental that modern democracy arose in the context of the history of the Western world. Many of the core ideas of modern democracy (such as liberty, equality, individualism, human rights, and rule of law) are Western ideas that had their genesis in the teachings of Judeo-Christianity.[4] The evidence of history would suggest that nations without a Judeo-Christian heritage are at a disadvantage when it comes to the development of successful democratic government. An excellent illustration of this is found among the nations of the Middle East.

With the exception of Israel (a nation with a Western religious and cultural tradition), democracy is nonexistent in the Middle East. While there are certainly a host of reasons why this is so, among the most important is the particular non-Judeo-Christian religious and cultural tradition that dominates tribally-based Islamic societies. These societies are closed societies in the sense that those outside the tribe are considered outsiders, strangers, enemies. The consequence for the development of democracy is described by British writer David Pyrce-Jones:

Arabs have . . . formed into states, each with its flag, its passport, its army, its airline, its postage stamps, and other appurtenances of sovereignty. [However], surviving as a tribal legacy down the centuries, the power-challenging dialectic (i.e., conflict between tribal insiders and outsiders) has everywhere perpetuated absolute and despotic rule, preventing the evolution of those pluralistic institutions that alone allow people to participate in the processes of the state. . . . Loyalty to tribe and religious affiliation obliges the Arab and the Muslim to defy and to reject true understanding and acceptance of the outsider and the unbeliever. The power-challenge dialectic continues to prevent the transformation of the collectivity of separate families into an electorate, of group values into rights and duties, of obedience into choice and tolerance, of arranged marriage into romantic love, of the power holder into a party system with a loyal opposition.[5]

Some non-Western societies, most notably in Asia, have seen democracy develop on their soil. Japan and South Korea, to cite two Asian examples, have successfully constructed democratic societies, although the path to democracy in South Korea has been rocky. While Asian nations do not have a Judeo-Christian heritage, their own unique (largely Confucian) traditions have given them cultural values that are amenable to the development of democracy.

The very success of Asian democracy demonstrates that certain aspects of Asian culture reflect Christian values. Since all truth comes from God, those aspects of Asian culture that are conducive to democracy—for example, respect for law and commitment to community—are ultimately Christian values. The experience of the Asian democracies, therefore, does not contradict the argument that God is the ultimate author of freedom.

Because of the long history of oriental despotism, the recent success of Asian democracy is noteworthy. It is certainly one of the major reasons for the international stability of the past half-century. Furthermore, the success of Asian democracy is an encouraging sign that democracy can be planted outside the Western world. And yet, the successes of Asian democracy should not blind us to its fragility in that part of the world. Democracy in the Philippines, South Korea, and Taiwan is incomplete and shaky, and Japanese democracy is much more authoritarian than that found in the West.[6]

On the other hand, it also needs to be acknowledged that Western traditions and the Judeo-Christian heritage do not alone guarantee that a society will be receptive to democracy. Once again the nations of Latin America provide evidence of this, as does a nation such as South Africa, where full democracy is a reality for only a minority of the population. In the case of Latin America, Michael Novak, among others, has persuasively shown that the unique mix of Spanish culture and Catholicism has stunted the growth of democratic values and institutions.[7] Fatalism and authoritarianism, for example, are important elements of the Hispanic worldview, and both are antithetical to democracy.

In short, the obstacles to the development of democracy throughout the world are many. And even if democracy does eventually reign everywhere, *perfect* peace and *perfect* justice will not. That reality, however, should not dissuade Christians from working hard for democracy. The path to peace and justice, short of Christ's return, is found in the cultivation and protection of democratic values and institutions.

WAR AND PEACE

International politics is unique from other kinds of politics. Unlike governmental affairs of an individual nation, international politics is characterized by an absence of authoritative institutions, as well as an absence of commonly-accepted standards of behavior. In most countries, including the United States, there exists a system of authoritative laws and governmental institutions that are generally accepted as legitimate and binding on all citizens. So, for example, in the United States (or in most other countries, with the exception of perhaps a Lebanon or Afghanistan) if a citizen breaks a law, he can expect to be held accountable. Both the law and the sanction are accepted as legitimate.

In contrast, the global system of nation-states (i.e., the international system) has no analogous body of authoritative institutions or standards. Every nation in the world—without exception—is a sovereign entity, bound by no law other than its own national interest. The situation that exists in the international system is akin to what it would be like in the United States if every single American citizen claimed to be sovereign, bound to no higher law and accountable to no higher institution than himself. If this were the case, anarchy would result. This is exactly how the international system has operated since the birth of the modern nation-state in the seventeenth century.

The very structure of the international system is a major factor contributing to the instability and conflict that characterizes international politics. We live in a world of over 160 nation-states, each claiming no obligation other than its own national interest. In such a world, conflict is inevitable as national interests clash.[8] The problem of conflict has always been one of the central problems of international politics.

Christians have always been troubled by the conflict that is unavoidably part of earthly politics.[9] The disquiet of Christians emerges from the Christian commitment to the Biblical message of reconciliation through Jesus Christ. Many early Christians believed that Biblical obedience required them to withdraw from the politics of the world, in large measure because of its conflictual nature. For this reason, many of these same Christians (for example, the Church Father Tertullian) believed that Christians must be pacifists. Later, as Christians moved away from separatism and pacifism, Christian involvement in the politics of the world remained fixed on peace. Writing in his immortal *The City of God*, Augustine reflected that "[earthly] peace is a good so great, that even in this earthly and mortal life there is no word we hear with such pleasure, nothing we desire with such zest, or find more gratifying."[10] Though they differ in important ways, both Christian pacifism and the Christian just war tradition have always shared a common commitment to peace and reconciliation.[11]

Profound differences exist among Christians, however, regarding the causes of war and peace. At the most basic level, Christians agree that the roots of war can be traced to man's sinful nature. Beyond this theological affirmation there is little agreement. In recent years some influential American Christians from the old mainline denominations, the Catholic Church, and the evangelical world have made peace and justice the centerpiece of their politics, and even of their theology.[12] Their concern has been precipitated in large measure by the advent of the nuclear age. The American Catholic bishops captured the anxiety of many when they wrote, in their now-famous Pastoral Letter *The Challenge of Peace*, that nuclear weapons have brought the world to "a moment of crisis," compelling us to look at war "with an entirely new attitude."

Furthermore, many of these same Christians identify four causes of war: mutual misunderstanding among nations; the arms race; imperialism; poverty. The ways to build international peace, therefore, involve discarding nationalism, stopping the arms race, eschewing imperialism, and ending global poverty.

None of these factors are unimportant in the overall ebb and flow of international politics. However, to concentrate on them is to miss the fundamental source of war and peace in the contemporary world: the monumental struggle between the forces of tyranny and freedom. The problem with much recent Christian thinking about war and peace is that it ignores and often belittles differences among political systems. This perspective derives from assumptions of moral equivalence between communism and liberal democracy and, relatedly, a critical aversion to American (and Western) history and values.[13]

PEACE AND JUSTICE

The challenge of peace today is twofold: to avoid war *and* to avoid the slavery of political tyranny. To address one and not the other is a sure recipe for disaster, bringing either war or the triumph of tyranny. Unfortunately, much of the recent religious discussion on war and peace tends to focus on the need to avoid war at *all* costs.[14] This perspective makes avoidance of war the ultimate goal, with no or little consideration given to the nature of peace itself. History clearly teaches us that not all states of peace are equal. Peace is more than the mere absence of war. The peace of a tyrant is not the peace of a freedom-loving society.

In the 1930s Hitler imposed his "peace" on the nations of France, Czechoslovakia, Austria, and Norway. Following World War Two, Stalin imposed a Communist "peace" on the nations of Eastern Europe. We need only compare, however, the peace of Hitler and Stalin with the peace that the United States helped to build in Europe and Japan after the war to see that there are profound and important differences between various states of peace.

Our own time is no different. For several years the Sandinistas in Nicaragua have been engaged in a campaign to end United States support of the *contras* who have been fighting against a Communist dictatorship. As part of their international campaign, the Sandinistas have presented themselves as peace-loving victims of a war they did not want. No one can doubt that the Sandinistas want to see an end to the *contra* war; in this sense the Sandinistas want peace. But what kind of peace? The ultimate objective of the Sandinistas is to end the *contra* war so they can get on with the business of consolidating their Marxist-Leninist revolution.

It is tragic, to say the least, that many—including many American religious leaders—fail to see that not all those who cry for peace want real peace. Real peace is a just peace, what Augustine called the "tranquillity of order" or a "well-ordered concord between those of the family who rule and those who obey." Such a just peace, as we have already noted, can only be the product of a just society—a free society. There is, therefore, a direct correlation not only between freedom and justice, but between freedom and peace.

PEACE AND FREEDOM

The association between peace and freedom is a strong empirical one which applies to both violence within nations as well as violence between nations. When talking about war and peace, we need to remember that government violence against its own citizens has been responsible for more violence than all of the international wars of this century. Stalin and Mao alone killed more of their own citizens than the total number of people who were killed during World Wars One and Two. A comparison of government violence between democratic nations and tyrannical nations demonstrates without question that democratic societies have been far *less* violent than tyrannies. The same is true regarding violence between nations. While democratic nations have participated in wars, in the past two centuries there is *no* example of war or violence between democratic states.[15] After an exhaustive historically-based statistical evaluation of the relationship between democracy and peace, political scientist R. J. Rummel concludes:

> As the degree of political and economic freedom increases in two states, their tendency toward mutual violence decreases. Liberal democratic states are least violent to one another [while] the least free, totalitarian states are most violent among themselves. . . . [Moreover], the more civil liberties, political rights, and economic freedom within a state, the less intense its foreign violence overall; the less such freedom, the more intense its violence.[16]

The bottom line is: freedom fosters peace, and a just peace at that. The values of institutions in democratic nations are conducive to international community-building in a way those of totalitarian governments are not. Conflict is still a part of the international relations of democratic nations; the interests of sovereign nation-states will always collide. But the conflict that does exist between democratic nations is addressed through peaceful channels. The post-World War Two interactions among the democracies of North America, Europe, and Japan illustrate and confirm the relationship between democracy and international peace.

To be sure, all of the Western democracies have had and will continue to have their differences, and not all of them insignificant. For example, the Western European nations do not always agree on common economic policies, and major differences exist between the United States and Western Europe over economic and security policies. Similarly, while the United States and Canada continue to clash over cultural, environmental, and economic policies, the two nations engage their differences peacefully and share the most open national border in the history of the world. Japanese-American relations have been tested time and again over a multitude of trade differences, but in every instance these conflicts have been approached or settled amicably.

Perhaps there is no more remarkable example of the role of democracy in fostering international peace than the post-war relationship between West Germany and France. Throughout most of the modern period they have vied for political control of Europe, often resulting in war between them. For this reason, the transformation that has taken place during the past forty-five years in Franco-German relations is nothing less than astounding—proof of democracy's power to build an international order of peace and justice.[17]

ENHANCING DEMOCRACY

As we relate our Christian faith to international politics, it is essential that we keep in mind the fact that developing and strengthening the institutions of democracy (i.e., freedom) will foster a more peaceful and just world. This goal can only be accomplished through the prudent use of national power. Because of its position as the world's oldest and most influential democracy, the United States has a special leadership role to play in fostering and sustaining democracy.

We have discussed the obstacles and threats to democracy, and we have cautioned against the misuse of national power. Nevertheless, a prudent and Biblically sound foreign policy cannot and must not avoid the exercise of power. And there is no more important use of national power than in the support of global democracy.

This task is not a simple one. Every nation presents its own unique set of circumstances that are conducive or destructive to democratic values and institutions. Therefore, American foreign policy must be flexible enough to deal with each unique situation, responding to the needs of each nation accordingly. Reflexive and impulsive policies born of ignorance or moralism are no substitute for carefully-thought-out policies. These policies may not always be popular with domestic constituencies, nor may they satisfy our desire for immediate results, but they will be more successful.

These points can be illustrated by looking at United States foreign policy toward South Africa, Panama, and China. A major American foreign policy goal toward these countries is to enhance democracy in each of them. This policy is motivated by American national interest as well as American disdain for tyranny, regardless of its degree or its source. These three nations, however, present unique challenges to United States policy. For example, South Africa does have a legacy of democratic values and institutions, but South African democracy is incomplete since the majority of its population cannot participate in the white-dominated political structures. China, on the other hand, has no democratic legacy, but an ancient one of despotic, authoritarian rule.[18] Panama's history is very different from that of either China or South Africa. Since its independence from Colombia in 1903, Panama has ostensibly tried to pattern its political system after that of the United States. Though a republic with a constitution and formal institutions of democracy, in practice Panama's political history has been a tortuous cycle of democratic government and military dictatorship.

Despite their different histories and their contrasting experiences with democracy, these three nations are similar in important ways. In the span of their respective histories, each has had a close, amiable relationship with the United States; each is strategically important to the United States;[19] each has tremendous positive potential given their respective natural and human resources; each is nondemocratic. In light of these things, how has the United States responded to the situation in these three nations?

In the case of Panama and South Africa, American policy has centered on economic sanctions. Sanctions represent one foreign tool among many others. They have the advantage of being politically popular because of their symbolism and because they are highly visible, are relatively easy to implement, and do not cost a great deal. This latter advantage is particularly germane in post-Vietnam America, where there has been a general aversion to the use of military force. The problem with sanctions is, there is scant evidence that they work. In spite of this, they are a preferred option of American policymakers.

If ever there were a situation where one would think sanctions would be effective, it would be American sanctions against Panama since the United States is Panama's primary trading partner (the Panamanians even use the United States dollar as their de facto currency!). Ronald Reagan imposed sanctions against the Noriega government in 1988, believing that Panamanian dependence on the United States would bring the swift ouster of Noriega. That did not happen. The Reagan Administration underestimated the willingness of a dictator like Noriega to endure economic hardship. Perhaps more tellingly, Washington underestimated the extent to which sanctions would actually affect Noriega personally. As in South Africa, the effects of sanctions have been felt primarily by the average person, and frequently by the poorest segments of society.

The Bush Administration turned up the heat on Noriega, keeping sanctions in place while intensifying diplomatic efforts against his government, even intimating that U.S. military intervention might be an option. Concerning South Africa, while Congress is unlikely to strengthen its 1986 sanctions package, there is certainly no general congressional support for the

removal of those sanctions either, even in light of their ineffec-
tiveness.[20]

In contrast to U.S. policy toward Panama and South Africa,
American policy toward China has aimed to encourage
American economic involvement in that country. On the surface
this situation is odd, given the fact that, according to Freedom
House, China is a more repressive society than either Panama or
South Africa, However, American policy toward China repre-
sents an attempt to encourage the forces of reform and openness
that characterized Deng Xiaoping's rule since 1976. However,
these forces were dealt a severe setback during the chaos of the
Summer of 1989.

The lessons that can be drawn from recent American
attempts to abet the development of democracy in Panama,
South Africa, and China must begin with the acknowledgment
that there is no easy path to democracy. Moreover, the situation
in those countries demonstrates that there are limits to what the
United States can accomplish. This does not mean that the
United States should forsake its role as leader of the Free World;
to do that would be disastrous both for the future of the United
States as well as democracy. Rather, it means that the United
States must assess how it can encourage the development of
democracy while realizing that its ability to influence the course
of events will vary from country to country. Where policies clearly do not work, as in the case of sanctions against South Africa,
those policies should be jettisoned. The wisdom of Socrates (if
you cannot do good, it is better to do nothing than to do evil) is
Biblically-sound advice that is especially pertinent to the conduct
of foreign policy.

What specific policies should the United States follow? As
an overall goal, a commitment to building global democracy
must be at the top of the American foreign policy agenda.[21] This
objective will be most effectively realized in different ways,
depending upon the specific situation of a given country. For
example, building democracy in Nicaragua requires a different
American response than in South Africa. Considerations of
national interest, available foreign policy options, and the means
that the United States has at its disposal to influence events must
all be carefully considered before policy is formulated. While the

American response to democratic development will differ from country to country, the United States has three major global responsibilities.

First, the United States must always be willing to assist, in whatever manner, those peoples who are fighting for freedom against tyranny. This principle is an old one and is implicitly found in the Monroe Doctrine and explicitly stated in the Truman and Reagan Doctrines. During the Reagan presidency, this doctrine was implemented with bipartisan support in aiding Afghanistan's *mujahadeen* in their successful ten-year struggle against direct Soviet domination. Less successfully, and with less bipartisan support, the United States aided the Nicaraguan *contras* and Jonas Savimbi's UNITA in Angola. While it may not always be prudent for the United States to directly aid those fighting for freedom, such an option must be left open; and when appropriate, it must be pursued.

Second, as an alternative to direct military aid, the United States should always be generous in its financial support of democratic movements wherever they may be found. A concrete expression of this kind of policy is the National Endowment for Democracy (NED). Initiated and funded by Congress, the purpose of NED is to assist individuals and organizations (e.g., labor unions, political parties, and publishing operations) that are struggling for freedom. For example, NED has been active in its support of Poland's Solidarity movement, democratic political parties in Chile, the free labor movement in El Salvador, and the Nicaraguan opposition newspaper *La Prensa*, providing the latter with ink and newsprint. The struggling movement for democracy in China illustrates how American monetary and material assistance can be used to encourage the budding of freedom.

Finally, the future of peace, justice, and freedom requires that the United States remain vigilant in its resolve to protect freedom. This resolve must be demonstrated through an American willingness to use military force if the need should arise. A strong, credible American nuclear deterrent is absolutely necessary if freedom is to survive the twentieth century.[22] Likewise, a strong conventional armed force is needed to meet challenges to freedom at whatever level they might arise. Diplomacy and other nonmilitary tools of foreign policy must usually be the front-line defense against the onslaught of tyranny;

however, should they fail, the enemies of freedom must know that their aggressive ambitions will be doomed.

The future of global peace and justice is dependent on the survival and growth of democracy. And the survival and growth of democracy is dependent on a strong, resolute American presence in the world. As freedom fosters peace, so it fosters prosperity.

THIRD WORLD DEVELOPMENT, HUMAN RIGHTS, AND FREEDOM

We have seen that if we care about peace in the world, we will pay close attention to the state of freedom in the world. There is a close, undeniable relationship between peace, justice, and freedom. A just social order is the precondition for real peace, and freedom is the the necessary precondition for a just social order. Freedom, expressed politically through the values and institutions of democracy, is a powerful antidote to tyranny.

Freedom is also a powerful antidote to global poverty. In spite of the tremendous progress that has characterized the past century of human history, multiplied millions of people in nearly every part of the world suffer the miseries associated with poverty: inadequate health care, poor sanitation, high infant mortality rates, decreased life expectancy, and illiteracy. While the Bible tells us that the poor will always be with us, the Bible also teaches through the life and work of Christ that we should have compassion on those who are hurting. The bane of poverty should be a major concern of all those who call themselves disciples of Jesus Christ.[1]

The record of the Christian Church in addressing problems of global poverty has been, on balance, a good one. No other private organization or movement can claim to have helped more of the world's poor over the past century and a half than various missionary movements. Even today, in addition to their evangelistic programs, missionaries and Christian relief organizations provide important educational and medical assistance to millions of the world's poor. In remote regions of the world and during acute crises associated with famine or natural disasters, these Christian relief efforts are often the only bulwarks separating people from life and death.

That Christians—especially Western Christians—have demonstrated compassion for the poor of the world is praiseworthy. At the same time, Christians have not always demonstrated keen discernment in their comprehension of the dynamics that are responsible for the poverty in the Third World. Very simply, compassion, no matter how well-intentioned, is not enough. Compassion must be shaped in the context of an understanding of the causes of global wealth and poverty. And such an understanding must begin with one undeniable fact of economics: freedom results in prosperity, equality, and respect for human rights, while political tyranny leads to impoverishment, inequality, and contempt for human rights.[2]

THE IDEA OF THE THIRD WORLD

Most of us identify global poverty with the Third World.[3] In turn, our popular conception of the Third World brings to mind a host of ancillary ideas such as imperialism, exploitation, and the quest for self-determination. Because the concept of the Third World is wrapped up in our understanding of global poverty and the role of the poor nations in world politics, it is imperative that we discuss the relationship between poverty, the idea of the Third World, and international politics.

Poverty predates the emergence of Western colonialism and the emergence of the Third World. Looked at in the broad sweep of history, poverty, like political tyranny, has been the normal condition of human existence. Only in the eighteenth century did people—in the Western world—begin to talk about human beings being lifted out of poverty.[4] Before that time, it was assumed that most people would always experience poverty. The notion of wealth having causes that could be deciphered and put into practice by anyone—in Adam Smith's words, by "the butcher, the baker, the candlestick maker"—was to revolutionize world history.

It is a mistaken idea, therefore, to assume that poverty is something new, born in the Third World following decolonization; it is not. What is new is the way in which the condition of poverty has been grafted onto a whole set of ideas that represent what is most accurately described as a Third World ideology. In other words, our contemporary understanding and approach to global poverty often reflects a set of assumptions that are part of a larger way of viewing the world. This worldview is Third Worldism.

The concept of the "Third World" has interesting roots which help us explain its peculiar ideological overtones. The phrase was first used by French intellectuals in the late 1940s or early 1950s.[5] What these French intellectuals meant to convey by their choice of words—*le tiers monde*—was that there exists a third option for humanity, void of the evils of modern industrial capitalism and slave-camp totalitarianism.[6]

The nascent ideological content of the concept was given political flesh in 1955 at the Bandung Conference of African and Asian nations. Here, in the former colony of Indonesia, Ghana's Kwame Nkrumah, Indonesia's Achmad Sukarno, India's Jawaharlal Nehru, and Egypt's Gamal Abdul Nasser assumed de facto leadership of the newly independent nations and articulated the themes that would come to define the essence of the Third World ideology in the following years. Their framing of the *idea* of the Third World exerted a significant impact on both the Third World's role in international affairs, as well the West's (i.e., the developed world's) response to it.[7]

The identifying definition of the Third World to emerge from Bandung was that of political nonalignment. The Bandung participants were in the main ex-colonies. Their call for nonalignment, therefore, was a form of "reactive nationalism," or a way of asserting national independence and self-identity. It should be kept in mind that political considerations, not economic ones, were the major concern of these founding fathers of Third Worldism. Decolonization of the remaining colonies around the world and an international role for the Third World, independent of the United States and the Soviet Union, were the targets that the Bandung leaders set for themselves.[8]

As important as these goals were, of equal importance were the means used to achieve them. As the goals of the Third World were political, so were its means. The path to political independence, equality, and self-determination lay—as it would later with respect to economic development—through politics. As Paul Johnson puts it, "What politics had done, politics could undo."[9] Specifically, this meant politics expressed through the aegis of a strong state whose interests and identity became virtually synonymous with a cult of personality surrounding the national leader. This type of politics was in some ways ideally suited to the nations of the Third World, where traditional political relationships were understandable only in terms of personal loyalty. So it was, for example, that Kwame Nkrumah referred to himself as *Osagyefo* or "the redeemer," while some years later Uganda's murderous Idi Amin would be called by some "Daddy."[10]

The problems with this type of political leadership soon evidenced themselves. Brutality, corruption, repression, and generally destructive political and economic policies sank most of what Paul Johnson has called the "Bandung Generation" deeper into misery. The promise of redemption that the Third World ideology originally spawned quickly deteriorated into political tyranny and economic chaos—in short, a condition of general human tragedy.[11]

This reality, however, has not discouraged the faith that many Western intellectuals and Third World elites have placed in the Third World ideology. This dissonance of reality and commitment can be explained in religious terms. Since its birth over thirty years ago, the idea of the Third World—and all the nuances that it entails—has become a religious affirmation among Western intellectuals and Third World elites. Sociologist Peter Berger describes the origins of this Third World faith:

[T]he religious associations evoked by the phrase Third World have deep roots in the eschatological tradition in the West . . . there are many antecedents in the imagination of the West positing the idea that somewhere on this earth there is or might be brought into being a place with salvific power.

[Since the 1950s some Western intellectuals have] sought out places that they deemed to be authentically "savage," and thereby "noble"—Africa, or the Pacific, or the wilder regions of South or Latin America. Others found redemptive nobility in the great non-Western civilizations of Asia and the Middle East. . . . What all of these [intellectuals] had in common . . . was the conviction that the West is sadly lacking in qualities to be found elsewhere.[12]

In other words, the sensitivity of Western intellectuals to the shortcomings of their own societies has produced a self-imposed alienation from those societies, while at the same time intensifying their commitment to finding that earthly locale where peace and justice embrace.[13] The logic runs something like this: We know the pervasive evils of Western culture; we know that a truly peaceful and just society must exist somewhere; therefore, it is likely that such societies exist in those ex-colonial nations of Africa, Asia, and Latin America—nations seeking to shape a better world out of their common experience of Western repression. The fact that the Third World is anything but a utopia is unimportant.

As Berger points out: "it is one of the basic propositions of the psychology of religion that faith in prophecy is strengthened, not weakened, by its empirical falsification."[14] For the true believer, the reality of the situation is not as important as the veracity of the faith and its concomitant political and economic agenda. Again quoting Berger,

It is as if the Crusaders, having failed to find the Holy Land where it was supposed to be, roamed all the shores of the *outremer* in search of a plausible landing place. If Jerusalem does not exist, it must be invented. [Western intellectuals] have demonstrated that the capacity to invent socialist utopias in the most unlikely regions of the Third World is sovereignly free of empirical restraint.[15]

THE CHRISTIAN FAITH AND THE NEW INTERNATIONAL ECONOMIC ORDER

Though the idealization of the Third World as a religious idea is primarily an expression of *secular* intellectuals, it is not limited to them. It also has been sympathetically received by some

Christians. Contemporary Christian concern for the poor of the world is often shaped out of compassion for those whom their missionaries have told them about for generations. However, there are other factors involved as well. Among the most powerful is the recent idea, popular among many Christians, that as Christians we are "World Christians." The idea of World Christian means many things to many people; frequently, however, it comes attached with a whole set of themes that are strikingly similar to those of the Third World ideology—assumptions about the evils of Western culture and, more specifically, American foreign policy (i.e., imperialism, ethnocentricism, racism, and exploitation).

What has emerged in recent years, therefore, is an unlikely alliance of Christians, Marxist (and Neo-Marxist) intellectuals, and Third World elites demanding social justice for the Third World.[16] The specific conception of social justice that is called for involves the original Bandung political agenda (i.e., nonalignment, self-determination, etc.), but also includes an economic agenda associated with the New International Economic Order (NIEO). The NIEO was the response of the Third World, or "Group of 77" as they later became known,[17] to their poor, underdeveloped status among the world's nations.

The NIEO resulted from a declaration adopted by a special session of the United Nations General Assembly in 1974.[18] The specific demands of the NIEO include trade reform, monetary reform, increases in economic aid by the developed nations of the West, the right of Third World nations to control multinational corporations, technology transfers from the West to the Third World, and cancellation of Third World debt.[19]

During the past two decades, the demands of the NIEO for a fundamental restructuring of the international system have achieved a prominent place on the overall agenda of international politics. North-South relations (i.e., relations between the developed nations of the northern hemisphere and the less-developed nations of the southern hemisphere) have joined East-West or American-Soviet relations as the major issues dominating the international agenda.

An important element of the Third World agenda includes assumptions about the nature of world politics. An amalgam of Marxist and anti-Western ideas, these assumptions represent the motivating force of much of contemporary Third World politics. These assumptions, as we have noted, are shared by Marxists and Marxist-leaning intellectuals, as well as by many Christian religious leaders in the United States and Europe. What is especially disturbing is that these assumptions are finding growing numbers of adherents among evangelical Christians. On evangelical college campuses, in particular, Third World ideology is warmly received and advocated by many faculty members and administrators.

What is troubling about this is that the ideology of the Third World is often equated with Biblical teaching. In reality, the assumptions undergirding the Third World ideology, though construed as Biblical, are extra-Biblical, masking an ideological agenda that has nothing to do with Biblical Christianity. Believing that the Bible teaches we should have compassion on the needy of the world does not mean that the assumptions associated with Third Worldism are Biblical (any more than slogans like "World Christian" are Biblical).

The call for social justice is not inconsistent with Biblical teaching, but to advocate policies that perpetuate human misery is. The commitment to the ideology of Third Worldism on the part of some Christians says more about their embracing a left-wing political agenda than it does about their desire to find a Biblical response to global poverty. Ideologically-driven moral outrage should never be confused with Biblical compassion. Addressing the problems of underdevelopment requires moral and intellectual integrity—that is, a sincere desire to understand the true causes of wealth and poverty.

THIRD WORLD IDEOLOGY AND ECONOMIC DEVELOPMENT

Those who embrace the ideology of what we have called Third Worldism begin their analysis of economic development with two assumptions: first, that poverty in the Third World is caused by factors external to the Third World countries themselves; and second, that economic wealth is fixed. In general terms, these assumptions are reflected in the credo that the poor are poor because the rich are rich. The wealth found in the nations of the "North" is caused by those nations taking more than their fair share from the poor nations of the "South." Since the economic pie of wealth is fixed, the only way for the Third World to get more is for the rich nations to do with less. The prescription for Third World development, therefore, requires redistribution of the world's wealth.

The agenda of the NIEO is built upon these two assumptions. The NIEO's call for a complete restructuring of the international system follows directly from its belief that the cause of Third World poverty is a direct consequence of the exploitation of the North: the North has gotten its wealth through theft and exploitation. The solution to underdevelopment is thus a radical revamping of the international system, a redistribution of the world's wealth.

The assumptions and agenda of the NIEO see the immediate causes and solutions of Third World underdevelopment as being Western imperialism.[20] Imperialism as a specific explanation for Third World poverty has an old history going back at least to the late-nineteenth- and early-twentieth-century writings of British journalist J. A. Hobson. In his book *Imperialism*, published in 1902, Hobson laid out arguments about the causes and nature of European imperialism which are still echoed today.[21] V. I. Lenin borrowed from Hobson and gave flesh to the argument that imperialism is the inevitable outgrowth of capitalism's insatiable quest for increased profits. The costs of imperialism, in turn, are borne by the poor peoples of Africa, Asia, and Latin America.[22] According to Lenin, imperialism is synonymous with plunder.

In the years since Lenin's death, the theory of imperialism has undergone numerous modifications. Though often stripped of explicit Marxist rhetoric, the theories of imperialism popular today are clearly indebted to Marxism-Leninism. Among the most influential of these is dependency theory.

Dependency theory was first given shape in the 1940s and 1950s by Latin American economists Raul Prebisch and Celso Furtado. In recent years it has become the economic orthodoxy of liberation theology. The theological premises of liberation theology have, in fact, been constructed on top of the economic premises of dependency theory. Logically and substantively, liberation theology stands or falls on the validity of dependency theory. Although it stands outside the mainstreams of economic thought, dependency theory, through liberation theology, has greatly influenced the thinking of many Christians, including many evangelicals in the United States.[23]

Dependency theory divides the world into two groups of nations—"core" or "center" nations, and "periphery" nations. The nations of the "core" are the wealthy nations of the North, while the nations of the "periphery" are the poor nations—the Third World nations—of the South. Dependency theory posits that the relationship between the "core" and "periphery" nations is inherently an unequal one. The central idea of dependency theory is that the international system has been designed to keep the rich nations rich and the poor nations poor. In other words, the nations of the "core" have created an international economic system to benefit themselves at the expense of the nations of the "periphery." The "periphery" is kept dependent (hence, the name dependency theory) on the "core" to provide it with cheap labor, natural resources, and raw materials. The villainous agents in this relationship are the rules and structures of the international capitalist system, as well as multinational corporations who act as surrogates for the interests of the "core" countries.

The logic used to describe the relationship between the "core" and "periphery" is derived directly from orthodox Marxism. Dependency theory views the world as divided between two classes: a capitalist oppressor class, and a pre-capitalist oppressed class. These two classes of nations are in perpetual conflict as the oppressor class of nations—the "core"—has one objective in its relationship with the "periphery"—to exploit it in order to increase wealth. Development—an important aspect, though not the totality of liberation—will come with the overthrow of the present international system. The remaking of the international system is accomplished through revolutionary activity in individual nations, as well as through the eventual triumph of the global agenda of the NIEO.

Like all theories, dependency theory is abstract in its formal expression. However, the practical meaning of dependency theory for the day-to-day affairs of international politics is evident enough. To the disciples of dependency theory, the capitalist nations of North America, Western Europe, and Asia are the bad guys, plundering the good guys of the Third World. Against such an onslaught of economic and military power, the Third World is helpless. The bottom line is: if it were not for imperialism (a product of capitalism), the Third World nations would be prosperous, peaceful, and just societies.

But capitalist-inspired imperialism is not the only factor to blame for the woes of the Third World. While it may be *the* major factor, its malicious effects are exacerbated by other Third World "realities": specifically, overpopulation and the lack of natural resources. According to the Third World ideology, the trio of imperialism, overpopulation, and dearth of natural resources explains Third World underdevelopment.

These factors and the assumptions that undergird them also provide justification for strong, intrusive state action. Since the forces "causing" underdevelopment are insidiously orchestrated from the outside, the state must take upon itself responsibility for the welfare of the people. A socialist state with tight control of political and economic life is thus seen as necessary to counteract the exploitative effects of capitalism.

How on target is this explanation of underdevelopment? Is imperialism the cause of Third World underdevelopment? Are imperialism, overpopulation, and lack of natural resources to blame? Does a radical restructuring of the international system (socialism) represent the Third World's salvation? These are important questions, with profound moral as well as economic and political implications.

A CRITIQUE

The answer to the above questions is quite easy: there is *no* evidence to support the argument that imperialism, overpopulation, and a lack of natural resources cause the poverty of the Third World. To the contrary, the empirical evidence is overwhelming in refuting dependency theory and other arguments which locate the sources of the Third World's problems in external factors.[24] Close scrutiny of several of the assumptions commonly held by Third World elites, leftist Western intellectuals, and even some Christians reveals the hollowness of their beliefs about the causes of underdevelopment.

In the first place, the developed, capitalist nations have relatively little economic contact with the underdeveloped nations of the Third World. The United States, for example, invests more in Canada than in all of the Third World. (Total U.S. investment in Central America is equivalent to the size of the economy of Springfield, Massachusetts.) The same is true of other developed nations. While the developed nations' investments in the Third World are not unimportant, they do not sustain the economies of the developed nations.

Likewise, the present wealth of the developed world is not the result of past colonialism. Modern scholarship demonstrates that nineteenth-century colonialism rarely repaid the costs to the colonial nation.[25] Moreover, many of the poorest and most troubled nations in the world, such as Afghanistan, Chad, Nepal, and Ethiopia, were never Western colonies and, until recently, had no external economic contacts with the developed world. On the other hand, some developed nations—the United States, Canada, and Australia—were once colonies themselves. Equally relevant, some wealthy nations, including Sweden and Switzerland, never had any colonies.

These *facts* confront head-on the development arguments of dependency theory and other theories of imperialism. Nevertheless, they are ignored by those true believers of Third Worldism who apparently are more concerned about ideological fidelity than discerning the real causes of underdevelopment. The reality is that imperialism is not the cause of the poverty and injustices of many Third World nations. The poor nations were poor before their first contact with the developed nations, just as today's wealthy nations were rich before colonialism.

In sum: the facts do not support the contention that the Third World is poor and oppressed because of contact with the West. To the contrary, the facts support the opposite argument; namely, that contact with the West has been the chief engine of progress for the Third World. P. T. Bauer, one of the world's most distinguished economists, concludes:

Far from the West having caused the poverty of the Third World, contact with the West has been the principal agent of material progress there. . . . The level of material achievement usually diminishes as one moves away from the foci of Western impact. The poorest and the most backward people have few or no external contacts. . . . [It has been] through these contacts that human and material resources, skills, capital, and new ideas including the idea of material progress itself (and, incidentally, that of Western guilt too) flowed from the West to the Third World.[26]

As the facts thoroughly discredit imperialism as a source of Third World poverty, so do they undermine other popularly held external explanations. For example, a comparative analysis of the development experience of the nations of the world quickly dispenses the argument that overpopulation is a major impediment to Third World development. Japan, France, and Great Britain, for example, are all more densely populated than Ethiopia, Kenya, and Indonesia. Moreover, Singapore and Hong Kong are two of the most densely populated nations in the world, and yet for the past thirty years they have experienced unprecedented economic growth. Moreover, the world's poorest countries do not have the fastest-growing populations. Ethiopia, the poorest nation in the world with a per capita GNP of $120, has a population growth rate equivalent to that of Hong Kong, which has a per capita GNP of $6910. To be sure, the relationship of population to development is a complex one,[27] but as an explanation for Third World poverty it is more accurately described as an alibi than an answer.

The same is true of other oft-cited explanations of Third World poverty. As far as natural resources are concerned, Japan has virtually none, while Mexico, with vast reserves of oil and other natural resources, is a far poorer nation. This same pattern is true throughout the world.[28] In recent years much attention has been focused on Western foreign aid as a means of redistributing global wealth. Increased foreign aid and forgiveness of the Third World's enormous debt are posited as necessary preconditions for Third World development. But again the evidence offers a very different conclusion. Foreign aid, as P. T. Bauer points out, does not

> go to the pathetic creatures pictured in publicity campaigns of the aid lobbies. The money goes to their governments: that is, their rulers. And all too often these rulers are directly responsible for the gruesome conditions that we wish to alleviate. [Foreign] aid helps, even enables such governments to

pursue policies which are extremely hurtful to their people. (1). Maltreatment of the most productive groups, especially minorities, and sometimes their expulsion. (2). Enforced movements of their population. (3). Coercive collectivization and other forms of expropriation. (4). Suppression of private trade. (5). Underpayment of farmers. (6). Restriction of the inflow of capital, enterprise, and skills. (7). Voluntary or compulsory purchase of foreign enterprises, thus absorbing scarce capital and depriving the country of skills which are helpful to development. (8). Massive spending on prestige projects or on the support of uneconomic activities, especially manufacturing. Such policies, even singly but much more so when pursued together, can undermine or cripple an economy. . . . This neglect of the basic functions of government amidst wholesale politicisation of life is widespread in [foreign] aid recipient countries.[29]

Similarly, the Third World's debt problems are not caused by forces beyond the control of the Third World leaders, but, in the words of Harvard University's Irwin Stelzer, "result from poor economic organization—bloated welfare states, dominated by inefficient state-owned enterprises and corrupt bureaucracies."[30]

In sum: explanations of Third World poverty that point to imperialism, overpopulation, and other factors external to the Third World are way off the mark. They are not totally useless, however; they serve to bolster an ideological agenda that is essentially anti-Western and socialistic. The poverty and oppression that continue to exist in the Third World are not products of Western malice, but of indigenous political and economic tyranny. As the empirical evidence is overwhelming in discrediting external factors as the cause of Third World underdevelopment, so the evidence is overwhelming supporting the contention that the real source of prosperity and justice is found through economic freedom—in other words, capitalism.

THE DEMOCRATIC CAPITALIST REVOLUTION

Despite its compassionate rhetoric, the Third World ideology of redistribution and state control has been unable to deliver on its promises. *There are no examples of successful development experiences among Third World nations that have adopted socialism.*[31] The euphoric optimism that greeted the independence of many Third World nations thirty years ago has given way to growing pessimism.

Examples of the failure of Third World socialism are found scattered from Cuba to Nepal, but particularly on the African continent.[32] Chad, Zaire, Uganda, Somalia, Niger, Madagascar, and Ghana, seven of the poorest countries in the world, are poorer today than they were twenty years ago. Three African nations—Ghana, Mozambique, and Uganda—have experienced dramatic *declines* in farm production during the same period, and none of these nations is located in the drought-stricken area of Africa. Julius Nyerere's Tanzania, once looked to as the hope of African development, is today an economic disaster.[33] The same is true of the former British colony of Ghana. The development experience of Ghana dramatically illustrates how the misguided development assumptions of Third Worldism have destroyed a nation with much potential.

Upon assuming power in 1957, the charismatic leader Kwame Nkrumah began to personally direct the Ghanaian economy. Declaring that "the social and economic development of Africa will come only within the political kingdom," Nkrumah brought Ghana's entire economy under state (i.e., political) control.[34] He fixed the price of Ghanaian cocoa at 40 percent of the world price, nationalized foreign-owned mines, cocoa processing plants, and industries, and fiddled with the Ghanaian currency. The effect of these "enlightened" policies was devastating: Ghana's cocoa production plummeted, 70 percent of Ghana's factories were shut down, the nation's trade balance sunk into the red, and, today only 1 percent of the nation's Gross National Product is devoted to new investment. Ghana's economic woes are not the result of external factors, but of three decades of gross economic mismanagement.[35]

Unfortunately, Ghana is the rule in the Third World, not the exception. The record of the past thirty years is clear: socialism has been a failure. What is equally clear from the experience of the past thirty years is that economic freedom—capitalism—works. The only successful cases of Third World development are found in East Asia, among the capitalist "Four Little

Dragons" of South Korea, Taiwan, Singapore, and Hong Kong. The development experience of these nations, Peter Berger observes, "is bad news for Marxism."[36] But it is not only bad news for orthodox Marxism, for "[t]he development of the capitalist societies of East Asia is the most important empirical falsification of dependency theory."[37]

On the eve of the 1960s, the Four Little Dragons *were* underdeveloped Third World nations. Since then, they have experienced tremendous economic growth and a commensurate rise in the standard of living for nearly all their citizens without any massive violation of human rights. All of this has been accomplished within a capitalist economic structure.

The ability of capitalism to generate economic growth has generally been accepted, even by Marxists.[38] (Karl Marx himself spoke approvingly of capitalism's capacity to produce.) The record of economic growth among East Asia's Four Little Dragons has been remarkable.[39] From 1965 to 1986 South Korea's economy grew at a rate of nearly 7 percent per year, while Hong Kong's grew 6 percent. Taiwan experienced a 9 percent growth rate from 1945 to 1975, and Singapore's economy grew at about the same rate from 1955-1975. Put in different perspective, South Korea's GNP tripled in the ten-year period from the mid-1960s to the mid-1970s, while Taiwan's GNP grew *eleven times* greater from 1952 to 1980! These impressive rates of economic growth have been accompanied by decreasing unemployment and a steady rise in wages.

The economic growth spawned by the capitalist nations of East Asia has not been matched by the Third World Socialist nations.[40] In thirty years the Four Little Dragons moved themselves from an underdeveloped status to the category of what the World Bank calls "upper middle-income" nations. Moreover, the economic growth potential of the Four Little Dragons show no signs of abating. It is quite possible, indeed likely, that by the early twenty-first century these nations—particularly South Korea—will be global economic powerhouses. (Of course, Hong Kong's becoming part of the People's Republic of China may very well reverse the economic gains there.)

The productive power of capitalism in East Asia is undeniable. But economic growth alone is not a sufficient measure of successful development.[41] Western and Third World critics of capitalism have generally been willing to grant capitalism the ability to breed economic growth. The fatal flaw of capitalism, they argue, is that capitalism is not compassionate; rather, it feeds man's baser instincts of greed and self-interest, benefiting a few at the expense of the masses. This is another myth of Third Worldism.

Contrary to common wisdom, a nation's economic system alone is not the major factor affecting equality of income distribution within that nation.[42] The strongest correlate of equality of wealth is the level of economic development: those nations that are more economically developed are most likely to have more equitable distributions of wealth. At the same time, however, there is a direct connection between equality and capitalism because capitalist nations are more successful at generating economic growth than are socialist systems. After an exhaustive comparative study of socialism and equality, political scientists Thomas Dye and Harmon Zeigler stated that "we find no discernible relationship between socialism and equality."[43] The individual experiences of the Four Little Dragons provides further confirmation of this conclusion. Quoting Berger,

> What the capitalist countries of Eastern Asia have achieved . . . is the eradication within one generation of all the dehumanizing traits we know as Third World misery. . . . The sharp contrast between the capitalist and socialist countries of [Asia], is a very instructive one indeed. . . . [The East Asian experience confirms] that policies favoring economic growth tend to improve the conditions of the poor more effectively than policies favoring redistribution.[44]

Not only is capitalism unsurpassed in its ability to stimulate economic growth, it is also unsurpassed in its ability to raise the condition of the masses of people to a decent standard of living. Socialism has not been able to do this.

Finally, the development experience of the capitalist East Asian countries, in contrast to Socialist Third World nations, has demonstrated that capitalism is closely associated with respect for human rights. As we noted in our previous chapters, a just order is the direct product of a just political order. Justice, or respect for the dignity and worth of every individual, does not simply happen. Justice—human rights—are the product of democratic political values protected by democratic political institutions.

The concept of human rights itself arose in the West and has been advanced and sustained through a commitment to political freedom. While capitalism as an economic system does not require democracy (i.e., political freedom), the very logic of capitalism, with its emphasis on economic freedom and its ability to create a dynamic middle class, exerts strong pressures toward political democratization. Recent events in South Korea bear out this relationship. As the South Korean middle class grew in numbers and economic power during the 1970s, it was inevitable that they would demand more political freedom. This is what happened, and the South Korea of the 1980s and the 1990s is a far more democratic society than it was just ten years before. This pattern has been repeated among the other Four Little Dragons and other capitalist nations as well.

The symbiotic relationship between capitalism and democracy is apparent in the fact that every democratic country in the world has a capitalist economy. Conversely, socialism and democracy are strangers. By virtue of claiming economic decision-making power for itself, the socialist state is inherently hostile toward individual liberty and, as a consequence, respect for basic human rights. In short, when a country opts for capitalism, it embraces an economic system that has consistently proven its ability to generate economic growth which in turn benefits the entire citizenry. Moreover, unlike socialism, the dynamic of capitalism is sympathetic to democracy. In fact, capitalism breeds pressures toward increasing democratization. In doing so, capitalism serves to protect and enhance fundamental human rights.

COMPASSION AND CAPITALISM

Peter Berger has written that "the issue of socialism should be put aside for good in any serious discussion of development; it belongs, if anywhere, to the field of political pathology."[45] There is an irony to Berger's observation. Democracy and capitalism *are* on the march throughout the world, while socialism is on the wane. Leaders of nondemocratic socialist nations from Eastern Europe to Africa are beginning to acknowledge that state dom-

ination of economic life leads to poverty.[46] Yet—and here is the
irony—at a time when the bankruptcy of socialism has never
been more apparent and more acknowledged, many religious
leaders and lay Christians still hold on to the myth of the superiority of socialism. The popularity of liberation theology and
dependency theory among many Christians, including evangelicals, provides disturbing evidence of this peculiar phenomenon.[47]
If these Christians really care about poverty and oppression as
they say they do, there is simply no longer any excuse for their
holding on to ideas that damage rather than help the world's
poor.[48]

Compassion for the Third World requires that we see the
genius and value of economic freedom. But, as with political
freedom secured through democratic government, the success of
capitalism is not automatic. Capitalism has taken root in East
Asia, but it has had a more difficult time in other parts of the
world, most notably Africa and Latin America.[49] Like democracy, to which it is so closely linked, capitalism requires a specific
moral-cultural framework, a framework historically associated
with Reformation-Protestant values.[50] The experience of Japan
and the Four Little Dragons suggests that those values are also
implicit in their own unique oriental traditions. While we should
not underestimate the difficulty of planting democratic capitalism in the Third World, compassion for the Third World mandates that American Christians support those policies that
nurture and build the values and institutions of economic freedom around the world.

ELEVEN

LOOKING AHEAD: AN AGENDA FOR THE BUSH YEARS

*T*he election of George Bush represented a resounding reaffirmation of the traditional American role in the world. Eight years of the Reagan presidency and the election of his vice president signaled a rejection of the indecision and near-paralysis that characterized American foreign policy in the immediate aftermath of the Vietnam War, culminating in the Carter presidency. The Bush Administration, like its predecessor, is committed to a strong American leadership role in the world. This is a role that Christians should support.

Of course, Christians should not blindly support just any foreign policy; Christians need to be discerning. But Christians should not hold back or hesitate in supporting a strong American presence in the world. In the previous pages, we have argued that on balance the United States has been a positive influence in the world. In recent years, there has been no more moving testimony to the hope that America holds for those living under tyranny than the image of courageous Chinese students defiantly erecting a likeness of the Statue of Liberty in Beijing's Tiananmen Square.

The message of this image from China and the central reality of our time is that the future of freedom is dependent on the future of the United States. The spread of freedom, through the nurturing of democratic values and institutions, is the only path (short of Christ's return) to a more peaceful, prosperous, and humane future.[1] While Christians must not confuse God's Kingdom with earthly politics, it is through earthly politics that human well-being is secured. Christians, therefore, have a stake not only in the survival of freedom, but in the perpetuation of a strong, free America.

A survey of the world in this last decade of the twentieth century offers much reason for optimism. Never has the future of freedom looked brighter, and tyranny's bleaker. And yet freedom is still precarious, its future uncertain. This will always be so, because tyranny is born of man's sinfulness. The speed and brutality with which the movement for more freedom in China was smashed should rid us of any sentimental belief that the ideologically-driven tyrant will bow to the wishes of "people power." Only democratic government, sustained by religious values, can effectively check the idolatrous pretensions of modern secular ideologies. The struggle against tyranny will end only when Christ returns. Until then, our Biblical faith requires that we do what we can to protect freedom against the ongoing threat of tyranny.

If we take our Christian faith seriously, we will support a powerful United States committed to protecting and enhancing global democracy. These twin goals represent the core interests of American foreign policy for the future. They need to be reflected in the foreign policy agenda of the Bush presidency.

THE SOVIET UNION

Despite the dramatic changes that have recently taken place in the Soviet Union, that nation remains the major foreign policy challenge for the United States. There are two reasons for this. First, it is by no means certain that Mikhail Gorbachev's reforms will succeed. In the early months of the Bush Administration, a flap arose when Secretary of Defense Richard Cheney was asked by a reporter if he thought Gorbachev would be successful in his attempt to restructure the Soviet system. Cheney replied that he did not think so, that it was likely that the Soviet Union would return to its pre-Gorbachev repression. Immediately a maelstrom of controversy arose, as the press reported that the Secretary of

Defense expected a return to the Cold War. The controversy was extinguished only when the president issued a statement saying that it was his hope (and therefore official U.S. policy) that Gorbachev's reforms would succeed.

Actually, the press misconstrued Cheney's point. Cheney did not say that he (or the United States) was opposed to Gorbachev's reforms. Rather, he simply expressed skepticism that they would be successful. Cheney's skepticism is indeed well-founded, as is the president's expression of support for Gorbachev. These two perspectives are not contradictory. As discussed in Chapter Two, positive changes have recently taken place in the Soviet Union. Nevertheless, the problems Gorbachev confronts are so many and so enormous, it is by no means certain that he will achieve what he has set out to accomplish. Moreover, Gorbachev certainly has domestic political enemies who would like nothing more than to see his policies fail.

In the second place, even if Gorbachev is successful, we do not know what Gorbachev's ultimate objectives are. Under Gorbachev the Soviet Union is a more open place than it has been at any time since the Bolshevik Revolution. But apart from the immediate goal of economic revitalization, what are the long-term objectives of *glasnost* and *perestroika*? What role does Gorbachev envision the Soviet Union playing in the world ten, twenty, fifty years from now?

The answers to these questions are not self-evident. The Soviet Union is still, even under Gorbachev, a tightly-controlled totalitarian society. There is no freedom of the press; freedom of speech is limited; there are no independent schools, trade unions, or political parties. Rule of law, expressed through an independent judiciary, is nonexistent. Marxism remains the official ideology. In short, all the institutions of totalitarian control remain in place.

Gorbachev should be applauded for all he has done. However, unless these gestures are accompanied by a dismantling of the instruments of Communist Party control, the Soviet Union will remain a repressive society. For instance, the new openness Christians have to practice their faith is good news; but there is always the danger that if this openness is not secured through a change in the institutional and legal structures of Soviet government, there will be a return to persecution.

Internationally, Gorbachev's "new thinking" promises an end to the export of Soviet-sponsored Communist revolution. The Red Army has withdrawn from Afghanistan, and there are other indications that Gorbachev is initiating a retrenchment of many of the Soviet Union's long-standing international commitments. But as encouraging as some of Gorbachev's foreign policies have been, there are also disturbing continuities with the past. Soviet defense spending has not appreciably slowed down under Gorbachev, and there is no clear evidence that offensively-minded Soviet military doctrines—governed by Marxist precepts—have been junked or significantly modified.

Perhaps most disturbing is evidence that Gorbachev has not turned his back on intimidation and deceit. For example, Moscow continued to supply the Nicaraguan Sandinistas with military aid long after Gorbachev promised President Bush that such aid would end. Similarly, Soviet Foreign Minister Shevardnadze's threat to violate the 1988 Intermediate Nuclear Forces Treaty if the United States modernized its short-range Lance missiles in Europe exhibits the same kind of intimidation long associated with Moscow's foreign policy.

In light of these realities, how should the Bush Administration approach the Soviet Union? First and foremost, the United States should be *cautiously* supportive of Gorbachev's reform efforts. It would be foolish for the United States to dismiss Gorbachev's reforms as a sham. Likewise, it would be imprudent for the U.S. to treat the Soviet Union as a member in good standing of the international community. Practically speaking, the United States cannot have normal political and economic relations with the Soviet Union until Moscow demonstrates that it is committed to institutionalizing reform through ending the monopoly power of the Communist Party and through enacting real constitutional restraints on the power of the state.

We cannot expect that this will happen overnight. But we should expect that the rhetoric of reform will be matched by the evolution of free and independent political, economic, and social institutions. Economic and technological cooperation with Moscow should only be incrementally agreed to, and then only as a reward for steady movement toward genuine democratization. Any regression in Soviet domestic or international behavior should trigger a punitive economic and/or technological response by Washington.

Second, because democratization will take years—if it succeeds at all—the United States must maintain a strong military posture. Even many of Ronald Reagan's critics are now willing to admit that his defense buildup played a major role in bringing about positive change in the Soviet Union's behavior. The old Roman maxim, "if you want peace, prepare for war" remains sound wisdom, even at a time when the threat of aggression by the Soviet Union appears unlikely. The best way to insure that Moscow does not threaten the peace in the future is to maintain a strong nuclear and conventional deterrent. Soviet leaders must be convinced that they can never achieve, at a conventional or nuclear level, military superiority. Even the perception that they can is a sure recipe for future international adventurism. In this regard, the United States should make it clear that it will not tolerate Soviet meddling anywhere, but particularly in those areas of the world, such as the Middle East and Central America, where the United States has major interests.

Finally, the United States must continue to woo away the nations of Eastern Europe. Since the end of the Second World War, Eastern Europe has been a strategic and economic insurance policy for Moscow. A Soviet Union devoid of puppet satellites would be a less dangerous Soviet Union. Reform in Poland and elsewhere in Eastern Europe has raised the possibility of the slow evolution of these nations away from Moscow's economic and political domination. The United States can carefully encourage this process, as it has in Poland, through financial support of groups such as Solidarity which are working for genuine democracy.

WESTERN EUROPE

Perhaps the most difficult challenge facing American foreign policy in coming years will be keeping the Western alliance together. For nearly half a century, the alliance of North American and Western European democracies has been the primary defense against Soviet aggression. The hub of the alliance has been the North Atlantic Treaty Organization (NATO). Through NATO, the Western democracies have projected a unified military and political posture toward the Soviet Union and the Warsaw Pact. Ironically, the very success of the Western alliance now threatens to be its undoing.

The first problem the alliance faces is political. Since the end of World War II, the common interest that all the Western democracies had in protecting themselves against Soviet aggression was the glue that united them. The post-War Western alliance is a remarkable phenomenon when we consider that for hundreds of years the nations of Western Europe were in continual conflict with one another. The fact that France and Germany, for example, have been allies for half a century is noteworthy, given their long history of mutual rivalry. Fear of Soviet invasion and the goal of deterring any Soviet belligerence has created a bond within the Western alliance that until recently held firm.

The reason for the appearance of the first cracks in the alliance are directly related to the improved relationship between the United States and the Soviet Union. Gorbachev's domestic reforms and his "new thinking" in foreign policy have significantly lowered the anxiety level among Europeans. Moreover, Gorbachev's charismatic personal style, coupled with the attention he has given to Europeans, has made him a very popular leader among the citizens of Western Europe. A poll conducted in West Germany in 1989 showed that 90 percent of the German public believed Gorbachev was a man who could be trusted. It is herein that the challenge to the unity of the Western alliance arises.

Because Europeans, and particularly West Germans, believe the threat of Soviet aggression has subsided, if not ended, many are beginning to question whether the Western alliance is still needed. This questioning of the alliance's continued viability is primarily directed at the leadership role of the United States. In West Germany, and to a lesser extent in the other major European powers, there are other forces disrupting the unity of the alliance as well.

West Germany has always felt uncomfortable with its separation from its other half—the Communist German Democratic Republic. The unification of Germany has been a goal of every West German government. With the thaw in the Cold War, many West Germans believe now is the time to begin a process leading to eventual unification. This yearning for national unity also reflects another major factor influencing the future of the Western alliance. German nationalism did not die with the defeat of Nazi Germany; it was simply muted. With so many Germans believing that the Soviet Union no longer poses a threat, some Germans are beginning to push for a more independent role for Germany in European affairs. The architect of this new strategy is West Germany's foreign minister Hans-Dietrich Genscher. The focal point of his strategy is to move Germany away from its dependence on the United States, while cultivating closer ties with the Communist nations of Eastern Europe.

There is a demographic factor influencing the future of the Western alliance as well. Recent years has seen the maturation of a new generation of Europeans who do not remember the war that was fought on their soil, and who do not remember a Soviet Union that threatened to swallow up their nations. This new generation of Europeans has known only peace and prosperity. For them, the fear of war and the threat of Soviet communism is only something they have read about in their history books.

In addition to these political forces pulling the Western alliance apart, there are economic forces working to the same end. In 1992 the twelve nations of the European Economic Community (often called the Common Market) will create a fully unified European economic market.[2] After 1992, Europe will be an integrated market with over 320 million consumers (50 percent larger than the United States) and a unified economy producing $4.5 trillion in goods and services, second in size only to the United States. The size and strength of this integrated European economy will inevitably generate strains in American-European relations.

The fluid nature of political and economic events among the nations of the Western alliance require deft handling by the United States. The United States must do everything it can to maintain the unity of the Western democracies. Again, Mikhail Gorbachev's intentions remain unclear. But historically the Soviet Union has time and again tried to drive a wedge between the Europeans and the United States. If this happened, the strategic position of the Soviet Union in Europe would be greatly enhanced, possibly even altering the global balance of power. For this reason, the United States needs to engage Gorbachev's European initiatives with a healthy dose of skepticism and caution.

Certainly the United States must be sensitive to the interests of Europeans as well as the dynamics of European history (e.g., West Germany's desire for a unified Germany). But the United States must make it clear to the Europeans that their future and that of democracy rests with the continuation of an unshakable, strong Western alliance. The United States should never agree to any proposal that would bring about the dissolution of the alliance.

For several years a major issue in Western European relations has been the presence of nuclear weapons on European soil. In 1988 the United States and the Soviet Union agreed to remove and destroy all of their intermediate-range nuclear weapons. This treaty was tremendously popular among the Europeans who know that if war were to break out in Europe, it would be *their* nations which would be devastated. Following the INF Treaty, the Soviet Union proposed, with enthusiastic West German support, that all short-range nuclear missiles (missiles with a battlefield range of forty to 100 miles) be removed from Europe as well. This proposal was greeted much less enthusiastically by President Bush.

The proposal for the elimination of short-range nuclear weapons illustrated the danger ahead for the Western alliance. Nuclear weapons are an emotional issue for the West Germans and for other Europeans as well. The problem with the proposal for the elimination of such weapons is twofold: It would further decouple European reliance upon the United States, while at the same time giving the Soviet Union and its Warsaw Pact allies an overwhelming conventional military superiority in Europe. The American nuclear forces in Europe have served the purpose of affirming American support for Europe and deterring Soviet conventional military superiority. President Bush understood this and rightly rejected the Soviet/West German proposal. In its place, the president made it clear that any reduction of short-range nuclear forces in Europe must be matched by a serious reduction of Soviet conventional forces.[3]

The issue of arms control cuts right to the heart of not only alliance relations, but also of America's role in the world. The Western alliance remains, even in this new era of U.S.-Soviet relations, an essential element in the defense of freedom. Furthermore, a credible Western military deterrent on the continent of Europe remains essential to the preservation of world peace.

On the economic front, the creation of an integrated European economy should be welcomed by the United States. Anything that strengthens the nations of Europe is good for the Western alliance. An economically strong Europe is in the United States' interest, just as it is in the interest of global democracy. While economic disputes will certainly arise, as they have over the past thirty years, these need not contribute to an increase in political tension between Washington and the European capitals. Above all, the Bush Administration must be vigilant in pressing the Europeans to make sure their new economic arrangements promote reciprocal free trade.

In sum: the future of the United States and of the nations of Europe are inextricably tied together. They share a common culture, common values, and a common interest in preserving freedom. Sensitivity to each other's interests, and a firm resolve to maintain an alliance that has guaranteed peace and prosperity for fifty years, are the necessary ingredients of American-European relations in the years ahead.

JAPAN

Along with Western European relations, the United States' relationship with Japan is of paramount importance. As a strong, free Europe is essential to U.S. interests, so is a strong, free Japan. Frequent squabbles between Tokyo and Washington over trade policy often obscure the fundamental interests which both countries share. Japan is the most powerful and influential democracy in Asia. As such, Japan has an important role to play in fostering peace and stability in that region of the world.

American policy toward Japan must be guided by several considerations. In light of the economic challenge Japan presents to the United States, there is a tendency on the part of Americans to seek retaliation in response to Japanese trade policies that do not seem fair. Domestically cultivated Japanese rice, for example, sells for twenty times that of American rice, and yet American rice producers have had a difficult time breaking into the Japanese market.[4] The proliferation of Japanese electronics products and automobiles, and also stories of massive Japanese purchases of American real estate help to fuel the resentment many Americans feel toward Japan.

In this instance, the facts do not fit the popular mythology. The reality is that Japan's tariff level is one of the lowest in the world, and that most of its non-tariff barriers have been removed.[5] While it may not be pleasant for Americans to admit it, the reason so many Japanese products are sold in the United States is because they are producing high-quality goods that Americans like. This is how a free market works: consumers vote with their pocketbooks. In recent years, Americans have been voting Japanese.

As far as exports are concerned, much of the difficulty that American manufacturers have in penetrating Japanese markets has to do with the way the Japanese economy functions. Unlike the market-dominated economies of the West, the Japanese economy is dominated by bureaucratic, industrial, and governmental networks. Consequently, the Japanese tend to buy directly from companies that are part of specific networks, even if the desired item can be purchased more cheaply from another firm inside or outside Japan.[6]

Certainly the United States needs to respond to unfair Japanese trade practices. However, it would be a mistake, politically and economically, for Washington to overreact. The voluntary automobile quotas that the Japanese recently adopted represent the kind of mutually beneficial agreement both countries should pursue in resolving other trade disputes. What the United States needs to avoid is inflammatory rhetoric and policies that hurt the American consumer and damage American strategic interests.

The number one priority of American policy toward Japan is to ensure that Japan remains a stable, prosperous member of the democratic world. Twice in the past century the Japanese military set out to conquer Asia; twice its imperialistic ambitions were thwarted. While the Japanese have proven themselves fast learners, it is not in the United States' interest to have Japan reemerge as a regional military power. The uncertainties that would be generated both inside Japan and in the other nations of Asia—particularly in China and South Korea, where the bitter memories of Japanese conquest are still alive—would not be conducive to the future stability of Japan or the rest of Asia. For this reason, the United States must be willing to bear the lion's share of the defense burden in Asia. In return, it is reasonable for the United States to expect that the Japanese will sincerely try to adjust those structural aspects of its economy which prevent American producers from competing equitably in Japan.

In dealing with Japan, the United States must remember that nothing is ever immutable in international politics. Forty years ago, for example, who would have thought that today Japan would be a stable democracy rivaling the United States in its technological and economic prowess? If history teaches us anything, it is that the future of international politics is difficult to predict. With these observations in mind, the Japanese must be assured that the American commitment to their security is firm and unwavering. Any economic controversies that arise between the two nations must be treated for what they are—disagreements between friends and allies.

CHINA

From 1949 until 1971, the United States had virtually no contact with the most populous nation in the world.[7] During those years, the People's Republic of China experienced great hardships brought about by the unpredictable and ruthless dictatorship of Mao Zedong. Mao's policies were directly responsible for the death of tens of millions of Chinese. His own brand of Marxism, known as Maoism, created a Chinese society which resembled Stalinism at its brutal worst.

Under these conditions, neither China nor the United States was interested in cultivating better relations. This was a difficult period for the United States because of its previous history of friendly relations with China. American merchants had begun trade contacts with China shortly after the American Revolution, and American missionary activity throughout the nineteenth and early twentieth centuries was a source of goodwill between the two peoples. In the early part of this century, Chinese democratic reformers Sun Yat-sen and Chiang Kai-shek were revered by Americans, even if their public image did not always fit the reality.

It was natural, therefore, that when changes began to take place in China at the end of Mao's life,[8] the United States sought to forge closer relations with Beijing. Since normalization of relations, the American relationship with China has been delicate and precarious because of the uncertainties of Chinese politics. The brutal crackdown on Chinese students in the Spring of 1989 illustrates the unpredictable nature of the Chinese political system. Who is in charge of Chinese politics and what policies the Chinese leadership is pursuing are both difficult to discern. This chronic uncertainty makes American relations with China difficult.

Nevertheless, the United States cannot turn its back on China. Apart from the impressive fact that one out of every five people in the world is Chinese, the United States has essential interests in China. In the broad picture of the global balance of power, China remains—even in the Gorbachev era—an important counterbalance to Soviet influence in Asia. It would be disastrous if China would ever revert to its pre-1950 alliance with the Soviet Union. Even though the Chinese Communist system remains an anathema to the United States, it is in America's interests, as well as the interests of freedom, that the United States not give the Chinese reason to turn to Moscow.

At the same time, the United States has an interest in seeing China continue its evolution away from totalitarianism. This process, started by Deng Xiaoping, was dealt a major setback following the Red Army's 1989 massacre of students in Tiananmen Square. The revival of repression, however, is likely to be short-lived. It is highly unlikely that the Chinese government will be able to permanently turn back the clock on the economic and cultural reforms of the past decade. The evidence is strong that Marxism is a spent force in China. Moreover, the legitimacy of the Communist government died with the students it killed. The sacrifice of those students and the economic and cultural openness that the Chinese people have enjoyed in the post-Mao years will inevitably bring pressure for more political freedom.

The United States cannot conduct business as usual with the Chinese government if it persists in the brutal repression of its people. However, it is not in the United States' interest to abandon China. Such a response might satisfy our moralistic instinct, but it would benefit neither the democratic movement in China nor American interests. As in the past twenty years, the

United States must prudently measure its response to China, rewarding Beijing for policies that promote democratization, and expressing our unequivocal condemnation of policies that retard democratization.

The experience of South Korea and Taiwan illustrates the tremendous economic potential of the Asian economies. Equally important, their experience illustrates that the road to democracy often has setbacks and detours, but that once the journey has begun, there is no turning back. These lessons need to frame U.S. policy toward China in the years ahead.

THE MIDDLE EAST

The Middle East today is a tinderbox. Its problems are complex, being aggravated by centuries of violence and mistrust. The fact that religion plays a central role in the politics of the region only further intensifies the difficulty of finding solutions. And yet, because of its geographical location and because of its abundant natural resources, the Middle East is a region of major interest to the United States.

The centerpiece of United States policy in the Middle East must continue to be built around American support for Israel. Since 1987, Americans have witnessed daily images of Israeli military action directed against Palestinians. The effect of these images has been to raise questions about continued American support for Israel. In spite of the tragic events in the West Bank and Gaza, the United States must remain firm in its support for Israel.

There are sound reasons for pursuing this policy. First, Israel is the only nation in the Middle East to share the cultural, legal, and political traditions of the West. Israel is the only democracy governed by the rule of law in the Middle East. The Israeli response to the Palestinian *intifada* (or uprising) has certainly strained its democratic institutions and traditions. Nonetheless, it would be completely imprudent for the United States to pursue policies that would threaten the security of Israel.

The second reason the United States should maintain close relations with Israel is that Israel has been a close ally of the United States and an important source of stability in the Middle

East. The destruction of Lebanon and its degeneration into anarchy illustrates the realities that characterize much of Middle Eastern politics. The idea of a unity of Arab and Islamic nations is a myth betrayed by the bitter internal factionalism and terrorism supported by nations such as Iran and Syria. Were it not for the existence of Israel, the fate of Lebanon could reasonably be expected to be the fate of other nations in the Middle East as well. Even with all of its own domestic and international problems, Israel is an important source of regional stability. Israel serves to protect the survival of democratic values in the region.

The final reason the United States needs to remain unwavering in its support of Israel is moral. The meaning of Israel is powerfully captured by the message of the Jewish holocaust memorial, located in the hills of West Jerusalem. The existence of Israel is a symbol of a people's survival of tyranny and their quest for freedom. Having helped to destroy Nazism, the United States has a moral obligation to ensure that a free Israel survives into the twenty-first century.

The Palestinian uprising has complicated the United States' relationship with Israel. There are no quick fixes to the Palestinian problem. At some point, under some formula, Israel will have to seriously negotiate with the Palestinians. This will not be easy, as evidenced by the deep political divisions which exist in domestic Israeli politics. The United States can play a constructive diplomatic role in facilitating the negotiation process. But this process will never seriously begin if Israel believes that the United States is less than fully committed to its future security.

On the other hand, the United States must not take the position that Israel must negotiate at any cost. The picture that Americans receive from the media concerning the Palestinian problem is not always fully complete. While the Palestinian people living in the West Bank and Gaza have suffered, their plight is not as unambiguous as the press would lead us to believe. For example, the only reason the West Bank and Gaza are occupied is because Arab nations unsuccessfully joined together to destroy Israel in 1967. Furthermore, for all their condemnation of Israel, the Arab nations' treatment of the Palestinians living in their own countries has been dismal.

Perhaps the major obstacle facing Israel is the nature of the

Palestinian leadership. In 1988 Yasir Arafat intimated that the Palestine Liberation Organization now respects Israel's right to exist. However, the PLO has not unequivocally renounced its long-standing objective of destroying Israel. Since the Palestinian uprising began, dozens of moderate Palestinians who have not marched in step with the leadership of the *intifada* have been executed by Palestinian radicals. Until this situation changes, Israel cannot be expected to negotiate.

Israel cannot begin the process of negotiation until it is absolutely assured of its security. Israel is a pariah in the Middle East, surrounded by nations committed to its liquidation. Three times in the past forty years Israel has had to shed the blood of its young men and women to protect its existence. American policy toward Israel must not be swayed by an emotional response to persistent television images. American policy must be concerned with finding a long-term solution that benefits both the legitimate aspirations of the Palestinian people and the nation of Israel.

As a first step, the United States should make clear its support for Israel's security. Second, the United States needs to use its influence to convince both the Israelis and the Palestinians that their interests are best served by good-faith negotiations. While American influence with the Palestinians is limited, Washington should express its willingness to work closely with moderate Arab nations such as Egypt, Saudi Arabia, and Jordan in an attempt to purge the Palestinian movement of its most radical elements.

The task of building peace in the Middle East will not be easy. A weighing of likely future outcomes in that part of the world does not give much reason for optimism. Animosities of all kinds are deeply embedded in the politics of the region. The realities of Middle Eastern politics are a bold reminder that perfect peace awaits Christ's return. In the meantime, American foreign policy needs to persevere, knowing that while its successes will be few, the stakes for America—and for democracy—are high.

CENTRAL AMERICA

Of all American interests in the Third World, none is more important than the cultivation and preservation of democracy in

Central America. Although the combined population of these seven nations is less than thirty million,[9] what happens there will have a significant impact on international politics in the years ahead.

The United States has always had an ambiguous relationship with the nations of Central America. Because of their geographical proximity and shared colonial histories, the nations of North and South America have felt a kinship toward one another. The United States' first major foreign policy doctrine, the Monroe Doctrine of 1823, proclaimed that the United States would act as the protector of the independence of the Americas.

For the nations of Latin America, most of whom gained their independence from Spain and Mexico around the time of the Monroe Doctrine, the United States was the model of democracy they sought to emulate. American heroes such as George Washington became the heroes of Latin American nations, while the institutions of United States democracy were copied into their constitutions. The two regions began to drift apart, however, in the latter half of the nineteenth century. While the United States prospered, Latin America was beset by poverty and political instability.

Acting out of genuine concern for its southern neighbors, although not always with appropriate sensitivity, the United States intervened frequently in Central America after the turn of this century. It is common for critics of American foreign policy to attribute U.S. intervention to economic motives. The explanation, while partially true, ignores the fact that U.S. intervention was motivated out of a sincere desire to foster stability in nations that were beset by chronic instability. Regardless of the intentions of U.S. policy, American economic and military involvement provided an easy scapegoat for those seeking to place the blame for Central America's troubles on external influences.

The prevalence of dictatorial rule in Central America has always presented problems for U.S. policy. But the United States has never turned its back on the region; Central America is too important to U.S. interests. In the previous chapter we saw that American economic interests in Central America are minimal. However, the political stakes in Central America are immense, for Central Americans as well as for the United States. In particular, the stakes in Central America were dramatically raised by the consolidation of a Marxist-Leninist regime in Nicaragua.[10]

Since coming to power in 1979, the Sandinistas have staged phony elections, curtailed basic freedoms, imposed a totalitarian network of control over all areas of Nicaraguan life, pursued economic policies that have wrecked the Nicaraguan economy, and built the largest military machine in all of Central America. The Sandinista army (it is the party army, not a national army) has received hundreds of millions of dollars of aid from the Soviet Union, in addition to logistical support from Cuba, Bulgaria, and Libya. The Sandinista facade of democratic legitimacy is betrayed by the kind of society they have built, as well as by their ongoing support of radical Marxist revolutions around the world.[11] In Central America, the Sandinistas have been the primary conduit of weapons to the Marxist guerrillas in El Salvador. The Sandinistas have even shipped vast amounts of arms to Panamanian dictator Manuel Noriega.

The domestic and international record of the Sandinistas provides compelling evidence that they pose a major threat to peace and democracy in Central America. During the Reagan years, U.S. policy combined diplomatic isolation and financial support for the *contras* (i.e., those Nicaraguans who have taken up arms to fight the Sandinistas) in an attempt to bring about democracy in Nicaragua. The Reagan policy was hampered by those in the U.S. Congress who were either unconcerned about the Sandinistas or who were interested in wresting control of foreign policy away from the president. Regardless of their motives, the eventual effect was to allow the Sandinistas to consolidate their revolutionary ambitions.

The Bush Administration is intent on building a bipartisan consensus that will allow a continuation of American humanitarian aid to flow to the *contras* as an incentive to force the Sandinistas to end their repression. The Sandinistas, however, show no evidence that they are interested in giving up their total control of Nicaraguan society. Judged by their actions—their suppression of freedom at home and their support of revolutionary movements elsewhere—there is no indication that the Sandinistas are interested in abandoning their radical Marxist agenda for Nicaragua and the rest of Central America. The Sandinista leadership is skilled at the public relations game; consequently, U.S. policy must be based on the Sandinistas' record, not their rhetoric.

The congressional defeat of the Reagan policy in Nicaragua has worsened the situation in Central America. Not only did Congress turn down the heat on the Sandinistas, but in doing so contributed to the deterioration of the situation in El Salvador. During the 1980s the United States provided $3.5 billion in aid—most of it economic—to the centrist government of Jose Napolean Duarte. Washington invested so much in the Duarte government because it represented a viable democratic alternative to the extremes of Left and Right in El Salvadorian politics. During his tenure, however, the Duarte government was besieged by a wave of terror carried out by the Sandinista-supported Communist movement known as the FMLN. These attacks, along with continued (though dramatically reduced) right-wing death activity, denied Duarte the ability to build a stable democracy in El Salvador.

In 1989 Duarte's Christian Democratic government was defeated in a free and fair election by the right-of-center ARENA party.[12] El Salvador's new president, American-educated Alfredo Cristiani, pledged to continue to build upon the democratic foundations laid by his predecessor. Herein lies the challenge to American foreign policy. There are some in the American Congress who are suspicious of Cristiani's political roots, fearing a return to power of those in control of the death squads. Because of this, some members of Congress have hinted that the United States should consider ending all aid to El Salvador. This would be a disaster. The experience of Nicaragua provides good reason for the United States to not forsake El Salvador, which would likely lead to a Marxist takeover there and in the process deal a fatal blow to freedom in Central America by endangering the shaky democracies of Honduras and Guatemala.

The existence of a permanent Marxist presence in Central America will perpetuate tyranny, poverty, and instability in the region. Communist regimes also provide a valuable stage for the export of revolution to the rest of South America, while giving the Soviet Union potentially valuable military outposts close to the U.S. border. For these reasons, the United States can never accept the Sandinista regime as part of the regional status quo. The Bush Administration should never give up American support for the democratic resistance in Nicaragua. Though restrained by Congress, President Bush should forcefully make the case to the

American public for continued American pressure on the Sandinistas.

In particular, the Bush Administration needs to aggressively counteract the disinformation spread by groups—particularly religious groups such as Witness for Peace—which are sympathetic to the Sandinistas. U.S. pressure should take the form of holding the Sandinistas publicly accountable for their actions, and of financially supporting opposition groups inside Nicaragua and in exile. As part of this overall strategy, the Bush Administration should not allow the *contra* movement to be destroyed until democracy returns to Nicaragua.

In El Salvador, the case must be made quickly for not abandoning that country. The United States must make it clear to ARENA that it will not tolerate a return to the days when the death squads ruled that country. Concurrently, Salvadorians must be assured that the United States will continue to support the construction of democracy in their nation. This support should be in the form of continued economic aid and support for the strengthening of independent organizations such as free trade unions and a free press. American aid to El Salvador should be tied to continued democratic reform, but the United States—and particularly Congress—needs to remember that the road to democracy is long and bumpy. Above all, it is imperative that El Salvador not become another Nicaragua.

SOUTH AFRICA

Perhaps no single American foreign policy issue has generated more emotional heat than South Africa. The future of that country is important to the United States for several reasons. It is a nation blessed with abundant natural and human resources, and its geographical location gives it major strategic value. In addition, South Africa shares many of the same traditions and values of the Western world. Finally, South Africa possesses the only fully-developed economy in all of Africa. Juxtaposed against these realities, South Africa's discriminatory racial policy of apartheid has torn South African society apart and made it an international pariah. No other nation in the world has been more vilified than South Africa.[13]

Without a doubt, apartheid is an egregious offense that

needs to be abolished. But in a comparative context, it is impossible to argue that the sins of South Africa are worse than the sins of most other African nations, not to mention many other nations around the world. Twenty-two African nations are military dictatorships, and in thirty-nine out of forty-one black African nations black populations do not have the right to vote.[14] According to Freedom House, the condition of political rights and civil liberties in South Africa is better than in Kenya, Chad, Algeria, Nigeria, and a host of other African countries. Moreover, political violence in South Africa is less than what is found in other African countries such as Ethiopia, Angola, and even Kenya.

As repugnant as apartheid is, the depth of hostility which South Africa elicits is greater than it should be given the fact that the injustices of South African society are no worse than what one finds throughout Africa, in the Communist world, and in much of the rest of the Third World, Indeed, the attack against South Africa is primarily ideological. Jacques Ellul perceptively points out that "South Africa is the good conscience the West buys on the cheap."[15] South Africa has become a symbol to many Third World dictators and Western intellectuals of all that they despise about the West. It is

> the incarnation of unrelieved evil . . . a splendid scapegoat! It has everything: racism, white exploitation of blacks, the production of such despicable goods as gold and diamonds, dictatorship, moralism, power based on religion, the union of church and state, capitalism in a pure form—everything![16]

Apartheid cannot be condoned. On the other hand, our distaste for apartheid is no excuse for distorting South African realities all out of perspective. Nor does it give us liberty to overlook similar or worse injustices committed by other nations.

In light of this, American policy needs to be based on a careful and fair analysis of the complex political realities in South Africa.[17] The most important goal of American policy must be to encourage South Africa to move toward a post-apartheid democratic society. It is not in the interest of the United States, nor the people of South Africa, to have apartheid replaced by a new form of oppression. For this reason, it is politically imprudent and morally unjustifiable to advocate the destruction of apartheid without considering what will replace it.

Also, the United States must realize the limits of its ability to influence events in South Africa. In dealing with South Africa, the United States must make clear its opposition to apartheid.[18] At the same time, the United States must affirm its commitment to a *democratic* future for South Africa. As apartheid is unacceptable to the United States, so is the agenda of the radical Left and the radical Right.

The Bush Administration must navigate a new course for American policy. During the 1980s the United States was not successful in influencing events in South Africa. While economic sanctions may make good domestic political sense for American legislators, it is a policy that has greatly reduced American influence with the Pretoria government. Just as importantly, economic sanctions have hurt the very South Africans the United States wishes to help. Contrary to the impression that is pervasive among Americans, the vast majority of South Africans—white as well as black—do not support sanctions; every major poll that has been conducted among South Africans has yielded the same conclusion.[19]

While the economic stick can be one effective tool in encouraging movement away from apartheid, the past ten years provides conclusive evidence that it is counterproductive if used alone. In formulating a new policy toward South Africa, Washington must help to nurture the democratic center, that majority of South Africans—white and non-white—who have rejected the radical solutions of the Left and Right. Walter Kansteiner has referred to this approach as "democratic enhancement." It is a strategy whereby the United States uses its influence to cooperate and encourage those businesses, labor unions, church groups, and political organizations who wish to build a democratic future for their country. Economic growth, stimulated by American investment, can also be—as it has been in the past—a particularly powerful vehicle for undermining the remaining pillars of apartheid.

There are no ultimate solutions that will satisfy everyone in South Africa. The complexities and paradoxes of South African society are so deep and so pervasive that South Africans will have to muddle through on their own, searching for a compromise solution. The prerequisite to an eventual solution is a realization on the part of all the relevant actors that no one will get everything they want; everyone will have to give in a little. American policy will not solve South Africa's problems, but American policy will either be irrelevant, a hindrance, or a help to the final outcome. American policy during the past decade, designed primarily by Congress, has been irrelevant at best and a hindrance at worst. The Bush Administration has the opportunity to build a new basis for U.S. policy toward South Africa, one that is helpful.

TWELVE

CONCLUSION: MAKING A DIFFERENCE

*T*he heart of the Christian faith is the resurrection of Jesus Christ. In that historical event God's redemptive plan for history finds its culmination, and in that event God's promise of the ultimate fulfillment of His Kingdom is foreshadowed. The Christian's hope for the future is derived directly from the resurrection of our Lord.[1] Because Christ rose from the dead, we know that our faith is real and that our labors on behalf of Christ and His Kingdom are not in vain.[2]

The reality of the resurrection has two implications for our approach to international politics. First, because Christ lives and reigns, we are assured that one day all human suffering will end. The world is filled with pain, and so it will be until Christ returns. But as Christians we live with the confidence that Christ will one day banish sin and restore all of creation according to His perfect will. This is the basis of the Christian hope for ourselves and for the world in which God has placed us. Our Christian faith is optimistic about the future precisely because we worship the sovereign Lord of the universe.

Our optimism is no excuse for complacency, however. It is a misreading of Biblical teaching to assume that because Christ will one day return we do not need to be concerned with the affairs of this world. To the contrary, a Biblical faith is an *active* faith, one that takes seriously God's evangelistic and cultural mandate. It is because of our hope that we desire to share our faith with others; and it is because of our hope that we should be involved in shaping the contours of our culture.

But how do we go about doing that in the realm of international politics? In the previous chapters we discussed the relationship of our Christian faith to international politics. But as individual Christians, how should we be involved in those issues that are a part of international politics? How can we make a difference?

In answering these questions we must first emphasize that God calls each of us to different tasks. As we look at the world's problems, we should not feel guilty because we cannot solve all of these problems ourselves.[3] The great problems of international politics are important; many are matters of life and death. But looked at from a Christian perspective, these problems are not *more* important than the day-to-day problems we confront in our own personal lives. God has called each of us to live our lives in different ways. We are members of different churches, we live in different places, we are part of different families, and we encounter different daily experiences. What God asks of us is that we be faithful to Him—that we serve Him and glorify Him wherever He has placed us.

The Bible also teaches that we are to be responsible citizens; among other things, we are to obey our government and pray for our leaders. Responsible citizenship also entails an appreciation of the value of democracy and an understanding of those forces that threaten freedom. In addition, we should understand the role our nation should play in enhancing democracy and challenging tyranny.

Beyond the basics of responsible citizenship, there are several ways Christians can influence international politics. We should vote for those individuals we think will most effectively promote freedom and fight tyranny. In addition to voting, we can help influence the course of our nation's foreign relations through such things as writing our elected representatives and writing letters to the editors of newspapers and magazines. We can become even more directly involved through participation in organizations that deal with international issues. These might be nonpartisan humanitarian organizations or organizations which focus their concerns on a particular region of the world or a particular international problem, such as religious freedom. Above all, it is important that we be as well-informed as possible. For this reason, it is imperative that we get in the habit of regularly reading newspapers and periodicals which provide accurate and comprehensive coverage of international affairs.[4]

For Christians who feel God's call to a career in international relations, there are a variety of vocations to consider. Careers in government, with the State Department, with intelligence organizations, or with a variety of other agencies responsible for foreign policy provide an excellent opportunity for those who want to have a direct impact on American foreign policy. There are also careers with international organizations (such as the World Bank) and international businesses which enable Christians to be directly involved in international relations.

Whether we simply seek to be responsible citizens or whether we work for the Secretary of State, international politics is important. This is a Biblical teaching, reinforced by the interdependent nature of our contemporary world. Regardless of the specific role God has chosen for us, however, all Christians share a common interest in maintaining the integrity of the mission of Christ's Church here on earth. Indeed, the most important contribution Christians can make to international politics is to ensure that the mission of the Church is never compromised. And that mission is to proclaim that Christ is Lord.

One of the greatest dangers facing the Church today comes from those who would replace this mission with a partisan political agenda.[5] Such an approach does not represent Biblical Christianity, but rather an ideologically-motivated impostor. Only by witnessing to a God who is greater than man and his earthly institutions is the Church faithful in being salt and light to a sinful world. By remaining true to its mission of proclaiming a Biblical gospel, the Church restrains the tyrannical pretensions of human sin and nurtures those values which are essential to democracy. Until Christ returns, it is our task as Christians to make certain that the Good News is proclaimed and that freedom endures.

NOTES

INTRODUCTION

1. John 18:36.
2. John 17:14.
3. Acts 1:6, 7.
4. Hebrews 11:13, 16.
5. Hebrews 11:10.
6. Matthew 28:19.
7. Matthew 6:10.
8. 2 Corinthians 6:17.
9. Genesis 1:28.
10. The classic discussion and typology of Christian responses to the world is H. Richard Niebuhr's *Christ and Culture* (New York: Harper & Row, 1951). A more recent and popularized version of Niebuhr's typology is Robert E. Webber's *The Secular Saint* (Grand Rapids, MI: Zondervan, 1979).
11. Romans 13:1–7; Luke 20:20–26.
12. Protestantism, of course, arose in reaction to the ecclesiology of the Catholic Church. Specifically, Protestantism rejects the authority structure of Catholicism whereby authority is exercised from the top down. The Protestant tradition, in contrast, stresses the priesthood of all believers, and thus authority is exercised from the bottom up. This is certainly an important reason why Protestants have never developed a tradition of social thought. The nature of American Protestantism, with its pietistic roots and emphasis on individual religious experience, has also contributed to this disinclination to systematically theorize about social life. Finally, American Protestants of all kinds have been influenced by the pragmatic tradition that is a part of the American character. As a generalization, it is fair to say that Americans are more interested in whether something works than they are in providing a systematic explanation of why it works. It also needs to be stressed that while the Catholic Church does have a long and rich tradition of social thought, such a tradition

does not guarantee clear thinking. For a brilliant and exhaustive treatment of this problem in the context of the American Catholic experience and war and peace issues, see George Weigel's *Tranquillitas Ordinas: The Present Failure and Future Promise of American Catholic Thought on War and Peace* (New York: Oxford University Press, 1987).

CHAPTER ONE *America in the World: The Role of Politics and Ideas*

1. William A. Galston and Christopher J. Makins, "Campaign '88 and Foreign Policy," *Foreign Policy* 71 (Summer 1988): p. 3.
2. Mark Noll persuasively argues that the roots of American "exceptionalism" are to be found in the Reformed Protestant culture which came to define English Protestantism during the late sixteenth and early seventeenth centuries. Writes Noll:

When events in England during the first third of the seventeenth century seemed to rule out the achievement of Puritan purposes in that land, a significant minority of Puritans came to the New World. Here they would establish godly commonwealths where the reform of self, church, and society could go forward. . . . The Reformed ideas that they brought with them as Puritans from England to America determined the early history of New England, exerted a compelling influence elsewhere in the American colonies, and became the dominant force in the shaping of religious attitudes toward public life in American civilization.

Mark A. Noll, *One Nation Under God? Christian Faith and Political Action in America* (San Francisco: Harper & Row, 1988), p. 19.
3. The intellectual origins of the Founders' understanding of American exceptionalism is thoroughly and brilliantly discussed in Forrest McDonald's *Novus Ordo Seclorum: The Intellectual Origins of the Constitution* (Lawrence: University of Kansas, 1985).
4. Reinhold Niebuhr, *The Irony of American History* (New York: Charles Scribner's Sons, 1952), p. 28.
5. The intermingling of Christian and Enlightenment themes in the historical development of U.S. foreign policy is profoundly evidenced in Woodrow Wilson's approach to U.S. responsibility in the world. Quoting historian Lloyd Ambrosius:

Christian faith undergirded Wilson's confidence in progress. He thought God had predestined victory for faithful men and nations. . . . He viewed the United States as the epitome of Christianity: "America was born a Christian nation. America was born to exemplify that devotion to the elements of righteousness which are derived from the revelations of the Holy Scripture. . . ." From his perspective, the United States appeared in the vanguard of world history, leading toward universal progress. [Therefore], Wilson justified American involvement in the [First World] as as a Christian crusade for democracy.

Ambrosius goes on to argue that Wilson's ill-fated quest to restructure international relations around a League of Nations represented an attempt to "enable the United States to provide leadership overseas without entangling itself in the Old World's diplomacy and wars." Lloyd E Ambrosius, *Woodrow Wilson and the American Diplomatic Tradition* (Cambridge, MA: Cambridge University Press, 1987), pp. x, 12.

6. The "new isolationism" has been the subject of a lively debate among its proponents and critics. See, for example, Robert M. Tucker, "Isolation and Intervention," *The National Interest* 1 (Fall 1985): pp. 16–25; and, Charles Krauthammer, "Isolationism: A Riposte," *The National Interest* 2 (Winter 1986): pp. 115–118.

7. Galston and Makins, p. 4; see also Norman J. Orstein and Mark Schmitt, "Foreign Policy and the Election," *The National Interest* 12 (Summer 1988): p. 4.

8. Murray writes that "The American Proposition is at once doctrinal and practical. . . . It is an affirmation and also an intention. . . . [And it is] a truth to be demonstrated." John Courtney Murray, *We Hold These Truths: Catholic Reflections on the American Proposition* (New York: Sheed and Ward, 1960), p. vii.

9. The first systematic study of the American political tradition was Alexis de Tocqueville's classic *Democracy in America*, published in 1835. In recent decades Richard Hofstadter's *The American Political Tradition* (New York: Vintage Books, 1974) and Louis Hartz's *The Liberal Tradition in America* (New York: Harcourt, Brace & World, 1955) have become the standard historical treatments of the American political tradition. Herbert McClosky and John Zaller's *The American Ethos: Public Attitudes Toward Capitalism and Democracy* (Cambridge, MA: Harvard University Press, 1984) empirically defines the contemporary nature of the American political tradition.

10. A commitment to the values and institutions of liberal (i.e., free, representative) democracy and capitalism have been at the core of the American political tradition. About conflict in the American experience, Hofstadter writes: "The fierceness of political struggles in America history has often been misleading . . . for above and beyond temporary and local conflicts there has been a common ground, a unity of cultural and political tradition, upon which American civilization has stood." Hofstadter, *The American Political Tradition*, p. xxxix.

11. It needs to be emphasized that what is commonly referred to in contemporary political parlance as "conservatism" and "liberalism" have not differed historically in their affirmation of those basic beliefs which underlay the American political tradition. In the early 1950s many conservatives, such as Robert Taft, were opposed to an active U.S. presence in world affairs, while the liberals of the time, such as Reinhold Niebuhr, supported a strong U.S. leadership role in the world. Nonetheless, both conservatives and liberals of that era accepted—and continued to do so until recently—the normative value of American democracy, particularly in its struggle against the tyranny of Marxism-Leninism. For most of the post-World War II period, both American conservatives and liberals were united in their fierce support of American democracy and in their opposition to Marxism-Leninism. That much has changed in the past decades is evidenced by how strange the words of Reinhold Niebuhr, written in 1952, sound today when he wrote with certitude that "*Everybody* understands the *obvious* meaning

of the world struggle in which we are engaged" (emphasis added). Niebuhr, *The Irony of American History*, p. 1.

12. Recent years have seen the publication of a host of books which tell the story of the rise and fall of Communist influence in America in the period from 1930 to 1950. See, for example, William Barrett, *The Truants: Adventures Among the Intellectuals* (Garden City, NJ: Anchor Press, 1982); Sidney Hook, *Out of Step: An Unquiet Life in the 20th Century* (New York: Harper & Row, 1987); William O'Neill, *A Better World* (New York: Simon & Schuster, 1982).

13. A historiography of the New Left has recently begun to emerge. Three of the most influential, and sympathetic, accounts of the origins of the New Left are: James Miller, *Democracy Is in the Streets: From Port Huron to the Siege of Chicago* (New York: Simon & Schuster, 1987); Maurice Isserman, *If I Had a Hammer: The Death of the Old Left and the Birth of the New Left* (New York: Basic Books, 1987); Todd Giltin, *The Sixties: Years of Hope, Days of Rage* (New York: Bantam Books, 1987).

14. Edward Shils, "Totalitarians and Antinomians," in *Political Passages: Journeys of Change Through Two Decades,* ed. John H. Bunzel (New York: The Free Press, 1988), p. 15.

15. *Ibid.*, pp. 16, 17.

16. William Phillips, "Partisan Review Then and Now," *Partisan Review* li (1984): p. 492.

17. See Shils, "Totalitarians and Antinomians," p. 25.

18. Peter L. Berger, *The Capitalist Revolution* (New York: Basic Books, 1986), pp. 66, 67.

19. For a thorough treatment of the value and belief system of the New Class, see Barry Bruce-Briggs, ed., *The New Class?* (New Brunswick, NJ: Transaction Books, 1979); Peter L. Berger, "Ethics and the New Class," *Worldview* (April 1978): pp. 6–11; Robert Lichter and Stanley Rotham, "The Media Elite and American Values," *Public Opinion* (October/November 1981): pp. 42–60; Marvin Olasky, *Prodigal Press: The Anti-Christian Bias of the American News Media* (Westchester, IL: Crossway Books, 1988).

20. The 1988 presidential election was certainly not the first to see a radical-Left challenge to what we have called the American Proposition. Eugene Debs's candidacies under the Socialist Party ticket in the years 1904, 1908, and 1912 were the first such challenges. In those three presidential elections Debs never received more than 6 percent of the popular vote. Henry Wallace's 1948 bid for the presidency through the Progressive Party also represented a radical challenge to the traditional values of American politics. Wallace, however, was only able to garner a little more than 2 percent of the popular vote in the general election. George McGovern's candidacy in 1972 was more successful than either Debs's or Wallace's (McGovern captured 37 percent of the popular vote); however, much of McGovern's support came from loyalists within the Democratic Party. McGovern's support was not broad-based, as evidenced by the significant number of Democrats who deserted the Democratic ticket to vote for Richard Nixon. Having said that, McGovern's candidacy was certainly more significant than that of Debs or Wallace, for while the latter two represented fringe movements whose

appeal was narrow and short-lived, McGovern's candidacy marked a turning away of the Democratic Party from its New Deal agenda that had characterized Democratic politics since the early 1930s, and an embrace of the values and agenda of the New Left. The popular euphemism "McGovern Democrat" reflects this transformation within the Democratic party.

21. See, for example, Maureen Dowd, "Bush, in Reagan Style, Drops Script and Assails Dukakis Foreign Policy," *The New York Times*, Tuesday, September 13, 1988, Section D; and Andrew Rosenthal, "Dukakis Stresses Defense, Ridicules Bush and Quayle," *The New York Times*, Tuesday, September 13, 1988, Section D.

22. While Dukakis changed his views on certain foreign policy issues—such as his initial criticism of the Grenada invasion and his support of the nuclear freeze—his understanding of the dynamics of international relations and the United States' role in the world reflect, in the words of *The New York Times*, "a lifetime of thought." See Andrew Rosenthal, "Dukakis' World," *The New York Times*, Friday, September 2, 1988, Section A.

23. Galston and Makins, pp. 17, 18.

24. See, for example, Rosenthal, "Dukakis' World"; Gerald F. Stein and Robert S. Greenberger, "Bush and Dukakis Stand Poles Apart on Ways to Promote U.S. Interests in the Third World," *The Wall Street Journal*, Thursday, September 8, 1988, Section II; Morton Kondracke, "The Best Case," *The National Review*, August 19, 1988, pp. 30, 31; Editorial, "Creature of the Caucus," *The Wall Street Journal*, September 13, 1988, Section I; Editorial, "For a Grand Foreign Policy Debate," *The New York Times*, August 28, 1988, Section A.

25. Paul Kennedy's *The Rise and Fall of the Great Powers* (New York: Random House, 1987) popularized this assumption (the book was a best-seller) and gave it academic legitimacy.

26. For an excellent discussion of the origins and nature of the American Framers' republican ideology, see Thomas C. Pangle, *The Spirit of Modern American Republicanism* (Chicago: University of Chicago Press, 1988).

27. See, for example, Ann Norton, *Alternative Americas: A Reading of Antebellum Political Culture* (Chicago: University of Chicago Press, 1986). Michael Novak perceptively argues that ideology and vision are inextricably related:

If human beings in their freedom have responsibility for the shape of the political, economic, and cultural institutions under which they live, then they clearly have need of a narrative vision. . . . Just as every human individual in action needs models, heroes, exemplars, types, as a sort of vision according to which to act and to shape his own character, so also assemblies of human beings need a vision of the good society. . . . In personal life, such a vision is called a story or a narrative. In secular social life it is called an ideology.

Novak believes that the concept of narrative or story better captures the nature of social vision than the concept of ideology. Ideology, writes

Novak, "has a profound social dimension, and makes special reference to matters of political economy and social order. Narrative stresses the dimension of human reflection and choice." See Michael Novak, "Narrative and Ideology," *This World* 23 (Fall 1988): pp. 69, 73.
28. James M. McPherson, *Battle Cry of Freedom* (New York: Oxford University Press, 1988), p. 56ff. A thoughtful and provocative contemporary defense of the Southern political tradition—void of any defense of chattel slavery—is Richard M. Weaver's *The Southern Tradition at Bay*, eds. George Core and M. E. Bradford (New Rochelle, NY: Arlington House, 1968).
29. Richard M. Weaver, *Ideas Have Consequences* (Chicago: University of Chicago Press, [1948] 1984), p. 3.

CHAPTER TWO *Freedom vs. Tyranny: The State of the World*

1. Historian Paul Schroeder points out that "[s]ince the second century A.D. under the Pax Romana, the Western world has known no long periods of general peace. The modern record was 38 years, nine months, and five days (June 22, 1815, to March 27, 1854), from the aftermath of Napoleon's defeat at Waterloo to the effective beginning of the Crimean War. . . . That record was broken . . . on May 15, 1984." Paul Schroeder, "Does Murphy's Law Apply to History?," *Wilson Quarterly* ix (New Year's 1985): p. 88.
2. The dynamics of Third World economic development—including the political, economic, and moral criteria for defining "successful" development, the relationship between equality and economic growth, and nexus between culture and development, among other things—are discussed in more detail in Chapter 10.
3. These figures are drawn from the World Bank's *World Development Report 1988* (New York: Oxford University Press, 1988) and from the United Nations' *World Population Prospects Estimates and Projections 1984* (New York: United Nations Department of International Economic and Social Affairs, 1986).
4. Critchfield regularly reports on his experiences for the British newsmagazine *The Economist*. His most recent book, drawn from his experiences, is *Villages* (Garden City: Anchor Press/Doubleday, 1981).
5. Critchfield believes that the use of contraceptives and scientific farming techniques are the prime reasons why the quality of village life has improved in recent decades. On the basis of his experience as an anthropologist, Critchfield concludes that "the more socially cohesive, hierarchical, self-confident . . . cultures are finding it easier to adapt to contraception and modern science than the less tightly knit [and] less secure . . . ones." *Ibid.*, p. 321.
6. Intellectual historian Robert Nisbet argues that the idea of progress has been *the* dominant animating intellectual idea of Western culture since the eighteenth century. See Robert Nisbet, *A History of the Idea of Progress* (New York: Basic Books, 1980). This Enlightment notion is anything but dead. In a well-publicized (and important) article that generated an enormous amount of controversy after it was published in 1989, Francis Fukuyama—a State Department official—argues that the

recent overspreading of democracy and capitalism around the world represents nothing less than "the end of history." Francis Fukuyama, "The End of History?," *The National Interest* 16 (Summer 1989): pp. 3-18. For an excellent overview of the stir caused by Fukuyama's article, see James Atlas, "What Is Fukuyama Saying?," *The New York Times Magazine*, October 22, 1989, p. 38ff.

7. The classic discussion of the sources of weakness and greatness of American democracy is Alexis de Tocqueville's *Democracy in America* (New York: The Modern Library, 1981). Though written over 150 years ago, this is still among the most insightful books ever written about democracy.

8. March 12, 1947, quoted in Alexander DeConde, *A History of American Foreign Policy*, 2nd ed. (New York: Charles Scribner's Sons, 1971), p. 670.

9. Contrary to the popular mythology which has surrounded Franklin Roosevelt's New Deal, a strong case can be made that it was the demand for goods and labor spawned by World War II, not FDR's New Deal programs, which brought an end to the Great Depression of the 1930s.

10. In hindsight, it may seem strange that the American people would have so easily changed their view of Stalin and the Soviet Union during the war; after all, anti-Bolshevik—anti-Communist sentiment ran high in the United States immediately following the Russian Revolution of 1917. The United States did not extend diplomatic recognition to the Soviet Union until 1934. (Having said this, it needs to be noted there were segments of American public opinion during the 1930s that thought very highly of Stalin and the Soviet Union. For example, *New York Times* Moscow correspondent Walter Duranty was a consistent apologist for Stalin. Likewise, Joseph Davies, the U.S. Ambassador to the Soviet Union in the 1930s, sent home glowing reports of Stalin's "successes." Davies's memoirs, *Mission to Moscow*, pictured Stalin as a Jefferson-style democrat. The book was later made into a movie. Generally speaking, however, apologists for Stalin in 1930s-America were a minority among the population at large.) While all of this is true, it is also important to note that the period of U.S. hostility toward the Soviet Union was rather short (twenty-three years, from 1917–1940) in terms of the overall history of Russian-American relations. When viewed in broader historical terms, going back to the early 1780s when the United States first forged a relationship with Russia, the history of U.S.–Russian relations has been more friendly than hostile. Therefore, the historical memory which Americans brought to their relationship with the Soviets during the Second World War was not all negative. Of course, the facts of the war—namely, that Hitler was bent on destroying both the United States as well as the Soviet Union—made friendship between those two nations easier to forge. For a discussion of the pre-World War II legacy of Russian-American relations, see John Lewis Gaddis, *The Long Peace: Inquiries into the History of the Cold War* (New York: Oxford University Press, 1987), pp. 3–19.

11. The classic "revisionist" expression of the origins of the Cold War—placing responsibility for its origins on the United States—is found in the work of American historian William Appleton Williams, most notably his *The Tragedy of American Diplomacy* (New York: Dell,

1972). Williams argues that throughout its history the United States has been driven by a quest to build an American empire. Since the Spanish-American War in the late nineteenth century, United States foreign policy has been motivated by the objective of finding cheap labor and markets for American goods. According to Williams, all subsequent American foreign policy can be explained by this desire to locate commercial markets for American goods. In short, American political control of the world is necessary in order for the United States to establish economic dominance over the world.

12. For example, Jim Wallis, editor of *Sojourners* magazine and one of the leaders of the so-called "new" or "neo" evangelicals, relies extensively on the analysis of New Left historiography to build his case for a putatively "Biblical" or "prophetic" politics. Interestingly, in his *Agenda for Biblical People* (San Francisco: Harper & Row, 1984) Wallis heavily relies on the analysis of David Horowitz in his 1964 New Left history of American foreign policy entitled *Free World Colossus* (New York: Hill and Wang, 1964). Horowitz, once a major leader in the New Left, has since renounced the arguments made in his 1964 book. See Peter Collier and David Horowitz, "From Left to Right," *The Washington Post Magazine*, March 17, 1985. That Wallis continues to cite Horowitz's 1964 arguments when Horowitz himself has repudiated those arguments illustrates a larger contemporary political phenomenon; namely, that the Religious Left continues to thrive while the secular Left has lost much—though not all—of its influence.

13. The historiography of the Cold War is vast. See, for example, John Lewis Gaddis, *The United States and the Origins of the Cold War, 1941–1947* (New York: Columbia University Press, 1972) and Hugh Thomas, *Armed Truce: The Beginnings of the Cold War* (New York: Atheneum, 1987). An important and devastating critique of the scholarship of the New Left historians is Robert J. Maddox's *The New Left and the Origins of the Cold War* (Princeton, NJ: Princeton University Press, 1973).

14. For a discussion of the impact of traditional Russian foreign policy objectives on contemporary Soviet foreign policy, see Adam B. Ulum's now-classic *Expansion and Coexistence: Soviet Foreign Policy 1917–1973*, 2nd ed. (New York: Praeger Publishers, 1974). A thorough history of pre-Bolshevik Russian foreign policy, with consideration of contemporary continuities, is found in Ivo J. Lederer, ed., *Russian Foreign Policy: Essays in Historical Perspective* (New Haven, CT: Yale University Press, 1967).

15. That the United States and the Soviet Union learned different lessons from the Cuban missile crisis is evident from a comparison of military capabilities in years after the crisis. For example, in 1967 the United States had 1,054 operational intercontinental ballistic missiles (ICBMs) to the Soviet Union's 460. Thirteen years later, the United States had the same number of ICBMs as in 1967, while the Soviet force had grown to 1,398 ICBMs. This same phenomenon was apparent in nearly every other nuclear weapons category and was accompanied by dramatic qualitative improvements in Soviet military capabilities.

16. For a thorough critique of the Carter foreign policy, see Joshua

Muravchik, *The Uncertain Crusade: Jimmy Carter and the Dilemmas of Human Rights Policy* (Lanham, MD: Hamilton Press, 1986).

17. President Reagan's understanding of the failures of the Carter foreign policy was shaped in great part by an article written by Georgetown University professor Jeane Kirkpatrick entitled "Dictatorships and Double Standards," *Commentary* 68 (November 1979): pp. 34–45. In it, Kirkpatrick accused Carter of pursuing an inconsistent foreign policy that punished friends of the United States while ignoring the greater dangers posed by Marxist-Leninist enemies of the United States. "No problem of American foreign policy," Kirkpatrick argued, "is more urgent than that of formulating a morally and strategically acceptable, and politically realistic, program for dealing with non-democratic governments who are threatened by Soviet subversion." After reading Kirkpatrick's article, President Reagan insisted that Kirkpatrick be given the position of United States Ambassador to the United Nations.

18. Ronald Reagan, "Promoting Democracy and Peace," address delivered before the British Parliament, June 8, 1982.

19. *Ibid.*

20. Robert G. Kaiser, "The U.S.S.R. in Decline," *Foreign Affairs* 67 (Winter 1988/89): p. 113.

21. *Ibid.*, p. 97.

22. Charles Krauthammer, "After the Cold War Is Won," *Time*, November 7, 1988, p. 34.

23. Seweryn Bialer and Michael Mandelbaum, *The Global Rivals* (New York: Alfred A. Knopf, 1988), p. 89.

24. Timothy J. Colton, "Gorbachev and the Politics of System Renewal," in *Gorbachev's Russia and American Foreign Policy*, eds. Seweryn Bialer and Michael Mandelbaum (Boulder, CO: Westview Press, 1988), p. 156. A literature on the Gorbachev era—most of it speculative—has begun to blossom. See, for example, Robert C. Tucker, *Political Culture and Leadership in Soviet Russia: From Lenin to Gorbachev* (New York: Norton, 1987); Jerry Hough, *Russia and the West: Gorbachev and the Politics of Reform* (New York: Simon and Schuster, 1988); Donald Kelly, *Soviet Politics from Brezhnev to Gorbachev* (Westport, CT: Greenwood, 1987). A critique of recent Sovietology as it relates to Gorbachev and recent events in the Soviet Union is found in Walter Laqueur, "Glasnost & Its Limits," *Commentary* 86 (July 1988): pp. 13–24.

25. Thane Gustafson, "The Crisis of the Soviet System of Power and Mikhail Gorbachev's Political Strategy," in *Gorbachev's Russia*, p. 191.

26. Colton, "Gorbachev and the Politics of System Renewal," in *Gorbachev's Russia*.

27. This and the following Gorbachev quotations are, unless noted otherwise, taken from *ibid.*, p. 153ff.

28. For a thorough discussion of the nature of the economic crisis confronting the Soviet Union, see Marshall L. Goldman, *Gorbachev's Challenge: Economic Reform in the Age of High Technology* (New York: W. W. Norton & Company, 1987). The specific economic failures of the Soviet Union are discussed by the distinguished Soviet physicist Yuri Orlov in "Before and After Glasnost," *Commentary* 86 (October 1988): pp. 24–34.

29. Quoted in Kaiser, "The U.S.S.R. in Decline," p. 102. Kaiser elaborates:

> Millions of Soviet workers have no idea of the difference between careful, high-quality work and what has traditionally been acceptable in their country. Soviet citizens have an utterly contemptuous view of Soviet workmanship. . . . Machinery that can only be produced under conditions of stringent quality control is simply not made. . . . What might be called the Soviet industrial culture has no tradition of quality control, cleanliness, attention to detail and the like. Only in special military plants have the Soviets regularly been able to produce high-quality, complicated machinery—and the costs of production in those enterprises are apparently enormous, because the principal method of assuring quality is simply to reject a large percentage of what is made.

30. *Ibid.*, pp. 106, 107.
31. Robert C. Tucker, "Giving Up the Ghost: The Gorbachev-Stalin Leadership Struggle," *The New Republic*, October 17, 1988, pp. 20, 33–35.
32. Quoted in *The Global Rivals*, p. 87.
33. Serge Schmemann, "Chasing That Hot New Account in Moscow," *The New York Times*, Sunday, October 30, 1988, Section E.
34. This is in remarkable contrast to the nature of the economic relationship which exists between the United States and the Republic of South Africa. While increased economic interaction with the Soviet Union has received the approbation of both the American business community and the American government, economic interaction with South Africa has become unacceptable. The very argument that is used to justify increasing economic contact with the Soviet Union—namely, that such contact will encourage moderation and reform—is precisely the argument that is rejected in dealing with South Africa. In addition to being inconsistent, this policy is truly ironic when one considers that according to human rights organizations such as Freedom House, the Soviet Union is more repressive, even under Gorbachev, than the Republic of South Africa.
35. These figures account for only a small portion of the overall loans which the Soviet Union has secured. For example, in 1986 the Soviet government received nearly $30 billion in loans from private Western sources.
36. Seweryn Bialer, "The Soviet Union and the West: Security and Foreign Policy," in *Gorbachev's Russia*, p. 469.
37. Angelo M. Codeville, "Is There Still a Soviet Threat?," *Commentary* 86 (November 1988): p. 27.
38. William E. Odom, "Soviet Military Doctrine," *Foreign Affairs* 67 (Winter 1988/89): p. 114.
39. These and the following statistics are taken from Odom, *ibid.*, and from Codeville, "Is There Still a Soviet Threat?"
40. Codeville, "Is There Still a Soviet Threat?," p. 24.
41. X (George Kennan), "The Sources of Soviet Conduct," *Foreign Affairs* (July 1947): p. 582.

CHAPTER THREE *International Politics: A Biblical Starting Point*

1. Since the early 1970s, scholars and policymakers have identified other forces that have been transforming world politics. Among these, nuclear weapons—with their unprecedented potential for global destruction—economic and ecological interdependence, the decolonization of the Third World, and the rise of so-called non-state global actors—such as terrorist groups and multinational corporations—have been viewed as revolutionary in their impact on global politics. The literature on how these forces have altered world politics is vast and growing. The best summary of this is found in Robert O. Keohane and Joseph S. Nye, *Power and Interdependence*, 2nd ed. (Boston: Scott, Foresman and Company, 1989).
2. Genesis 3:1-6.
3. Genesis 3:16-24.
4. Isaiah 53:6; Romans 5:12.
5. Romans 5:15-21.
6. Romans 8:18-25.
7. Romans 3:21-24; Ephesians 2:4, 5.
8. Below I discuss further the relationship between the earthly kingdom and the Heavenly Kingdom. Suffice it to say at this juncture that the earthly and the heavenly should not be confused. The final and complete restoration of all of creation (Romans 8:20) awaits God's extra-historical work.
9. Romans 13:1-7.
10. Genesis 1:27, 28.
11. Psalm 8:4-6.
12. Psalm 24:1.
13. One of the most powerful and beautiful statements of God's sovereignty over His creation is found in Job 38—41.
14. The distinction between the earthly and the heavenly has roots deep in church history. The classic statement of this distinction and its implications is found in Augustine's *The City of God*, where he distinguishes between two invisible cities, the city of God and the city of man. Augustine did not, however, argue that the state was part of the city of man. According to Augustine, both the Church and the state are divinely ordained. Both exist to do good. The specific purpose of the state is to obviate the effects of sin as it relates to man's interaction with man. The state is not an agent of spiritual salvation, but exists to restrain sin while concurrently healing and restoring man's earthly condition. Furthermore, the state is comprised of citizens of both the city of God and the city of man; it is common to both the regenerate and the unregenerate. As both the regenerate and unregenerate participate in the state, and the state exists for their common good, what distinguishes the Christian participation in politics—or in the state—is that the non-Christian seeks no higher good than this life, while the Christian's ultimate objective is to further the Kingdom of God. It needs to be emphasized that Augustine, like the great Reformers who followed him, in no way denigrated the task of politics, or any of the other tasks of the earthly kingdom such as education or aesthetics. To

acknowledge the existence of two kingdoms is not to imply the goodness or superiority of one and the evil or inferiority of the other. Both
were created by God for His glory. In his *Institutes of the Christian
Religion*, John Calvin further spells out the difference of purpose
between the two kingdoms:

I call "earthly things" those which do not pertain to God or his
Kingdom, to true justice, or to the blessedness of the future life; but have
their significance and relationship with regard to the present life and are,
in a sense, confined within its bounds. I call "heavenly things" the pure
knowledge of God, the nature of true righteousness, and the mysteries of
the Heavenly Kingdom. The first class [or the former] includes government, household management [i.e. economics], all mechanical skills, and
the liberal arts. In the second [or the latter] are the knowledge of God
and of his will, and the rule by which we conform our lives to it.
(II.II.13)

15. See Gustavo Gutierrez, *A Theology of Liberation* (Maryknoll, NY: Orbis
    Books, 1973).
16. Many of the political and theological themes of liberation theology are
    reflected in the approach to theology and international politics of evan-
    gelicals such as Ronald J. Sider and Jim Wallis, and through their orga-
    nizations and publications, including Evangelicals for Social Action and
    Sojourners magazine. Sometimes these themes are implicit, although
    evangelicals associated with the political Left have become increasingly
    forthright in their explicit defense of liberation theology. See, for exam-
    ple, Ronald J. Sider, *Rich Christians in an Age of Hunger* (Downers
    Grove, IL: InterVarsity Press, 1977) and Jim Wallis, *Agenda for a
    Biblical People*, 2nd ed. (San Francisco: Harper & Row, 1984).
17. Two thorough and critical discussions of the themes of liberation theol-
    ogy are: Michael Novak, *Will It Liberate? Questions About Liberation
    Theology* (New York: Paulist Press, 1986) and Ronald H. Nash, *On
    Liberation Theology* (Milford, MI: Mott Media, 1984). A good discus-
    sion of recent developments in the evolution of liberation theology is
    found in Michael Novak, ed., *Liberation Theology and the Liberal
    Society* (Washington, D.C.: American Enterprise Institute, 1987).
18. See, for example, Robert McAfee Brown, *Unexpected News: Reading
    the Bible with Third World Eyes* (Philadelphia: Westminster Press,
    1984).
19. This approach to theological thinking is often referred to as "contextual
    theology," by which it is meant that theology reflects its class, race, and
    gender context. In postulating this approach, contextual theology denies
    the power of the Holy Spirit to witness to every person regardless of
    time, place, ethnicity, or socioeconomic status.
20. Liberation theology has had a major impact on theological and political
    thinking among the Left in each of these countries. Of the three,
    Nicaragua provides us with the most fully developed example of the
    marriage of politics and theology found in liberation theology. See
    Humberto Belli, *Breaking Faith* (Westchester, IL: Crossway Books,
    1986). While the political and religious situation in South Africa and the

Philippines is quite different than that in Nicaragua, the fact of the matter is that liberation theology has had a major impact on leftist religious leaders in both countries. For an example of this in the South African context, see Allan A. Boesak, *Black and Reformed: Apartheid, Liberation, and the Calvinist Tradition* (Maryknoll, NY: Orbis Books, 1984).

21. The role of politics generally in redefining American religion is discussed from a sociological perspective in Robert Wuthnow, *The Restructuring of American Religion* (Princeton, NJ: Princeton University Press, 1988).

22. See James Davison Hunter, *American Evangelicalism: The Coming Generation* (Chicago: University of Chicago Press, 1987), p. 44; and, George M. Marsden, *Reforming Fundamentalism: Fuller Seminary and the New Evangelicalism* (Grand Rapids: Eerdmans, 1987), p. 309.

23. For a succinct yet incisive theological critique of liberation theology, see Carl F. H. Henry, "An Evangelical Appraisal of Liberation Theology," *This World* 15 (Fall 1986): pp. 99-107.

24. H. M. Kuitert, *Everything Is Politics But Politics Is Not Everything* (Grand Rapids: Eerdmans, 1986), p. 4.

25. In the first century after Christ, a heresy arose called Gnosticism. Its name derived from its root meaning ("knowledge)." According to the Gnostics, the human body and all other physical matter is evil. Only the spirit is good and real. Accordingly, human appetites and impulses should be surpassed while humans seek salvation through the cultivation of the invisible world of knowledge. The early Christians were aware of the dangers of this heresy, as evidenced by the warnings of Paul to the Colossian Christians and the strong arguments of John for both the full humanity and full divinity of Christ. See Colossians 2 and 1 John.

26. Genesis 1:31.

27. Psalm 19:1; Psalm 24:1.

28. Kuitert, *Everything Is Politics But Politics Is Not Everything*, p. 120.

CHAPTER FOUR *International Politics: A Biblical Framework*

1. Allan Bloom, *The Closing of the American Mind* (New York: Simon and Schuster, 1987).

2. Much of the media and the educational establishment in the United States has tried to belittle the term "secular humanism"—characterizing it as a hokey invention of fundamentalist Christians. This attempt to discredit the term is disingenuous. The fact of the matter is that there is good reason to conclude that secular humanism *is* a religion. See James Davison Hunter, "America's Fourth Faith," *This World* 19 (Fall 1987): pp. 101-110.

3. While Bloom's book has been attacked primarily by the educational establishment, his argument is about the future of democracy in America. Bloom makes a compelling case that there is an inextricable nexus between Judeo-Christian values, Western culture, and the survival of democracy. To the extent that American education no longer teaches those values, or relativizes them, the very foundations of American democracy are undermined. Similar arguments are made in William J.

Bennett, *Our Children and Our Country: Improving America's Schools & Affirming the Common Culture* (New York: Simon and Schuster, 1988).

4. Romans 12:2.
5. 2 Timothy 3:16, 17.
6. Genesis 12:2; 18:18; 22:18; Deuteronomy 28:49; Jeremiah 27:6, 7.
7. Psalm 110:6.
8. Proverbs 14:34.
9. Henry Van Til, *The Calvinistic Concept of Culture* (Grand Rapids: Baker, 1972), p. 162.
10. *Ibid.*
11. A thorough historical and theological discussion of common grace is found in Bruce Demarest, *General Revelation: Historical Views and Contemporary Issues* (Grand Rapids: Zondervan, 1982).
12. 1 Corinthians 15:58.
13. Matthew 22:37.
14. C. S. Lewis, "On Living in an Atomic Age," in *Present Concerns: Essays by C. S. Lewis*, ed. Walter Hooper (New York: Harcourt Brace Jovanovich, 1986), p. 80.
15. John 20:21.
16. Matthew 25:31-46.
17. This has been the position of traditional Anabaptist theology, which posits a sharp dichotomy between the Heavenly Kingdom and the earthly kingdom. A more common manifestation of this approach is an increasingly familiar one which argues that Christians should not worry about whether their earthly actions are deemed responsible because as Christians we are called to be "faithful," not responsible. This is a variation of Anabaptist theology in that it implies that Christians do not need to be concerned with what happens in the world because as Christians we are no longer part of the earthly kingdom. This approach is both irresponsible as well as unfaithful to Biblical teaching.
18. See Paul Seabury and Walter A. McDougell, eds., *The Grenada Papers* (San Francisco: Institute for Contemporary Studies, 1984), and Geoffrey Wagner, *Red Calypso: The Grenadian Revolution and Its Aftermath* (Washington, D.C.: Regnery Gateway, 1989).
19. For a good overview of various philosophies of history, including the Christian view, see John Warwick Montgomery, *Where Is History Going?* (Grand Rapids: Zondervan, 1969).
20. See Anthony Hoekema, "God's Game Plan," *Christianity Today* (May 1980): pp. 26-29.
21. This promise is beautifully expressed by John in his apocalyptic vision contained in Revelation 21:1-6:

Then I saw a new heaven and new earth, for the first earth had passed away, and there was no longer any sea. I saw the Holy City, the new Jerusalem, coming down out of heaven from God, prepared as a bride beautifully dressed for her husband. And I heard a loud voice from the throne saying, "Now the dwelling of God is with men, and he will live with them. They will be his people, and God himself will be with them and be their God. He will wipe every tear from their eyes. There will be no more death or mourning or crying or pain, for the old order of things has passed away." He who was seated on the throne said, "I am making everything new!" Then he said, "Write this down, for these words are trustworthy and true."

22. This ethic of survivalism became popularized in the early 1980s through the arguments of Jonathan Schell in his best-seller *The Fate of the Earth* (New York: Alfred A. Knopf, 1982). Carl Sagan's predictions of "nuclear winter" have also been influential in nurturing survivalism.
23. See Genesis 1:26, 27; 2:7.
24. See Matthew 10:28.
25. Joshua 1:9; Psalm 139:7-10; Matthew 28:20.
26. Revelation 22:12-21.
27. The notion of a Biblical third-way approach to foreign policy is especially commonplace among evangelical social activists and academics. When their specific positions on foreign issues are scrutinized, however, it is evident that there is little that is "distinctive" about them. In reality, the concept of a distinctively Biblical foreign policy is used to legitimize foreign policy positions that are, for the most part, run-of-the-mill Left-liberal. For a further discussion of this reality, see James Davison Hunter, "The New Class and the Young Evangelicals," *Review of Religious Research* 22 (December 1980): pp. 155-169; Dean C. Curry, "Evangelicals, the Bible, and Public Policy," *This World* 16 (Winter 1987): pp. 34-49.
28. To be sure, there are examples of Christians supporting extreme right-wing movements and governments; however, that problem is now less evident than Christian leaders and organizations supporting leftist, Marxist-Leninist regimes. What is particularly distressing is that these Christians of the political Left frequently praise Marxist regimes as paragons of Christian virtue—as just, peace-loving societies. For a hard-hitting discussion of this problem, see Lloyd Billingsley, *The Generation That Knew Not Josef* (Portland: Multnomah Press, 1985).
29. Reading Valladares's prison memoirs is a shocking but invaluable experience. *Against All Hope* (New York: Alfred A. Knopf, 1986) has not only become a classic piece of literature, it is must reading for what it tells us about man's capacity for evil and the enduring power of Christian hope.
30. Armando Valladares, Presentation to the Institute on Religion and Democracy, July 11, 1983.
31. In 1988 Dr. Carl Lundquist, president of the Christian College Consortium—an association of elite evangelical colleges—interviewed Fidel Castro in Cuba. Upon his return, Lundquist spoke glowingly of Castro and his revolution. Apparently Lundquist had not bothered to read Valladares. See Carl Lundquist, "Face to Face With Castro," *The Standard* (February 1988): pp. 4-7.
32. 1 Kings 3:7-9.
33. 1 Kings 3:10.
34. Alberto R. Coll, "Christian Realism and Prudence in Foreign Policy: A Challenge to Evangelicals," in *Faculty Dialogue* (forthcoming).
35. Carter also believed that human rights should receive priority attention

because, so he argued, his predecessors—Nixon, Kissinger, and Ford—pursued a *realpolitik* (or national interest) approach to foreign policy. Carter saw this approach as a betrayal of the noble American tradition of idealism. To date, the best and most thorough discussion of Carter's human rights policy is Joshua Muravchik's *The Uncertain Crusade: Jimmy Carter and the Dilemmas of Human Rights Policy* (Lanham, MD: The Hamilton Press, 1986).

36. The whole panoply of tragedies surrounding the Shah and American policy toward Iran during the Carter years is engagingly discussed in William Shawcross, *The Shah's Last Ride: The Fate of an Ally* (New York: Simon and Schuster, 1988).

CHAPTER FIVE *International Politics: A Christian Agenda*

1. Idealism as an approach to international politics emerged with the secularization of society during the Middle Ages. By the eighteenth century, utopianism was well-defined and influential. This was an inevitable outgrowth of Enlightenment thought, which placed man's reason above God's revelation as the source of knowledge. Dependent upon himself, not God, man naturally assumed that he had the ability to control his own destiny. Consequently, in the words of the great British historian E. H. Carr, the "Enlightenment was the royal road to the millennium." Carr's *The Twenty Year Crisis, 1919-1939*, originally published in 1939, remains the best and most thorough discussion of idealism as an approach to international politics.

2. Earlier in the twentieth century, American evangelicalism closely identified the Christian faith with anti-Catholicism, Prohibition, and opposition to evolution.

3. Richard V. Pierard, *The Unequal Yoke: Evangelical Christianity and Political Conservatism* (Philadelphia: J. B. Lippincott, 1970).

4. *Ibid.*, p. 104.

5. *Ibid.*, p. 99. Pierard's discussion of why people are attracted to communism is instructive in terms of the assumptions that he brings to his opposition to anti-communism. Among other things, Pierard states that "the hostility of the system, *especially as it has developed in the United States*, and the highly individualistic free enterprise economy is distasteful since it seems to be selfish and cruel." Pierard also says that communism is appealing because of its "sense of community. It enables the individual to find self-realization apart from self-seeking in group action and in service to others." Pierard notes, too, that "Soviet achievements have made a profound impression on many, especially those in developing nations." All of these features of communism are, in Pierard's words, "definite positive achievements" that are "to its credit" (emphasis added). See *ibid.*, pp. 74-99.

6. One of the most influential books arguing for a reawakening of evangelical social responsibility was David O. Moberg's *Inasmuch: Christian Responsibility in the Twentieth Century* (Grand Rapids: Eerdmans, 1965).

7. See George Marsden, ed., *Evangelicalism and Modern America* (Grand Rapids: Eerdmans, 1984).

8. James D. Hunter's scholarship dealing with American evangelicals demonstrates the extent to which these "radical" evangelicals were influenced by the political orientation of the secular New Left.

9. *The Post-American* was later renamed *Sojourners*. It remains, along with *The Other Side* magazine, a major voice of radical evangelicalism.

10. Jim Wallis, *Agenda for Biblical People* (San Francisco: Harper & Row, 1984), p. 63.

11. Ronald J. Sider, ed., *Cry Justice* (Downers Grove, IL: InterVarsity Press, 1980), p. 3.

12. See, for example, Ronald J. Sider, *Rich Christians in an Age of Hunger* (Downers Grove, IL: InterVarsity Press, 1977); Nicholas Wolterstorff, *Until Justice and Peace Embrace* (Grand Rapids: Eerdmans, 1983); Stephen Monsma, *Pursuing Justice in a Sinful World* (Grand Rapids: Eerdmans, 1984).

13. Kenneth A. Myers, *Christianity, Culture, and Common Grace* (Powhatan, VA: Berea Publications, 1989), p. 16.

14. The Exodus story—or "paradigm," as it often called—is central to the theological system of liberation theology.

15. Sider, *Rich Christians*, p. 60.

16. *Ibid.*

17. *Ibid.*

18. *Ibid.*

19. *Ibid.*, p. 61. Sider, in a 1984 revised edition of *Rich Christians*, tempered somewhat this categorical statement.

20. For example, Sider frequently cites the "Jubilee Principle" of Leviticus 25 as evidence that "God requires radically transformed economic relationships among his people." See *ibid.*, pp. 88-90. Perhaps Sider's book *Cry Justice* best illustrates his approach to Biblical interpretation. In that book Sider has compiled hundreds of Biblical quotations that relate to themes of justice, poverty, and peace. Sider allows these quotations to stand alone without interpretation, except for an occasional chart describing such things as national infant mortality rates. It is clear that Sider believes these quotations speak for themselves—that their meaning and relevance to contemporary politics and economics is obvious.

21. 2 Samuel 22:7-43.

22. See Ronald H. Nash, *Social Justice and the Christian Church* (Milford, MI: Mott Media, 1983). This little book is an excellent primer. Nash clearly spells out the philosophical and theological meanings of justice. He also renders intelligible the often arcane contemporary controversies surrounding the concept.

23. Gordon Spykman, *et al.*, *Let My People Live: Faith and Struggle in Central America* (Grand Rapids, MI: Eerdmans, 1988).

24. *Ibid.*, p. 221.

25. *Ibid.*, pp. 20, 21.

26. *Ibid.*, pp. 215, 216.

27. See Nash, *Social Justice and the Christian Church*, Chapters Three and Six.

28. Wallis, *Agenda for Biblical People*, p. 60.

29. *Ibid*, p. 62.

30. Wolterstorff, *Until Justice and Peace Embrace*, p. 72.

31. Luke 4:5-8.
32. Luke 23:36-43.
33. Matthew 5:3-11.
34. Wolterstorff, *Until Justice and Peace Embrace*, p. 72.
35. See Peter C. Cragie, *The Problem of War in the Old Testament* (Grand Rapids, MI: Eerdmans, 1978), pp. 85-91.
36. In addition to misreading the meaning of *shalom*, such an argument for pacifism must be reconciled, among other things, with the Old Testament image of God as a warrior. See Myron Augsburger and Dean C. Curry, *Nuclear Arms: Two Views on World Peace* (Waco, TX: Word, 1987), pp. 78-106.
37. Wolterstorff writes: ". . . shalom is intertwined with justice. In shalom, each person enjoys justice. . . . There is no shalom without justice." Wolterstorff, *Until Justice and Peace Embrace*, p. 69.
38. Stanley Hauerwas, *Against the Nations: War and Survival in a Liberal Society* (Minneapolis: Winston Press, 1985), p. 129.
39. Stanley Hauerwas, *The Peaceful Kingdom* (Notre Dame, IN: University of Notre Dame Press, 1983).
40. Clark Pinnock, "A Pilgrimage in Political Theology," in Ronald H. Nash, ed., *On Liberation Theology* (Milford, MI: Mott Media, 1984), p. 109.
41. *Ibid.*
42. Wallis, *Agenda for Biblical People*, p. 57.
43. See *ibid.*, pp. 56-72.
44. Reinhold Niebuhr, *Christianity and Power Politics* (New York: Charles Scribner's Sons, 1946), pp. 15-17.

CHAPTER SIX *Tyranny and the Modern Crisis of Faith*

1. See Allen Weinstein, *Perjury: The Hiss-Chambers Case* (New York: Alfred Knopf, 1978).
2. Whittaker Chambers, *Witness* (New York: Random House, 1952), p. 25.
3. *Ibid.*, p. 83. *Witness* remained out of print for many years. Recently a new edition has been issued by Regnery Press and the University Press of America.
4. *Ibid.*, p. 4.
5. *Ibid.*, p. 17.
6. *Ibid.*
7. *Ibid.*, pp. 9, 10.
8. Fifty million is a conservative estimate. Estimates for Hitler's deaths range from three to ten million; for Stalin, twenty to sixty million; for Mao, twenty to over fifty million. Altogether, totalitarian regimes—primarily Communist regimes—are directly responsible for killing over 110 million people this century. See R. J. Rummel, "War Isn't This Century's Biggest Killer," *Wall Street Journal*, July 1986.
9. James Turner Johnson, *Without God, Without Creed: The Origins of Unbelief in America* (Baltimore: The Johns Hopkins University Press, 1985), p. xii. Johnson's book is an engaging discussion of how unbelief in God became possible. Johnson points out that before the seventeenth century, the option of not believing in God simply did not exist.

10. *Ibid.*
11. The triumph of a secular, naturalistic worldview first took place in the western nations of Europe and later the United States. Through the nineteenth century, the worldviews of the rest of the world remained traditionally religious in the sense that modern secular naturalism had not yet begun to undermine traditional religious assumptions about man, nature, and the universe. Certainly the traditional religious expressions were different in such places as Africa, Asia, and Latin America; but in each of these, traditional religious worldviews continued to frame people's thinking about life.
12. Quoted in Paul Johnson, *Modern Times: The World from the Twenties to the Eighties* (New York: Harper & Row, 1983), p. 48.
13. See *ibid.*, p. 48.
14. This is not to say that nonideological considerations of national interest are irrelevant to twentieth-century international politics. What I am arguing is that in our century, international politics has been driven by ideology as well as by nonideological national interests. The ideological factor in twentieth-century international politics distinguishes it from previous international history when considerations of national interest alone (what is called *realpolitik*) determined the dynamics of the politics among nations. So, for example, in the nineteenth century European nations would shift alliances solely on the criterion of the need to maintain a stable balance of power. For most of this century, certainly since 1945, alliances have been centered around ideological considerations. Hence, alliances are much more rigid today because it would be unthinkable for a nation to ally itself with an ideological adversary. The injection of ideological factors into international politics has arguably also made international politics more dangerous, since the fundamental issues that divide nations are now defined in absolute terms—i.e., good and evil.
15. For a discussion of the personal lives of Marx and Hitler and how these affected their politics, see John Toland, *Adolf Hitler* (New York: Doubleday, 1976) and Thomas Sowell, *Marxism* (New York: Morrow, 1985). A particularly incisive and devastating indictment of Marx's life and scholarship is found in Paul Johnson, *Intellectuals* (New York: Harper & Row, 1988), pp. 52-81.
16. Marx referred to dialectical materialism as "scientific." However, Marx's frequent use of the term "scientific" to describe his ideas should not be interpreted to mean that these ideas met some objective and rigorous criterion of truth. In violation of the basic tenets of science (and logic), Marx simply proclaimed that his ideas were true because they were "scientific."
17. Paul Johnson points out that Marx's later political writings reflect eschatalogical themes that were pervasive in the poetry he wrote as a young man. While Johnson concludes that Marx's poetic gift well served his later writing, of more significance is the fact that his mature political writings, which we identify as Marxism, reflect themes of destruction, hatred, and violence that were central to his mind-set well before he started writing about politics and economics. Writes Johnson: "The point is that Marx's concept of Doomsday, whether in its lurid poetic version or its eventual economic one, is an artistic not a scientific vision." Johnson, *Intellectuals*, p. 55.

18. Though the major expression of fascism, Hitler's National Socialism was not the only Fascist movement in the 1930s and 1940s. Mussolini's Italy was also a Fascist state, but not nearly as influential as Hitler's Germany. In addition to being an extreme expression of nationalism, fascism has also been viewed as a nihilistic reaction against the individualism of modernity. "Mankind is tired of freedom," Mussolini said. To the Fascists, communism and democracy were both degenerate expressions of modern individualism.

19. Immediately after his death, Marx's ideas began to be modified. For example, during the late nineteenth century, British and German Socialists such as George Bernard Shaw and Edward Bernstein accepted Marxism, but without the revolutionary component. Their "variety" of Marxism eventually became identified, respectively, with the British Labor Party and the German Social Democratic Party. The most significant modification in Marx's thought came with the Russian Vladimir Ilyich Ulyanov (alias V. I. Lenin), who saved Marxism from irrelevance while demonstrating that Marx's revolutionary insights could be applied to a pre-capitalist nation like Russia. In the first instance, Lenin explained why countries such as Great Britain and Germany did not experience, as Marx predicted, a revolution of their proletariat. According to Lenin, the capitalists in these countries wisely postponed the inevitable Communist revolution by building welfare states at home while exploiting the poor in what is today called the Third World. Lenin believed this stalling strategy would give the capitalist nations time, but that it would eventually fail as the Communist revolution inevitably marched through history. Had Lenin not provided such an explanation, it is unlikely Marx's ideas would have survived into the twentieth century. Through the idea of the "Party" as the "vanguard" of the revolution, Lenin also demonstrated how a Communist revolution could be brought about in a peasant (pre-capitalist) nation. When one considers that all of the Communist revolutions which have taken place have been in such countries, one understands the significance of Lenin's innovation. As a reminder of the debt of Marxism to Leninism, Marxism has subsequently become known as Marxism-Leninism. There have been other modifications of Marxism through the years as well. Among these, Mao Zedong's (known as Maoism) and Fidel Castro's (known as *Fidelista* or Castroism) stand out in terms of their influence. The important point to remember is that even with the evolutionary changes which have taken place in Marxist thought, the core orthodoxy remains. It begs the question, therefore, to ask whether, for example, the Sandinistas in Nicaragua are Marxists simply because their worldview is not *identical* to that of Marx himself or the Soviet Union in 1935. More important are the essential worldview continuities that exist within Marxism, such as the affirmation that "the history of all . . . existing society is the history of class struggles." That there are a variety of Marxisms and that Marxism has evolved, there can be no doubt. That this is so does not demonstrate that orthodox Marxism is a thing of the past; rather, it demonstrates that Marxist orthodoxy has the ability to adapt as the need arises. This reality is discussed in an important but neglected book by Tufts University political scientist Tony Smith, entitled *Thinking Like a Communist* (New York: W. W. Norton, 1987).

20. Peter Berger states that Marxism's theoretical appeal can be traced to what he calls Marxism's "mytho-poetic" nature—i.e., its promise of a remade man and human society.

21. In all Marxist nations, society is organized according to the principle of "democratic centralism." This principle ordains that Marxist societies must be centrally controlled by the Party from the top down. The institutions of society—schools, youth organizations, labor unions—are controlled by the Party and act as the transmissions belts through which the policies of the Party are carried out in every area of social life. The democratic component to "democratic centralism" is illusion, not fact.

22. The murderous crimes of Stalin have been condemned with unprecedented candor by Gorbachev. (Criticism of Lenin is still strictly off-limits.) Conservative Sovietologists in the West are finding that what they have been saying for years about Stalin's rule is being borne out in official statements by the Gorbachev regime. For example, Soviet officials have admitted that Stalin is responsible for the death of at least twenty million innocent citizens during his nearly thirty-year rule. The Soviet government has even gone so far as to allow the erection of monuments honoring the victims of Stalin. Moreover, Gorbachev has been equally candid in his exposure of corruption within the Communist Party. In the Spring of 1989, Gorbachev made the shocking admission that the Soviet Union's collectivized agricultural system has been an utter failure. In making this admission, Gorbachev has called for the decentralization of agricultural decision-making and the private leasing of agricultural lands. These reforms strike at the very heart of Marxist dogma in the Soviet Union.

23. Many students of the Soviet Union argue that the movement of Eastern European nations out of the Soviet orbit will dramatically—even fatally—weaken the latter politically and economically. See Zbigniew Brzezinski, *The Grand Failure: The Birth and Death of Communism in the 20th Century* (New York: Charles Scribner's Sons, 1989).

24. According to the World Bank, Ethiopia is the poorest nation in the world. Ethiopia's per capita GNP is $120 (compared to $1,100 in Turkey and $6,900 in Hong Kong). Average life expectancy in Ethiopia is forty-six years (compared to sixty-five in Turkey and seventy-six in Hong Kong). Mozambique's per capita GNP is $210, average life expectancy eighteen. Both Ethiopia and Mozambique have experienced *no* growth in their per capita GNP since 1965. (By comparison, Turkey's per capita GNP has grown an average of 2.7 percent and Hong Kong's 6.2 percent.) Moreover, agricultural production in both African nations—both heavily dependent on subsistence agriculture—has *dropped* since 1980 an average of 3.8 percent and 15.9 percent respectively. Source: *World Development Report 1988.* These economic statistics tell us little about the terrible human suffering that has taken place in these nations. It has been estimated, for example, that hundreds of thousands of Ethiopians have died during the past decade as a direct result of the political and economic policies of the Marxist government of Colonel Mengistu.

25. Ironically, one of the only places where Marxism still thrives is in the universities of the West.

26. Paul Johnson, "Christianity and Ideology in the Late 20th Century," presentation to The James Madison Foundation, December 1988, Washington D.C.
27. *Ibid.*

CHAPTER SEVEN *The Sources of Contemporary Tyranny*

1. Robert A. Nisbet, *The Quest for Community* (New York: Oxford University Press, 1953), p. 98.
2. *Ibid.*, p. 99.
3. Leo Strauss, "Niccolo Machiavelli," *History of Political Philosophy*, eds. Leo Strauss and Joseph Cropsey (Chicago: University of Chicago Press), p. 289.
4. Most historians date the birth of the modern nation-state system with the Treaty of Westphalia in 1648. The treaty ended the religious conflicts that had ravaged Europe for decades and redrew the political map of Europe along nonreligious lines. Thus was born the secular nation-state system. The emergence of secular nation-states was legitimated by the philosophical ideas developed by men such as Machiavelli and Bodin. It needs to be pointed out that these factors coalesced at the same time as the emergence of nationalism, which was also a unique expression of modernity. Nationalism, or mass identification with the territorial nation-state, resulted at least partially from the growing secularization of European life. With the collapse of traditional loyalties and bonds, people more and more began to identify themselves with the nation. Henceforth the nation would compete with the Church, the family, and other traditional associations for the loyalty of the individual. The classic discussion of nationalism remains Hans Kohn's *The Idea of Nationalism* (Toronto: Collier Books, 1967).
5. Nisbet, *The Quest for Community*, pp. 143, 151.
6. A century and a half after Rousseau, Benito Mussolini proclaimed the essence of fascism to be "Everything within the state, nothing outside the state, nothing against the state."
7. Nisbet, *The Quest for Community*, pp. 140, 141.
8. In this regard, it is interesting that Rousseau referred to the state as the "*patrie*" or father.
9. Furthermore, Iran is often assumed to be an Arab nation; it is not.
10. The term "Muslim" refers to the followers of Islam. *Muslim* literally means "those who do Islam."
11. A fascinating discussion of the uses and meanings of language by Islam is found in Bernard Lewis, *The Political Language of Islam* (Chicago: University of Chicago Press, 1988). Lewis discusses the roots and Islamic understanding of *umma* on p. 32ff.
12. *Ibid.*, p. 29.
13. *Ibid.*, p. 31.
14. The ways in which Muslim peoples have attempted to adapt themselves to the modern world of sovereign nation-states is the subject of James P. Piscatori's penetrating study, *Islam in a World of Nation-states* (Cambridge, MA: Cambridge University Press, 1986).
15. See Bernard Lewis, "The Map of the Middle East," *The American Scholar* (Winter 1989): p. 37.

16. *Ibid.*, p. 86. Also, Piscatori identifies three different "conformist" approaches on the part of Muslims to the modern nation-state system. First, there are those Muslims who believe that Islam and the modern nation-state may be theoretically incompatible, but the latter is a fact of life that must be accepted. The second group argues that the nation-state is a natural institution, reflecting the pluralism of the world. These Muslims believe "that pluralism is sanctioned by the Islamic texts and desirable because it allows for diverse cultural contributions within the loosely conceived *umma*." The third group accepts the nation-state system, but believes it needs to be reformed because "Islam has much to offer the prevailing system of nation-states." Piscatori, *Islam in a World of Nation-states*, pp. 76-100.

17. Islam is divided into two groups: the majority Sunnis and the minority Shi'ites. Historically the division between them is rooted in a different understanding of who represents the legitimate leadership within Islam. Islamic fundamentalism is most closely associated with the Shi'ite Muslim nation. The divisions between Shi'ites and the more modern, pragmatic Sunnis are a major source of conflict and instability in the Middle East. The Iran-Iraqi War, which ended in 1988 after seven years and over one million deaths, was a war fought in large part by the Shi'ite Iranians against the Sunni elite who govern the majority Shi'ite population of Iraq. Relations between Iran and Saudi Arabia have never ruptured into war, although the fact that the Saudi monarchy is Sunni and controls the Muslim holy sites of Mecca and Medina has been a source of great tension within Saudi Arabia and between it and Iran.

18. The Muslim population in the United States is estimated to be between four and eight million, and growing. (The current Jewish population is six million.) By the turn of the century it is quite possible there will be more Muslims in the United States than Jews. What effect this might have on future United States foreign policy is the source of much speculation.

19. R. Hrair Dekmejian, *Islam in Revolution* (Syracuse, NY: Syracuse University Press, 1985), p. 4. Dekmejian argues that Islamic fundamentalism is pervasive, polycentric (in the sense of not having a single revolutionary leadership), and persistent.

20. Piscatori, *Islam in a World of Nation-states*, p. 26.

21. *Ibid.*, p. 31.

22. *Ibid.*, p. 36.

23. While moderate accommodationist Muslims interpret *jihad* spiritually, the classic meaning of the concept—and the one embraced by Islamic fundamentalists—is military in nature. See Lewis, *The Political Language of Islam*, p. 72.

24. *Ibid.*, p. 73.

25. The Soviet Union has the fifth-largest Islamic population in the world.

CHAPTER EIGHT *Christianity and Democracy*

1. The specific responsibilities the individual Christian has toward international politics are discussed in Chapter Twelve.

2. See Michael Novak, *The Spirit of Democratic Capitalism* (New York: Simon and Schuster, 1982), pp. 16-18.

3. The antecedents of American democracy can be traced to the Magna Carta (1215 A.D.) and the ancient Greek writings of Plato, Aristotle, and Cicero.

4. See Forrest McDonald, *Novus Ordo Seclorum: The Intellectual Origins of the Constitution* (Lawrence, KS: University Press of Kansas, 1985).

5. The American Framers reached this conclusion on the basis of their reading of classic political philosophy as well as their own experience. For example, Shays' Rebellion of 1786 (a riot of Massachusetts farmers whose farms had been foreclosed) convinced many Americans of the dangers of "liberty run mad." See Catherine Drinker Bowen, *Miracle at Philadelphia* (Boston: Little, Brown, and Company, 1986), p. 10. Certainly the near-anarchy and violence associated with the French Revolution (1789) demonstrated the dangers of unrestrained, mass democracy. Interestingly, many of the American Framers—including Thomas Jefferson—saw a great affinity between the American and French Revolutions. Indeed, the issues of whether or not Americans should support the latter almost tore the young America apart during its first decade. A highly readable and insightful history of the French Revolution—and, among other things, its relationship to the American Revolution—is Simon Schama's *Citizens: A Chronicle of the French Revolution* (New York: Alfred A. Knopf, 1989).

6. The literature on formal democratic theory is vast. See, for example, Giovanni Sartori, *The Theory of Democracy Revisited*, 2 vols. (Chatham, NJ: Chatham House, 1987) and David Held, *Models of Democracy* (Stanford, CT: Stanford University Press, 1987).

7. This thesis that religion supports democracy was, during an earlier time in American history, a noncontroversial one; not so today. Political scientist William Galston writes:

Early liberal [i.e., democratic] theorists . . . assumed that civil society needed morality and publicly effective morality rested on religion. . . . This understanding of the proper relation among politics, morality, and religion dominated the American Founding. . . . In clearly recognizable form, it survived well into the twentieth century. In the past generation, however, this understanding came under attack. . . . Influential forces equated liberty with the absence of all restraints . . . [and] many influential philosophers argued that the essence of liberalism [i.e., democracy] was public neutrality on the widest possible range of moral issues.

William A. Galston, "Liberalism and Public Morality," in *Liberals on Liberalism*, ed. Alfonso J. Damico (Totowa, NJ: Rowman and Littlefield, 1986), p. 129. Three particularly influential contemporary proponents of this new understanding are John Rawls, Ronald Dworkin, and Michael Sandel. Three contemporary traditionalists—and critics of the aforementioned—are Alasdair MacIntyre, Harvey Mansfield, and Richard John Neuhaus.

8. To be sure, these values are reflected in some non-Judeo-Christian societies, especially in Asia. The success of democracy in Japan, for example, would seem to negate the proposition that Judeo-Christian values are essential for democracy. Traditional Japanese culture is imbued with a strong sense of duty and virtue, thus providing the necessary base for the development of

democracy. However, two points need to be stressed. First, because of the peculiarities of Japanese culture which manifest themselves in tremendous pressures to conform, Japanese democracy—and Japanese society—is much more authoritarian than what one finds among the democratic societies of the West. Second, as Japan has become more modern, there are signs that those traditions which have given Japan its unusual degree of stability are beginning to erode. For all the resiliency of its traditions, it appears that Japan, too, is not immune to the secularizing pressures of the modern world. Today Japan is a remarkably stable democracy, Whether Japan will be able to *sustain* its democracy as its cultural traditions erode is arguable. For an excellent discussion of Japanese tradition and the impact of modernization on Japanese society, see Robert Smith, *Japanese Society: Tradition, Self, and the Social Order* (Cambridge, MA: Cambridge University Press, 1987).

9. Richard John Neuhaus, *The Naked Public Square* (Grand Rapids: Eerdmans, 1984).

10. The specific relationship between democracy and international peace, justice, and freedom is discussed in Chapter Nine.

11. Matthew 28:18.

12. The Williamsburg Charter, subtitled "A National Celebration and Reaffirmation of the First Amendment Religious Liberty Clauses," was an official part of the celebration of the Bicentennial of the United States Constitution. The complete text of the Charter, along with commentary on it by several of the distinguished individuals who helped prepare it, is found in *This World* 24 (Winter 1989): pp. 40-101. See also Richard John Neuhaus, "The Upside Down Freedom," *Christianity Today*, December 9, 1988, pp. 24-26.

13. Peter L. Berger, "The First Freedom," *Commentary* (December 1988): p. 64. Berger argues elsewhere that because religious liberty is so fundamental, the status of religious liberty is a good litmus test of the general condition of rights and liberties in a country. Richard Neuhaus refers to religion as "freedom's shield." See Richard John Neuhaus, *Christianity and Democracy* (Washington, D.C.: The Institute on Religion and Democracy, 1981).

14. Berger perceptively writes:

In this quality of relativizing, unmasking, debunking the pretensions of human power we can see a deep, if rarely noted, affinity between the religious and the comic, between the prophet and the clown. The prophet proclaims that God laughs at all the kings and emperors of the earth; the clown makes a joke and reveals that the emperor has no clothes. No wonder, then, that tyrants are afraid both of prophecy and of jokes. No wonder that the tyrants of modern totalitarianism have been equally assiduous in controlling the institutions that may bring forth prophets and in persecuting anyone who has dared to make jokes about their grim agendas. Which explains why churches have become the last refuge of dissenters in all totalitarian societies, and why the same societies have produced a luxurious growth of underground humor.

Ibid.

15. *Ibid.*, p. 65.
16. Neuhaus, "Christianity and Democracy," p. 8.

CHAPTER NINE *Power, Justice, and Freedom*

1. The best single summary of the state of freedom in the world is Freedom House's annual *Comparative Survey of Freedom*. See also Raymond D. Gastil, *Freedom in the World: Political Rights and Civil Liberties, 1986-1987* (New York: Greenwood Press, 1987).
2. Jacques Barzun, "Is Democratic Theory for Export?," *Ethics and International Affairs* I (1987): p. 54.
3. *Ibid.* p. 57.
4. Statements such as this one are increasingly coming under attack for being "ethno-centric" and "imperialistic." These sentiments reflect a broader assault on the part of many Western and Third World intellectuals against Western values and history. A good discussion of this multifaceted phenomenon is found in: Jacques Ellul, *The Betrayal of the West* (New York: The Seabury Press, 1978); Pascal Bruckner, *Tears of the White Man* (New York: The Free Press, 1986); William J. Bennett, "Why the West," *The National Review*, May 27, 1988, pp. 37-39.
5. David Pryce-Jones, *The Closed Circle: An Interpretation of the Arabs* (New York: Harper & Row, 1989), pp. 26, 33.
6. Indeed, there is a revisionist school of thought which maintains that Japan is not a democratic society, but a highly regulated and authoritarian one governed by an oligarchy of government bureaucrats and business executives. This thesis is well-developed in Karel van Wolferen's *The Enigma of Japanese Power: People and Politics in a Stateless Nation* (New York: Alfred A. Knopf, 1989).
7. Michael Novak, *The Spirit of Democratic Capitalism* (New York: Simon and Schuster, 1982). See also Lawrence E. Harrison, *Underdevelopment Is a State of Mind* (Lanham, MD: University Press of America, 1985), pp. 132-148.
8. The structure of the international system is such that we must reasonably expect anarchy to characterize international politics. However, this has never been the case. The reason for this is that the politics among nations has historically been managed through a variety of mechanisms that have prevented international politics from degenerating into chaos. These mechanisms include war, diplomacy, international law, and balance of power arrangements. Each of these mechanisms, in different ways and with varying degrees of success, have been effective in providing a modicum of stability to the international system. These mechanisms are discussed in more detail in Hans Morgenthau, *Politics Among Nations* (New York: Alfred A. Knopf, 1967).
9. Conflict and violence involving physical harm are not identical. To say that all politics—from that of the local school board to the international variety—is characterized by conflict is not to say that all politics is characterized by a state of physical violence. Conflict of all kinds represents a continuum from the more benign, controlled conflict to all-out physical violence. The Christian aversion to political conflict tends to focus on the latter end of the continuum.

10. Though considered the father of the just war doctrine, Augustine made it clear that his doctrine of just war was a celebration of peace; e.g.: "It is therefore with the desire for peace that wars are waged."

11. While traditional, separatist pacifism survives today, recent years have seen the rise of a new activist variety that tends to be motivated by a Leftist political agenda. The roots and beliefs of this new type of pacifism are discussed in Guenter Lewy, *Peace and Revolution: The Moral Crisis of American Pacifism* (Grand Rapids, MI: Eerdmans, 1988) and Myron Augsburger and Dean C. Curry, *Nuclear Arms: Two Views on World Peace* (Waco, TX: Word, 1987), pp. 98-124.

12. A refreshingly thoughtful consideration of war and peace with a quite different emphasis than that presented in most mainline Protestant statements is the National Association of Evangelical's *Guidelines* for its Peace, Freedom, and Security Studies Program.

13. Moral equivalence and the New Left critique of traditional American values are discussed more fully in Chapters Two and Five respectively.

14. This is the view of the United Methodist bishops who in their 1986 Pastoral Letter *In Defense of Creation* argued that "when governments themselves become destroyers of community and threats to Creation, when they usurp the sovereignty which belongs to God alone, they are rightly subject to protest and resistance." It is certainly troubling that the bishops of the United Methodist Church have embraced a theology which allows for man's actions to thwart God's sovereignty.

15. R. J. Rummel, "On Fostering a Just Peace," *International Journal on World Peace* I (Autumn 1984): p. 10. Rummel states that there are two possible exceptions to this record, both minor. The one involved the Roman Republic War of 1849, the other Finland's alliance with Nazi Germany against the European democracies in 1941. For a number of reasons, both exceptions are marginal and in no way undermine the remarkable fact that democracies do not go to war against each other.

16. *Ibid.*, p. 12.

17. The relationship between freedom and peace is obvious and irrefutable. Yet, it has been ignored by many Western intellectuals. Rummel suggests why this is the case:

[L]iberalism [i.e., democratic capitalism] has been for over a century under siege by socialists. . . . Moreover, there has been a clear movement of political scientists, historians, and other intellectuals to the left and at least a partial adoption of the socialist critique of individual freedom and free market economics. Many, if not most, claim that democratic institutions fail to deal with poverty and racism, and argue that these institutions lead to spiritual malaise, alienation, a rapacious hunger for profit, and domestic and foreign violence. Indeed, the dominance of one flavor or another of socialism among academics and intellectuals has required some personal courage for those still believing in capitalism to speak out professionally.

Ibid., p. 13.

18. The Chinese experience earlier this century under the ostensibly democratic Republic of Sun Yat-sen and Chiang Kai-shek demonstrates the

difficulty of planting real democracy in a nation such as China. And yet the slow but successful evolution of democracy since 1949 in Chinese-governed Taiwan suggests that democracy can be planted in the People's Republic of China as well.

19. South Africa because of its vast mineral resources and its geographical location; Panama because of the Canal; China because of its sheer size as well as its relationship with the Soviet Union.

20. The most thorough analysis of the impact of economic sanctions upon South Africa is Merle Lipton's *Sanctions and South Africa* (London: The Economist Intelligence Unit, 1988).

21. How this should be done is discussed in detail in Chapter Eleven.

22. See Myron Augsburger, and Dean C. Curry, *Nuclear Arms: Two Views on World Peace*, pp. 125-146; Dean C. Curry, "Beyond MAD: Affirming the Morality and Necessity of Nuclear Deterrence," *Transformation 5* (January/March 1988): pp. 8-17.

CHAPTER TEN *Third World Development, Human Rights, and Freedom*

1. It needs to be emphasized at the outset of this discussion that the concept of poverty is a difficult one to define. As people who are well-fed, well-clothed, healthy, and have secure dwellings to call home, we have an intuitive understanding of what poverty is. We know, for example, when we see frightful television images of swollen-bellied, hungry African children that such hunger and malnutrition is a symptom of poverty. Likewise, when we travel through certain rural areas of the American South or in the ghettos of urban America, we experience that which we call poverty. Several important observations need to be made, however, about our understanding and definitions of poverty. First, conditions of poverty are relative. The urban poor in America, using any local indicator, are not poor by Haitian or Ugandan standards. Second, to be poor is no sin; nor does poverty *necessarily* or *always* imply personal unhappiness or misery. Third, poverty is a complex, multidimensional idea. Poverty is more than a low personal income or a low per capita Gross National Product. For this reason, social scientists prefer the concepts of development and underdevelopment rather than poverty. A nation that is underdeveloped—for example, Mali, Chad, or Nepal—is poor more than in the sense that its population has low income levels. Such countries are also beset by problems of inadequate health care, illiteracy, high levels of infant mortality, etc. Hence, the process of development involves more than economic growth alone. Development involves a process of economic growth coupled with rising income levels, increased investment, expanding life expectancy, improved health care, social mobility, etc. The issue of development is a major concern among the world's economists and policymakers; yet, while there exists a consensus of sorts concerning a general definition of development, there is much diversity regarding the specific meaning of development. H. W. Arndt, an Australian economist, writes in this regard:

[A]nyone who asked articulate citizens in developed or developing countries what they meant by this desirable objective of "development" would get a variety of answers. High living standards. A rising per capita income. Increase in productive capacity. Mastery over nature. Freedom through control of man's environment. . . . Catching up with the developed countries in technology, wealth, power, status. Economic independence, self-reliance. Scope for self-fulfillment for all. Liberation, the means to human ascent. [In sum], development in the vast literature on the subject, appears to have come to encompass almost all facets of the good society, everyman's road to utopia.

H. W. Arndt, *Economic Development: The History of an Idea* (Chicago: The University of Chicago Press, 1987), p. 1. Arndt's book is an indispensable discussion of the evolution of the idea of economic development.

2. The empirical evidence supporting this conclusion is simply overwhelming. See, for example, Peter L. Berger, *The Capitalist Revolution: Fifty Propositions About Prosperity, Equality, and Liberty* (New York: Basic Books, 1986) and Nick Eberstadt, *The Poverty of Communism* (New Brunswick, NJ: Transaction Books, 1988). Political scientists Thomas Dye and Harmon Zeigler argue that the penchant of many—perhaps most—academics and intellectuals (including religious leaders) to ignore the overwhelming empirical evidence that capitalism fosters prosperity, equality, and respect for human rights "must be attributed to the pernicious effects of ideology." Reflecting on their own professional discipline, Dye and Zeigler conclude that "there are few examples of political scientists asserting propositions with so little evidence as they do in describing the economic consequences of socialism." Thomas R. Dye and Harmon Zeigler, "Socialism and Equality in Cross-national Perspective," *PS: Political Science and Politics* xxi (Winter 1988): pp. 55, 56.

3. Some Christians prefer the term "Two-Thirds World" as a more accurate demographic description of the Third World.

4. This is the central argument of Adam Smith's seminal *An Inquiry into the Nature and Causes of the Wealth of Nations*, published in 1776. Smith's book (commonly referred to as *Wealth of Nations*) revolutionized the way people looked at wealth and poverty.

5. Peter L. Berger, "The Third World as a Religious Idea," *Partisan Review* 50 (Spring 1983): p. 163.

6. Paul Johnson, *Modern Times* (New York: Harper & Row, 1983), pp. 476, 477.

7. Paul Johnson eloquently describes the thematic tone of the Bandung Conference as articulated by its host, President Sukarno:

"This is the first inter-continental conference of coloured peoples in the history of mankind," said Sukarno in his opening oration. "Sisters and brothers! How terrifically dynamic is our time! . . . Nations and states have awoken from a sleep of centuries!" The old age of the white man, which has ravaged the planet with its wars was dying; a better one was dawning, which would dissolve the Cold War and introduce a new multi-racial, multi-religious brotherhood, for "All great religions are one in their message and tolerance." The coloured raced would introduce the new morality: "We the people of Asia and Africa . . . far more than half the human population of the world, we can mobilize what I have called the *Moral Violence of Nations* in favour of peace."

Johnson trenchantly points out that the high-sounding moralism and optimism reflected in the rhetoric of the Bandung Conference was not reflected in the reality of the situation, either before or after:

It was calculated that 1,700 secret police were in attendance. Some of those present were subsequently to plot to murder each other; others were to end their lives in gaol, disgrace or exile. But at the time the Third World had not yet publicly besmirched itself by invasions, annexations, massacres and dictatorial cruelty.
Ibid.

8. Since it was first articulated as a goal of the Third World, non-alignment has been more of a myth than a reality. Suffice it to say that the leader of the Third World non-aligned movement (known as the Group of 77) in the early 1980s was Cuban. The fact that Daniel Ortega, Fidel Castro, and Muammar Qaddfi all consider themselves part of (and are accepted as part of) the "non-aligned" movement speaks volumes.

9. Johnson, *Modern Times*, p. 512.

10. Amin, who among his other claims to infamy is a reputed cannibal, was responsible for the deaths of at least 200,000 Ugandans in the 1970s. The distance between the moralistic rhetoric of the Third World leadership and the reality is boldly evidenced in the fact that the Organization of African Unity (OAU) elected him its chairman in the mid-1970s. In a speech before the General Assembly of the United Nations in October 1975, Amin was given a standing ovation after calling for the "extinction" of Israel. *Ibid.*, p. 536.

11. See *ibid*, Chapter Fifteen, entitled "Caliban's Kingdom."

12. Berger, "The Third World as a Religious Idea," pp. 188-191.

13. Sociologist Paul Hollander discusses the dynamic of the intellectual class's alienation from Western values and institutions in his penetrating study *Political Pilgrims* (New York: Oxford University Press, 1981). Hollander's book is also an excellent discussion of how bright, rational, and otherwise thoughtful people are easily blinded to the horrors of totalitarianism.

14. Berger, "The Third World as a Religious Idea," pp. 191, 192.

15. *Ibid.*, p. 193.

16. Arndt, *Economic Development*, pp. 168-173.

17. The term "Group of 77" was first applied to the Third World nations in the early 1960s. Today there are over 120 nations that are part of the "Group of 77." In contrast, twenty-nine African and Asian nations participated in the 1955 Bandung Conference.

18. The United Nations was the product of Franklin Roosevelt's and Winston Churchill's dream for a new-world order of collective security following World War II. In the early years of the organization, the General Assembly was generally sympathetic to the American (and the Western) view of the world. However, as the rhetoric of the leaders of the Third World became more strident in the early 1960s, the General Assembly became a hostile forum in which the agenda of the Third

World—a predominantly anti-Western agenda—was formulated and articulated. Another organ of the United Nations, the United Nations Conference on Trade and Development (UNCTAD), created in 1964, has been the primary vehicle through which the economic agenda of the Third World (i.e., the NIEO) has been perpetuated.

19. In 1988 Third World debt totalled $1.25 trillion.

20. Or, more accurately, using today's jargon, Northern imperialism.

21. Hobson's argument was based on the premise that Western capitalists had to turn to Africa and Asia in order to use up the excess production of their industries. In other words, the Western capitalists produced so much they had to export capital in order to maintain and increase profits. This argument became known as the theory of under-consumption. The sinister side of Hobson's theory was that the export of capital to Africa and Asia involved the conscious exploitation of the native peoples who lived in those places.

22. Lenin's argument is found in his *Imperialism: The Highest Stage of Capitalism* (1916). This little book not only develops the orthodox Marxist-Leninist view of imperialism, it also lays out the Marxist-Leninist theory of international relations— specifically, that war is the inevitable outcome of competition among capitalist nations for colonies. Such competition is inevitable precisely because capitalists are driven to increase profits at all costs.

23. Certainly religious groups opposed to United States policy in Nicaragua played a major role in thwarting the Reagan Administration's policy toward that country. At the same time, the role of the Religious Left in influencing overall American foreign policy, and in particular American foreign policy toward the Third World, has been negligible. Nevertheless, to the extent that the Religious Left is successful in—albeit slowly— shaping the American public's understanding of foreign policy issues (El Salvador, for instance), its influence is likely to grow.

24. The following represent a sampling of important works which convincingly refute the argument that Third World underdevelopment is caused by capitalism, imperialism, or any other external force: P. T. Bauer, *Equality, the Third World, and Economic Delusion* (Cambridge, MA: Harvard University Press, 1982); P. T. Bauer, *Reality and Rhetoric: Studies in Economic Development* (Cambridge, MA: Harvard University Press, 1984); Peter L. Berger and Michael Novak, *Speaking to the Third World: Essays on Democracy and Development* (Washington D.C.: American Enterprise Institute, 1985); Peter L. Berger, *The Capitalist Revolution: Fifty Propositions About Prosperity, Equality, and Liberty* (New York: Basic Books, 1986); Lawrence E. Harrison, *Underdevelopment Is a State of Mind* (Lanham, MD: University Press of America, 1985); Thomas Sowell, *The Economics and Politics of Race: An International Perspective* (New York: William Morrow, 1983); Hernado de Soto, *The Other Path: The Invisible Revolution in the Third World* (New York: Harper & Row, 1989).

25. Sowell, *The Economics and Politics of Race*, p. 219.

26. Bauer, *Equality, the Third World, and Economic Delusion*, pp. 70, 71. Elaborating on this conclusion Bauer writes:

Since the middle of the nineteenth century commercial contacts established by the West have improved material conditions out of all recognition over much of the Third World. . . . The transformation of Malaya
[the present Malaysia] is instructive. In the 1890s it was a sparsely populated area of Malay hamlets and fishing villages. By the 1930s it had
become the hub of the world's rubber and tin industries. By then there
were large cities and excellent communications in a country where millions of Malays, Chinese and Indians now lived much longer and better
than they had formerly.

Bauer demonstrates that the Malayan experience was not unusual.
Similar transformations took place in nearly every Third World area that
had contact with the West.

27. See Nick Eberstadt, "Population and Economic Growth," *The Wilson Quarterly* x (Winter 1986): pp. 95-127.

28. It also needs to be noted that natural resources do not instantaneously appear. Resources are created. Oil, for example, lay beneath the ground for centuries before man—i.e., human resources—figured out how it could be used. The origins of natural resources and their relationship to the ultimate resource—man himself—is discussed in detail in Julian Simon, *The Ultimate Resource* (Princeton, NJ: Princeton University Press, 1981). Simon's book is also an excellent discussion of, *inter alia*, the rela-tionship of population growth to the ability of the world to feed itself.

29. P. T. Bauer, "Creating the Third World: Foreign Aid and Its Offspring," *Encounter* (April 1988), p. 67.

30. Irwin M. Stelzer, "Third World Deadbeats," *The American Spectator* (April 1989), p. 34. Hernado de Soto discusses in great detail how the economic experience of Peru provides powerful support for this argu-ment. See de Soto's *The Other Path*.

31. Indeed, there are no examples *anywhere* of successful socialism. Apologists for socialism frequently point to the Scandinavian nations to support their belief in the superiority of socialism. However, using the generally accepted definition of socialism (state control of the means of production) the Scandinavian nations are not socialist, for the means of production are not state-controlled as they are in socialist economies such as the Soviet Union and Angola. Though not socialistic, the Scandinavian nations are well-developed welfare states. Of the truly socialistic nations, East Germany, with a per capita GNP estimated at $11,000, has been the most successful. However, East Germany's relative economic success is anomalous in the socialist world and is not equal to that of West Germany, which has a per capita GNP of $12,000.

32. According to the World Bank, twenty-two of the world's thirty-nine poorest nations are found in Africa. Ironically, the Republic of South Africa has the only fully developed economy on the continent of Africa.

33. Per capita GNP in 1988 stood at $250, having declined steadily since 1965. Life expectancy in 1986 stood at fifty-three years.

34. Eberstadt, "Population and Economic Growth," pp. 108, 109.

35. *Ibid*, p. 109.

36. Peter L. Berger, *The Capitalist Revolution*, p. 157. Berger's book is important both for its conclusions and for the rigor of its argumentation.

37. *Ibid.*, p. 128.
38. Modern technology, regardless of the economic system that utilizes it, is a major factor generating economic growth. Having said that, it is also true that capitalism is still unsurpassed in its ability to produce economic growth.
39. The following data is drawn from the World Bank and from Peter Berger's *The Capitalist Revolution.*
40. The economy of the People's Republic of China, a Marxist-Leninist socialist nation, grew at an annual rate of about 11 percent from 1979-1989. However, this growth spurt was unleashed by a freeing-up of state control on the Chinese economy.
41. Peter Berger has made this point with great elegance in a number of his recent writings, including *The Capitalist Revolution.* See also, "Underdevelopment Revisited" in Berger and Novak, *Speaking to the Third World,* pp. 21-30, and Peter L. Berger, "Human Development and Economic Alternatives," *Crisis* (November 1987), pp. 18-23.
42. See Dye and Zeigler, "Socialism and Equality in Cross-National Perspective," pp. 45, 56.
43. *Ibid,* p. 54.
44. Berger, "Human Development and Economic Alternatives," p. 21.
45. Berger and Novak, *Speaking to the Third World,* p. 29.
46. We have already noted that this reality is what has driven many of the reforms of Mikhail Gorbachev and Deng Xiaoping. In the Third World, cracks in the once-impenetrable walls of socialism show signs of appearing as well. For example, in early 1989 the one-party socialist nation of Zimbabwe announced a major revision of its investment code. The purpose of the revision is to encourage more outside investment. Since independence in 1980, the socialist government of Zimbabwe has only been able to attract $50 million in outside investment, this for a nation that is rich in natural resources and has a sophisticated infrastructure (i.e., transportation systems, etc.). Though strongly criticized by Zimbabwean leftists as a betrayal of its socialist ideals, the Zimbabwean finance minister has responded that "the direction of socialism is clear. There is no inherent contradiction between socialism and market forces" (see "Zimbabwe Shifts Investment Rule," *The New York Times,* Monday, May 15, 1988, Section D). Despite the foreign minister's assertion, Zimbabwe confronts the dual dilemma that all socialist nations face as they move toward more free economic arrangements: the difficulty of justifying socialism in the midst of its obvious failures, and containing increasing pressures for more political freedom to go along with growing economic freedom.
47. Peter Berger has quipped that ten years from now the only Marxists left in the world will be four Brazilian nuns.
48. A personal anecdote illustrates part of the problem. In the Spring of 1989 a Washington D.C. "think tank" sponsored a conference at which a leader of Evangelicals for Social Action, a left-leaning evangelical organization sympathetic to liberation theology, stated that it was imperative that Christians listen to the Latin American people. Another participant at the conference asked the ESA leader if he meant people like Peru's Hernado de Soto, probably the most influential person in contemporary

Latin America who has made a persuasive case for capitalism in his best-selling book *The Other Path*. In response to the question, the ESA leader sat in silence and then admitted that he had never heard of de Soto!

49. See Lawrence E. Harrison's *Underdevelopment Is a State of Mind*.
50. The role of cultural values, particularly Reformation Protestant values, in sustaining democratic capitalism is argued with force by Michael Novak in *The Spirit of Democratic Capitalism* (New York: Simon and Schuster, 1982). Similar arguments are made by Berger and Harrison. Thomas Sowell has described in fascinating detail how differences in cultural values affect differences of economic performance among ethnic groups in the United States and elsewhere.

CHAPTER ELEVEN *Looking Ahead: An Agenda for the Bush Years*

1. See Gregory A. Fossedal, *The Democratic Imperative: Exporting the American Revolution* (New York: Basic Books, 1989).
2. The dream of an economically and politically unified Europe brought about the creation of the European Economic Community in 1957. From the original six members, the EEC has grown to its present membership of twelve: Portugal, France, Ireland, Great Britain, Spain, Luxembourg, West Germany, Netherlands, Denmark, Belgium, Italy, Greece.
3. The Soviet Union/Warsaw Pact enjoys overwhelming superiority at every level of conventional forces. In tanks, the Warsaw Pact has 59,000 to NATO's 22,000; in artillery, the Warsaw Pact has 57,000 to NATO's 17,000; in aircraft, the Warsaw Pact has 7,000 to NATO's 4,000; and in troops, the Warsaw Pact has 3.6 million compared to NATO's 2.2 million.
4. The Japanese attitude toward rice is a good illustration of the influence that traditional cultural values exert on all areas of Japanese life. As a product of the soil so essential to the survival of the Japanese throughout history, rice has a sacred aura about it. This is certainly a major reason why Japanese rice production is so heavily subsidized.
5. See Stephen D. Krasner, "A Trade Strategy for the United States," *Ethics and International Affairs* 2 (1988): pp. 17-35.
6. *Ibid.*, pp. 32, 33.
7. After the Communist revolution in Mainland China, the United States officially recognized the Republic of China (Taiwan) as the legitimate Chinese government. When full diplomatic relations with the People's Republic of China were resumed during the Carter Administration, the United States broke its formal diplomatic ties with the Taiwan government. Nevertheless, the United States still maintains close economic and *de facto* political relations with Taiwan.
8. President Nixon's overture to China in the early 1970s corresponded to the exhaustion of the Mao-instigated Cultural Revolution that all but destroyed civilized life in China. The relatively more moderate policies of Mao's successors are correctly viewed as a reaction against the chaos, hysteria, and destruction that characterized Mao's policies, and the Cultural Revolution in particular. For an informative and shocking history of the Cultural Revolution, told by one who participated in it, see Gao Bang, *Born Red: A Chronicle of the Cultural Revolution* (Stanford, CA: Stanford University Press, 1987).

9. The seven nations of the region are Costa Rica, Guatemala, Honduras, Belize, Panama, Nicaragua, and El Salvador.
10. The best account of the Sandinista revolution and its Marxist ideology is Shirley Christian's *Nicaragua: A Revolution in the Family* (New York: Random House, 1985).
11. It is instructive that Nicaragua, along with Cuba and Vietnam, were the only nations in the world to explicitly approve of the 1989 Communist Chinese massacre of students in Tiananmen Square.
12. The Democratic Convergence Party—the political wing of the FMLN—received less than 5 percent of the vote.
13. Denis Worrall, a leader of South Africa's anti-apartheid Democratic Party, points out:

> World War II marked something of a revolution in South Africa's position within the community of nations. . . . The reasons for this change have less to do with race relations in South Africa (which remained more or less constant), than with the very changed circumstances of the international system. Before the war the structure of the South African governmental system was oligarchic and official policy with respect to race relations was discriminatory. That did not, however, prevent South Africa, and white South Africans, from playing a normal role in international affairs. Conflict was inevitable in the greatly altered postwar world, with its commitment to individual human rights . . . and with the coming to independence of the countries of Asia and the rest of Africa.

Denis Worrall, "The Real Struggle in South Africa: An Insider's View," *Ethics and International Affairs* 2 (1988): p. 116.
14. Only Botswana and Senegal allow their own black people the right to vote in free, fair elections.
15. Jacques Ellul, *The Betrayal of the West* (New York: The Seabury Press, 1978), p. 6.
16 *Ibid.*, pp. 6, 7.
17. For a thorough and fair analysis of South African political realities, see Richard John Neuhaus, *Dispensations: The Future of South Africa as South Africans See It* (Grand Rapids: Eerdmans, 1986); Walter H. Kansteiner, *South Africa: Revolution or Reconciliation?* (Washington, D.C.: Institute on Religion and Democracy Press, 1988); Peter L. Berger and Bobby Godsell, eds., *A Future South Africa: Visions, Strategies, and Realities* (Boulder, CO: Westview Press, 1988).
18. An excellent discussion of American policy toward South Africa is found in Kansteiner, *South Africa: Revolution or Reconciliation?*, pp. 119-130.
19. For example, a 1989 Gallup poll of South Africans showed that nearly 80 percent of South Africans oppose sanctions. Among blacks, a sizable majority of nearly 60 percent opposes sanctions. When it comes to Western disinvestment in South Africa, 90 percent of whites and an almost equal percentage of blacks are opposed. This poll was the most comprehensive taken in South Africa, and the Gallup organization stood fully behind its accuracy. See *The Star* (Johannesburg), May 17, 1989. That Americans have come to believe that nonwhites in South Africa support sanctions and disinvestment is attributable to the influence of South

African clerics Desmond Tutu and Allan Boesak. The reality is that Tutu and Boesak do not represent all of South Africa's nonwhites; their voice is one among many. In allowing the impression to be perpetuated that they speak for the majority of South Africa's nonwhites, Boesak, Tutu, and their publicists in the West act with less than full integrity. Among the interesting conclusions of the Gallup poll cited above is the fact that only 1 percent of South Africa's total population considers Rev. Boesak the country's most popular leader. See *The Star* (Johannesburg), May 24, 1989.

CHAPTER TWELVE *Conclusion: Making a Difference*

1. 1 Corinthians 15:12-19.
2. 1 Corinthians 15:58.
3. Neither should our motivation for concern about the world be guilt-driven. God does not hold us personally accountable for the world's problems. We are accountable to God for our own personal relationship with Him and for the way in which we live our lives. Of course, if we are aware of evil, we must never condone it. But there are many ways we can respond to evil and still be faithful to Biblical teaching. For example, the soldier who took up arms against Hitler and the citizen who prayed for those living under Hitler's tyranny were both Biblically faithful. Neither person was responsible for Hitler's tyranny.
4. *The New York Times* and the *The Christian Science Monitor* are particularly good sources for following current international events. The editorial pages of *The Wall Street Journal* and *The Washington Times* also provide excellent commentary on current events. *The National Interest*, *Orbis*, and *Foreign Affairs* are three informative and influential quarterly journals of international politics. *The New Republic*, *The National Review*, and *Commentary* are three opinion periodicals that generally provide excellent analyses of a variety of issues relating to international politics and U.S. foreign policy.
5. One of the major reasons denominations long-associated with the National Council of Churches have experienced dramatic declines in membership in the past twenty years is that they have replaced the proclamation of the Biblical gospel with the proclamation of a leftist political agenda. For many in these "mainline" (or, more accurately, "old-line" or "sideline") denominations, political orthodoxy is more important than theological orthodoxy. It is often more important, for example, whether one supports the Sandinistas than whether one believes in the historicity of Christ's virgin birth. Recently, the old-line denominations have seen renewal movements emerge within them which seek a return to Biblical orthodoxy. Whether or not these efforts will be successful remains to be seen. The problem of politicizing the gospel and the mission of the Church is beginning to be found even among more traditionally conservative evangelicals. The battle against this kind of compromise of the Biblical message is being responsibly (and successfully) fought by organizations such as the Institute on Religion and Democracy (729 15th Street NW, Suite 900, Washington, D.C. 20005) and the Peace, Freedom, and Security Studies Program of the National Association of Evangelicals (1023 15th Street NW, Suite 500, Washington, D.C. 20005).

INDEX